UNDERSTANDING CHINA

Introduction to China's History, Society and Culture

JIN BO

CHINA INTERCONTINENTAL PRESS

图书在版编目（ＣＩＰ）数据

阅读中国：历史、社会和文化　　　英文／金帛编著；
王国振 李萍译.
—北京：五洲传播出版社，2008.6
ISBN 978-7-5085-1214-3

Ⅰ.阅...　Ⅱ.①金...②王...③李...
Ⅲ.中国－概况　Ⅳ.K92
中国版本图书馆 CIP 数据核字（2007）第 171790 号

Photos courtesy of China Foto Press, Wang Yan, Wang Yi'e, Cai Cheng

Map drawn by Gao Rui

Diagrams drawn by He Jie with Beijing Jinxiushengyi Cultural Development Co., Ltd.

Approval number for use of maps:(2007) No.1593

Understanding China: Introduction to China's History, Society and Culture

Published and Distributed by China Intercontinental Press

Writer: Jin Bo	Finalizers: Wang Jide
Executive Editor: Zheng Lei	Translators: Wang Guozhen, Li Ping
Layout by Miao Wei, He Jie	

Add: 25th Floor, Huatian Plaza, 6 Beixiaomachang, Lianhuachi Donglu, Haidian District, Beijing, China 100038

Telephone: 86-10-58880244　　Fax: 86-10-58891281　　Website: www.cicc.org.cn

Layout and designer: Beijing Jinxiushengyi Cultural Development Co., Ltd.

Printed by Beijing Langxiang Printing Co., Ltd.

Format:787 × 1092, 1/16

ISBN 978-7-5085-1214-3　　　　　　　　　　　　　　Price: 92.00 RMB

Preface

Many people regard China as a distant, ancient and mysterious country simply because the history and culture of their own countries are so different from that of China.

China may be far away from some countries in terms of distance, but this does not mean China is mysterious and difficult to get to.

With an over 5,000-year-old civilization, China has developed a unique culture which has greatly enriched world civilization. This makes China a country worthy of being understood.

China is one of the countries experiencing the fastest economic growth and social change. The development of China, with the largest population in the world, provides opportunities for other countries to develop; and this in turn brings China increasingly closer to the outside world. China's development calls for a peaceful international environment, and the world's prosperity needs China's development. In this environment it is necessary that China be understood.

China is not difficult to understand. Currently the country is going full steam ahead to open its door to the outside world and learn from others. China is dedicated to peaceful endeavors, and is sincere in dealing with others.

For thousands of years people have come to explore China. Some of them gained a good understanding of the country. Of course, impressions of China varied according to the period.

Some 400 years ago, Alvaro Semedo, a Portuguese missionary who came to China, described China in the following way in his book *1645 History of China*:

It is a big country with a large population, with endless villages and towns, each in close proximity to the next. Houses fill the horizon. China has varied climates according to latitude and region. The country abounds in fruit, giving the impression of being a warehouse of fruit gathered from around the world. It is self-sufficient in food production, and in fact produces a surplus to trade with other countries. Many countries yearn for the chance to visit China. Many countries consume mainly wheat or rice, and China grows both in large amounts.

When talking about the Chinese society more than 30 years ago, the famous American Sinologist, John King Fairbank said in his book *China: Tradition and Transformation:*

In viewing China, however, foreign advisors must remember the following: First, the Chinese society has families, instead of individuals, government or churches, as its basic unit. Each family provides its members with major support for their financial needs, education and recreational activities. China's ethic system also has families as its center, instead of God or country. The family system calls for its members to be faithful in social behavior. Law is the indispensable tool for management while individual morality constitutes the foundation of the society. In China, there will never be anarchy due to a lack of importance being attached to the law in mind; Chinese society is closely united under Confucianism.

Three years ago, William Overholt, Director of the Center for Asia Pacific Policy at the RAND Corporation, made the following comment in his article *China and Globalization* on the changes in China:

Adoption of the rule of law, of commitment to competition, of widespread use of English, of foreign education, and of many foreign laws and institutions are not just updating Chinese institutions but transforming Chinese civilization... It is hard to overstate the social adjustment Chinese are experiencing. But because China has been willing to accept such adjustments, no large country in human history has ever experienced such rapid improvements in living standards and working conditions.

With the deepening of the reform and opening-up, and with more efforts made to become deeply involved in economic globalization, China becomes more closely connected with the rest of the world. Under this situation, getting to know more about China has become the order of the day. This book is created with the expectation of being of some help in this regard.

Author
Beijing, January 2008

CONTENTS

I. Geography and Civilization of China

China, being a united multi-ethnic country, is blessed with a special geographical environment. In the process of its formation and evolution, China became a country featuring readily identifiable and cohesive characteristics.

II. Unification of China in History

In the long historical development of Chinese culture it was inherited and carried forward continuously. In spite of foreign invasion, it was never replaced by other cultures. The ancient history of China is mainly different from the histories of other countries in its length, continuity and unification.

III. The Traditional Ideology, Culture and Society

The traditional Chinese ideology and culture are the foundation of the spirit and character of the Chinese nation and lie behind all the achievements of China's historical development.

IV. Developed Country of the Agricultural Civilization Era

Ancient China represented the agricultural civilization, whose productivity and social development led the world for a fairly long time. For more than 2,000 years the Chinese ancestors worked hard and were creative, hence enriching and developing the civilization of human beings.

V. End of Feudal Power and Establishment of a Modern Country

China experienced Westernization in the aspects of technology, social system and culture until the New Democratic Revolution led by the Communist Party of China. Thanks to more than 100 years of unremitting efforts, the nation finally found its way onto a new road of development.

VI. Endeavors of New China and Reform and Opening-up

The year 1978 marked a turning point in the history of New China through the introduction of reform and opening up. Since then, the Chinese people and the Communist Party of China have both undergone huge changes, and the relationship between China and the world has entered a new period of development.

CONTENTS

VII. The Largest Developing Country in the World

China is the most populous developing country in the world.China's modernization drive calls for efforts of more than ten and even scores of generations. At present, the Chinese people are striving to build a well-off society.

VIII. China and the World in the Era of Economic Globalization

China has become an important member of the contemporary international system and plays a significant role in international affairs. As a large, responsible, developing country, China has committed itself, along with the other nations of the world, to building a more harmonious global environment with long-lasting peace and common prosperity for all.

I. GEOGRAPHY AND CIVILIZATION OF CHINA

As an old Chinese saying goes, "Man is conditioned by the natural environment he lives in". It emphasizes the significance of the environment for the development and survival of a country.

China, being a united multi-ethnic country, is blessed with a special geographical environment. In the process of its formation and evolution, China became a country featuring readily identifiable and cohesive characteristics.

(I) The Geography and Climate Features

Situated to the east of the Asian continent, the northern part of the Eastern Hemisphere, as well as forming a shoreline along the edge of the Pacific Ocean, China is a country exhibiting both maritime and continental topography. Its territorial area of approximately 9.6 million square km accounts for one-fifteenth of the terrestrial globe, or a quarter of the landmass of Asia. To put this in a global perspective, its terrestrial area is smaller than that of Russia and Canada, but larger than that of the United States and Australia, and approximately equal to that of Europe. With its land borders extending more than 22,000 km, and over 18,000 km of mainland coastline, China is adjacent to 14 countries and has six neighbors across the sea.

China has a terraced terrain, which descends, through a series of gradations, from the west to the east before meeting the shores of the sea. Thanks to various landforms, the Chinese topography consists of mountains, plateaus, basins, plains, lakes and hills. China has many mountains, with mountainous areas accounting for two-thirds of the country's total landmass. Its major mountain ranges include the Himalayas, Kunlunshan, Tianshan, Qilianshan and the Altay Mountains in the west, and the Hengduanshan, Dabashan, Taihangshan and Yinshan Mountains in the central part, as well as the Wuyishan and Changbaishan Mountains in the east. These towering and majestic natural features comprise a network, ranging from hundreds of meters to thousands in height, giving shape and perspective to the entire country. China also has many basins, mainly distributed in the west; major ones include the Zungar Basin, the Tarim Basin, the Chaidamu Basin and the Sichuan Basin. There

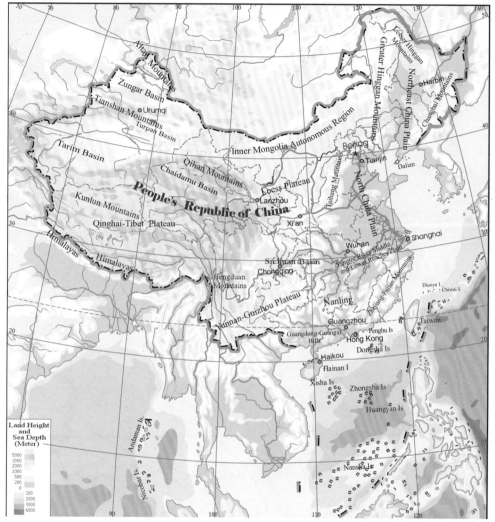

Sketch Map of China's Geography.

are also famous plateaus which can be found in the west and the north, and these include the Qinghai-Tibet Plateau (often called "The Third Pole" or "The Roof of the World"), the Yunnan-Guizhou Plateau, the Loess Plateau and the Inner Mongolia Plateau. In addition, China's three major plains are all situated in the low-lying area in the eastern part of the country; they are the Northeast China Plain, the North China Plain and the Middle and Lower Yangtze Valley Plains. So far as the hills are concerned, these are mostly to be found in the southeast. After comparing the topography of China with that of Europe, North America and India, Fei Zhengqing (John King Fairbank), the famous American Sinologist, concluded:

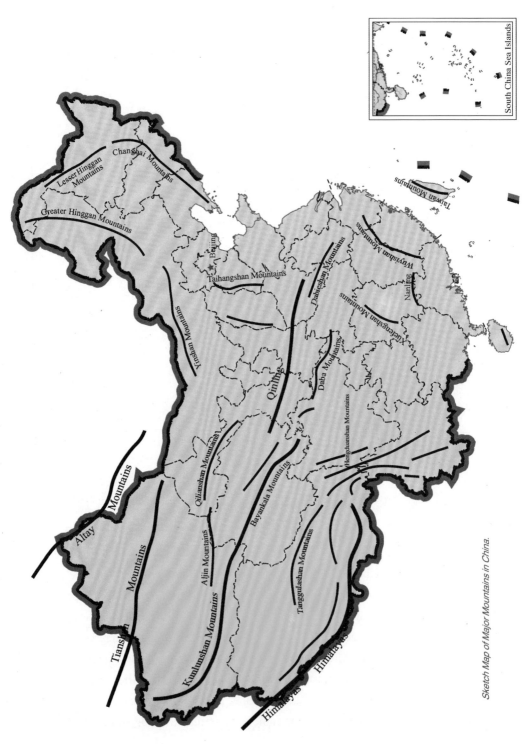

Sketch Map of Major Mountains in China.

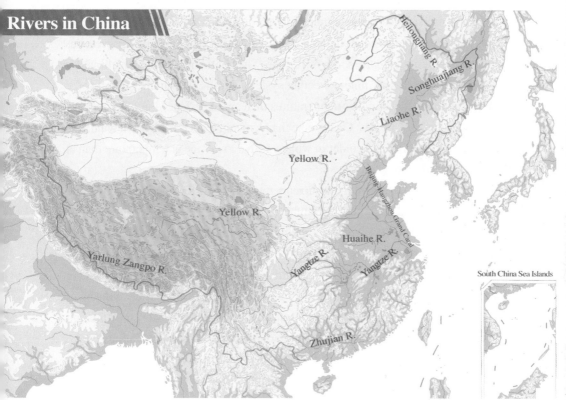

Rivers in China

Sketch Map of Major River Systems of China.

China has a disunited topography, with a subsequent lack of good transport access. On the other hand, its North China Plain, although certainly very large, is in fact significantly smaller than the north plains in India, let alone the large plains in Northern Europe and middle-west plains of North America.

China has numerous rivers. Principle among these are the Yangtze River, ranking first in terms of length and water volume, the Yellow River, Pearl River and Heilongjiang River. Whereas rivers in the rest of Central Asia and North Americas tend to flow either north to south or south to north, Chinese rivers, due to the terraced topography mentioned earlier, mainly flow from the west to the east or southeast. There is also a significant drop in elevation during a river's course, resulting in tremendous water resources.

China's territory extends south of the Tropic of Cancer from 50 degrees of northern latitude. As a consequence of this vast size, its climate is wonderfully diverse, although the majority exhibits temperate, warm and subtropical zones with a generally mild range of temperature and four distinct seasons. The greater part of China's territory, an area approximately the size of the United States of America, lies at a degree of latitude to the south of Europe. The continental monsoon climate is the major feature of the Chinese weather system. During the summer months, the southeast wind leads to higher temperatures than are experienced in other parts of the world at similar latitudes. On the other hand, owing to the severe north wind, this same area is both drier and colder in winter, with a lower mean temperature than at the same latitude elsewhere.

As the cooler continental air currents meet the moister air currents over the Chinese landmass, a great deal of rainfall is the inevitable result. In the southeast area covering the Huaihe River, the Qinling Mountain Range and the Qinghai-Tibet Plateau, the annual precipitation is over 800 mm in its east and south; the annual precipitation is less than 800 mm in its north and west. And this figure decreases the further north-west one travels: by the time we reach the Tarim Basin we discover that the annual rainfall has reached an upper limit of just 50 mm. Most precipitation occurs during the summer, although there are important regional variations due to the topographical features to which we have previously referred. In the south, there is a long rainy season from May to October, but in the north a shorter season from July to August.

(II) Geographical Environment and Inward Movement

China faces the Bohai Sea, the Yellow Sea, the East China Sea and the South China Sea in the east and southeast. These vast seas were taken as the end of the land by the ancient Chinese.

In the northern part of China lies the vast Mongolia Plateau which is bisected into Inner Mongolia (south of the desert) and Outer Mongolia (north of the desert) by the vast sweep of desert, the Gobi Desert and the Yinshan Mountains. To the north of the Mongolia Plateau are mountains stretching thousands of km from east to west. Further north of these mountains is chilly Siberia. The special geographical environment forced various ethnic groups on the grasslands to turn to the area south of the plateau, namely the Central Plains in the valleys of the Yellow River and the

Tian Ya Hai Jiao in Hainan was regarded as the end corner of China.

Sky-scraping Himalayas in Tibet.

Yangtze River, to seek opportunities for development. In ancient times, the ethnic groups living on the Mongolian Plateau were mostly nomadic tribes. They, being attracted by the culture of the Central Plains, kept moving southward. Some of them established regimes in the Central Plains.

In the northeastern part of China, the Greater Hinggan Mountains screen the Mongolian Plateau off in the west; the Lesser Hinggan Mountains lay in the north; the Changbaishan Mountains extend in the east; further east is the vast Pacific Ocean; and the vast Northeast China Plain covers the area between these mountains and the ocean. A long narrow corridor winds its way from the south of northeast China along the coastline of the Bohai Sea, serving as an extremely important route connecting northeast China with the Central Plains. Historically, it was the corridor used by most of the ethnic groups in northeast China to move westward or southward to the affluent Central Plains. Also, it is the same corridor used by the Han people of the Central Plains to spread into the Northeast China Plain for a new life, bringing advanced civilization there with them.

In the northwestern part of China, the border areas are covered with steep high mountains and the desolate Gobi desert, forming a natural barrier. The Tangnushan and Altay Mountains sit in the north; the Pamirs Plateau, tucked away at an elevation of above 4,000 meters, is located in the west; the lofty Kunlunshan Mountain Range towers in the south; further south is the Qinghai-Tibet Plateau, a lonely area. For local ethnic groups longing for a better life, the best choice was to turn eastward. The Central Plains in the east possessed the material conditions necessary for the development of the northwest. In old times, various races here maintained very close relations with the Central Plains by way of the Mongolia Plateau and the Hexi Corridor. Located west of the Yellow River, it is called the He (river) Xi (west) Corridor. It lies to the north of the Qilianshan Mountains in west Gansu Province.

In the southwestern part of China, the Himalayas with an elevation of 5,000 meters and the Hengduanshan Mountains with deep ravines and rapids extend along the border area; these mountains join the Qinghai-Tibet Plateau and the Yunnan-Guizhou Plateau in making the region the most inconvenient in terms of transportation in ancient times. Dozens of ethnic minority groups inhabit the region, making it the most heavily populated area by ethnic minority groups. In history, many of these ethnic minority groups moved northeastward to the Central Plains.

Such a geographical environment restrained the ancient ethnic groups from expanding outward; the terrain even formed impassable natural barriers in some places. Thus, various ethnic groups in remote border areas were forced to turn to inland areas, especially the Central Plains which boasted proper conditions suitable for human existence, such as mild climate, plenty of natural resources and flourishing culture, and enjoyed political stability and followed ethnic policies good for them. This helped promote the migratory trend.

(III) Source and Connotation of "China"

Many think our country is called China because the country was famous for its chinaware in the ancient times. There are also some who believe the word China evolved from the word Chin, the name of the ancient Chin (Qin) Dynasty (221 BC-207 BC). Chin (Qin), the first feudal dynasty in the Chinese history, was formidably powerful.

No matter how people argue, it is indisputable that the word China appeared some 3,000 years ago to refer to the area under the control of tribes in the middle reaches of the Yellow River. With the passing of time, the word expanded to mean mainly the Central Plains. The word China even found its way into the classic titled *Spring and Autumn* created some 2,500 years ago, but it was used to mean the capital of the country which exercised jurisdiction over areas other than the Central Plains, including the border areas where ethnic minorities lived.

In ancient times, people in East Asia described their countries with words such as "Under the Heaven," "Four Seas" and "Within the Four Seas." These terms existed alongside "China" and refer to areas including the minority regions. This is why ancient Chinese people created phrases such as "those who win popular support will eventually win all" and "all under the heaven belong to the same family" as well as "all men are brothers within the four seas." At that time, the emperors were deemed superior to all and "all under heaven."

In the Chinese history, all dynasties had dynastic titles to distinguish one rule from another, and these include "Great Han" (206 BC-220 AD), "Great Tang" (618-907), "Great Song" (960-1279), "Great Yuan" (1271-1368), "Great Ming" (1368-1644) and "Great Qing" (1644-1911). The Western countries once referred to China as the "Ming State" or "Qing State", and referred to the people as the "Tang people" or "Qing people."

This situation lasted until the Qing Dynasty was toppled in 1911 and the

Festive scene of Tian'anmen Square in Beijing.

Republic of China was founded in the following year. From then on, China was the name of the country.

Today, China is short for the People's Republic of China founded in 1949. Composed of 56 ethnic groups, it is administratively divided into the following:

The whole country is divided into provinces, autonomous regions and municipalities directly under the Central Government;

The provinces and autonomous regions are divided into autonomous prefectures, counties, autonomous counties, and cities;

The counties and autonomous counties are divided into townships, ethnic townships and towns.

At present, China has 34 administrative units at the provincial level, including 23 provinces, five autonomous regions, four municipalities directly under the Central Government, and two special administrative regions.

Beijing is the capital of the People's Republic of China.

Provincial-level Administrative Divisions of China

Name	Shortened Form	Administrative Center	Area (10,000 square km)	Population (10,000)
Beijing Municipality	Jing	Beijing	1.68	1,581
Tianjin Municipality	Jin	Tianjin	1.13	1,075
Hebei Province	Ji	Shijiazhuang	19.00	6,898
Shanxi Province	Jin	Taiyuan	15.60	3,375
Inner MongoliaAutonomous Region	Meng	Hohhot	119.75	2,397
Liaoning Province	Liao	Shenyang	14.57	4,271
Jilin Province	Ji	Changchun	18.70	2,723
Heilongjiang Province	Hei	Harbin	46.90	3,823
Shanghai Municipality	Hu	Shanghai	0.62	1,815
Jiangsu Province	Su	Nanjing	10.26	7,550
Zhejiang Province	Zhe	Hangzhou	10.18	4,980
Anhui Province	Wan	Hefei	13.90	6,110
Fujian Province	Min	Fuzhou	12.00	3,558
Jiangxi Province	Gan	Nanchang	16.66	4,339
Shandong Province	Lu	Jinan	15.30	9,309
Henan Province	Yu	Zhengzhou	16.70	9,392
Hubei Province	E	Wuhan	18.74	5,693
Hunan Province	Xiang	Changsha	21.00	6,342
Guangdong Province	Yue	Guangzhou	18.60	9,304
Guangxi Zhuang Autonomous Region	Gui	Nanning	23.77	4,719
Hainan Province	Qiong	Haikou	3.40	836
Chongqing Municipality	Yu	Chongqing	8.20	2,808
Sichuan Province	Chuan, Shu	Chengdu	48.40	8,169
Guizhou Province	Gui, Qian	Guiyang	17.00	3,757
Yunnan Province	Yun, Dian	Kunming	39.40	4,483
Tibet Autonomous Region	Zang	Lhasa	127.49	281
Shaanxi Province	Shaan	Xi'an	20.50	3,735
Gansu Province	Gan, Long	Lanzhou	45.00	2,606
Qinghai Province	Qing	Xining	72.00	548
Ningxia Hui Autonomous Region	Ning	Yinchuan	6.28	604
Xinjiang Uygur Autonomous Region	Xin	Urumqi	165.58	2,050
Hong Kong Special Administrative Region	Gang	Hong Kong	0.1104	694
Macao Special Administrative Region	Ao	Macao	0.0028	48
Taiwan Province	Tai	Taipei	3.60	2,277

Note: Population of various provincial-level administrative areas in China's hinterland comes from the sample survey at the end of 2006. Population of Hong Kong, Macao and Taiwan refers to the population of 2005.

(IV) Different Parts of China

China is blessed with a diverse topography and also exhibits an enormous range of climate across its various regions. These two factors not only shape the country's various modes of production, such as crop cultivation, livestock breeding, fish farming and hunting, but are furthermore responsible for the development of distinct life styles, customs and entertainments in different regions. They even influence the physical attributes and character of the people in various areas.

The Chinese are also usually spoken of as being either southern, northern, northeastern or northwestern people. In the past, the people's modes of production varied greatly between the south and north, between the east, west and central parts of China. Some of this diversity can still be found today. On the whole, speaking in terms of natural conditions, the south and east of China are particularly suitable for the development of agriculture, with relatively less emphasis on fishery, while the north and west of the country have tended to be more dependent on livestock breeding, with relatively less emphasis on crop cultivation.

The south and east China consist mainly of hills, plains, and lakes, as well as some big mountains, although these are relatively modest when compared with those of the more rugged north and west of the country. Taken as a whole, the area boats a moderate climate, with many hours of sunshine and plentiful rainfall. It is particularly suitable for the cultivation of rice, which can be harvested twice a year. Furthermore, its abundant rainfall enables efficient water

Ancient town of Xitang in Jiashang County, Zhejiang Province: Representative of the area south of the Yangtze River.

transportation and fishery; indeed the southeastern part of China has always been known as "The Land of Fish and Rice". Crisscrossed by many rivers, it has, throughout history, been more affluent than the north. People in this region enjoy a comfortable life, despite the threat of floods, and the consequence is a large population with densely peopled towns and cities. People here are noted for their mild and temperate disposition, combined with qualities of diligence and goodness, thus forming the distinguishing cultural feature of the inhabitants south of the Yangtze River.

The north and west of China, by contrast, is characterized by numerous mountain ranges and high plateaus. The climate is typically continental, being significantly colder than that of south China, the natural environment much harsher. Historically, the people here had always lived primarily on animal husbandry, combining this with growing wheat, corn and *kaoliang* (Chinese sorghum) in the places which were suitable for crop cultivation. Many rivers in north China are seasonal: in the summers, some of them become so shallow that only paddle boats can navigate them and most are never suitable for heavier shipping. In ancient times, animals were the only practical conveyance for passengers or freight throughout the entire region. Although the northwestern part of China boasts a vast area, it has a small population. Due to the tough natural conditions, famine was a constant danger in the past and, as a consequence, the people of this region are noted for their hardiness and courage in the face of adversity.

Hulun Buir Grassland in the Inner Mongolia Autonomous Region.

The differences inherent in the character of the people of north and south China finds full expression in the ancient literature of China. Consider, for example, this traditional folk song dating from the Southern Dynasties (420-589):

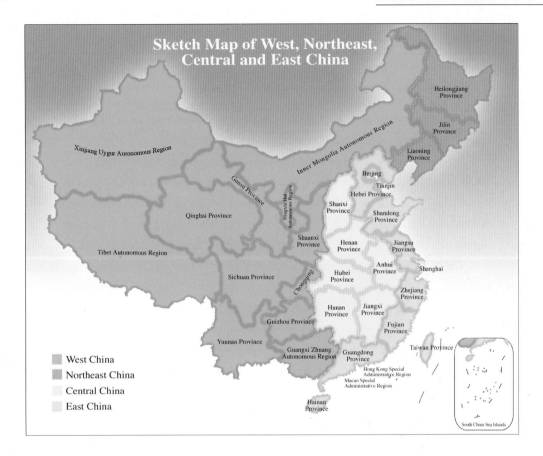

I am like the Northern Star

Whose position in the topmost hemisphere.

Is constant and unchanging

For thousands of years.

You are like the sun

Which rises in the east at dawn.

But in the evening

Disappears into the west.

The song delicately depicts a woman who is firmly loyal to her lover and blames her husband for his betrayal.

Here, too, is a folk song produced in the Northern Dynasties (386-581) in approximately the same period, which acts as a counterpart to the one quoted above:

Beneath the vault of sky, under the Yin Mountains,

Far and wide are spread the wide Chinese plains.

Beneath the heaven blue, over the vast country below,
A passing wind discloses the herds amid the grasses low.

It gives expression to a most characteristic and attractive scene of the vast, magnificent steppe where the nomadic peoples in north China still live.

In China today, to achieve a coordinated development among different regions, the State initiates and carries out various development programs, including pushing forward the development of the western regions, revitalizing the old industrial bases of northeast China, promoting central China's modernization, as well as encouraging the eastern region to lead the country in development.

West China includes Sichuan, Guizhou, Yunnan, Shaanxi, Gansu and Qinghai Provinces, Chongqing Municipality directly under the Central Government, as well as the Tibet, Ningxia Hui, Xinjiang Uygur, Inner Mongolia and Guangxi Zhuang Autonomous Regions. It covers 6.85 million square km, making up 71 percent of the total area of China. Its 2004 population was 371.27 million, accounting for 28.6 percent of the national total population. Its GDP hit 2,758.5 billion Yuan, or 16.9 percent of the national total.

Northeast China encompasses Liaoning, Jilin and Helongjiang Provinces. It covers an area of 790,000 square km, or 8.2 percent of the country's total. The region had a population of 107.43 million, or 8.3 percent of China"s total, in 2004. Its GDP was 1,513.39 billion Yuan, accounting for 9.3 percent of the national total.

Central China comprises Shanxi, Henan, Hubei, Hunan, Anhui and Jiangxi Provinces, covering 1.027 million square km, or 10.7 percent of the national total area. In 2004, it had a population of 365 million, accounting for 28.1 percent of China's total. Its GDP reached 3,208.8 billion Yuan, accounting for 19.7 percent of the national total.

With an area of 913,000 square km, or 9.5 percent of the national total, east China is composed of Hebei, Shandong, Jiangsu, Zhejiang, Fujian, Guangdong and Hainan Provinces, as well as Beijing, Tianjin and Shanghai Municipalities directly under the Central Government. It had a population of 450.34 million in 2004, or 34.6 percent of the population in China. Its GDP was 8,843.3 billion Yuan, making up 54.2 percent of China's total.

(V) Origin of the Chinese

There is no evidence to show that Chinese ancestors migrated to China from elsewhere.

In the 1960s, *Homo erectus Yuanmouensis* remains, dating back 1.7 million years, were found in Yuanmou County of Yunnan Province in southwest China. Two incisors from the upper jaw of the *Yuanmouensis* were discovered then. Animal bones with traces of cuts, and the relics of possible use of fire were also unearthed. Also in the 1960s, the remains of *Homo erectus Lantianensis*, which lived about 800,000 years to 600,000 years ago, were found in Lantian, Shaanxi Province in central western China.

Another major study about ancient Chinese started in 1927, when the remains of *Homo erectus Pekinensis* (Peking Man), which lived between 500,000 and 200,000 years ago, were found in the Longgushan (Dragon Bone) Hill at Zhoukoudian, about 50 km southwest of Beijing. Years of systematic excavation of the site produced six almost complete skulls, as well as fragments of skulls, pieces of femur, teeth, and so on. With narrow teeth and jaw bone, and

Monument to the 30th Anniversary of the Discovery of Yuanmouensis.

Restored image of Peking Man.

Restored image of Cave Man.

a larger skull, Peking Man is more similar to that of modern man in terms of its skeletal morphology, such as bone size, shape, proportion and muscle attachment points. With a height of about 156 cm, Peking man has shovel-shaped incisors characteristic of the Mongoloid race. Besides Peking Man fossils, some 100,000 pieces of stone artifacts, rock fragments and large amounts of mammal fossils were also found at the site. They are evidences showing Peking Man could do simple work with stone tools. Signs of fire found in the Peking Man Cave tell the importance of fire in the life of the Peking Man. Due to low productivity and poor living conditions, life spans were very short. In 1937, Japan launched a war of aggression against China, and unfortunately the Peking Man skulls were lost.

Early *Homo* sapiens existed between 200,000 and 100,000 years ago. The human fossils from this period include the Maba Man found in Qujiang in Guangdong Province in south China, the Changyang Man found in Changyang of Hubei Province in central south China, and the Dingcun Man found in Xiangfen in Shanxi Province in north China. From the Dingcun site, some 2,000 pieces of stone artifacts were found, the most representative being stone cores and triangular pyramid shaped tools, which were technologically more advanced than that of Peking Man.

Human fossils and relics of activities of later *Homo* sapiens, who lived 100,000 to 10,000 years ago, were found in southwest, northwest and north China. The Upper Cave Man was found in the early 1930s in the Upper Cave of the Longgushan

Hill at Zhoukoudian, where the Peking Man was found. The Upper Cave Man lived 18,000 years ago, and in physical form was basically devoid of ape-like characteristics, and basically the same as modern people. Stone artifacts produced were quite delicate, and bone needles were used for decoration and repair, proving that drilling, grinding, and other technologies had been mastered to meet their own aesthetic need. Fish and other animal bone fossils unearthed prove that the Upper Cave Man's life involved fishing, hunting and gathering.

(VI) Primitive Chinese Civilization

After more than 1 million years of evolution, humans left the caves and moved to settle down in the plains and bottomland some 8,000-5,000 years ago. They began living on farming. And Chinese civilization entered its primitive period.

Water is the origin of life, and also the source of civilization. When the major life-sustaining activities of humans evolved from fishing and gathering into farming, water played an even more important role in their lives. The Tigris River and the Euphrates River were major sources of irrigation for the Mesopotamian civilization, the Nile River for ancient Egyptian civilization, the Indus River for ancient Indian civilization, and the Aegean Sea for ancient Hellenic civilization, and similarly Chinese civilization was nourished by two rivers—the Yellow River and the Yangtze River.

The Yellow River is the second longest river in China. It runs through north

Lanzhou of Gansu Province by the Yellow River.

China, flowing through nine provinces and autonomous regions and covering a drainage area of 750,000 square km. Known as the birth place of Chinese civilization, the Yellow River is regarded as the Mother River in China and it contains many cultural relics throughout its drainage area. These sites were named according to the cultures they represented, including the Yangshao Culture (in Henan Province), Qijia Culture (in Gansu Province), Dawenkou Culture (in Shandong Province) and Longshan Culture (in Shandong Province).

The Yangtze River is the longest river in China, covering a drainage area of more than 1.8 million square km, nearly one-fifth of the Chinese territory. Many cultural sites are found in its middle and lower reaches, and most famous ones include the Hemudu Culture and Liangzhu Culture (in Zhejiang Province), and Qingliangang Culture (in Jiangsu Province) . The Hongshan Culture was discovered in the Liaohe River Valley in northeast China. All these sites indicate that ancient Chinese people made constant progress not only in production and livelihood, but also in enlarged area of their activities.

Pottery basin bearing patterns including human face and double fish lines of the Yanshao Culture, unearthed from the Banpo Village in Xi'an of Shaanxi Province.

The farming economy was representative of the primitive Chinese civilization. A primitive farming civilization is the main feature of all culture relics mentioned above. At that time, people lived on farming, and they also engaged in livestock breeding, fishing, hunting and gathering. During the period of Yangshao Culture (5,000-6,000 years ago), maize was the main crop. From the ancient site of Banpo Village of this period, some 100 kg of maize were found in a pit. From the Dawenkou Culture site, tracing back to between 4,300 BC and 2,500 BC, one cubic meter of maize was discovered. Rice was found from a relic site of the Hemudu Culture (5,000-3,300 years ago). All these discoveries show

Jade Pig Partly in the Shape of a Dragon of the Hongshan Culture, some 5,000 years ago, discovered from Jianping of Liaoning Province.

much progress made in farming tools, especially stone implements.

During the period, handicrafts saw enormous progress. The stone implements found from the relic sites were more delicate and included stone axes, stone shovels, stone knives, and stone sickles.

There was also pottery created to meet the need of daily life. Some pottery excavated from sites of these periods bear symbols which represented certain meanings to their producers. As they were similar to the later ancient Chinese characters carved on tortoise shells or animal bones, these symbols are considered to be the embryonic form of the Chinese characters.

The development of agricultural civilization made it possible for the ancient people to put down roots and form communities. This created opportunities for marriage between different groups. Then some related groups united to form a phratry, close phratries formed a tribe, and friendly tribes made up a tribal union. Emperor Yandi and Emperor Huangdi in Chinese mythology were leaders of such tribes or tribal unions. They organized an army and fought to protect their territory and their survival. They established a rudimentary organizational system necessary to administrate activities. Some of these tribes and tribal unions grew in strength and formed the rudiments of states in China.

II. UNIFICATION OF CHINA IN HISTORY

Xia (21st Century B C-16th Century BC), Shang (16th Century BC-11th Century BC), Zhou (770 BC-221 BC)··· Qin (221 BC -207 BC), Han (206 BC -220 AD)··· Wei (220-265), Jin (265-420)··· Sui (581-618), Tang (618-907)....Song (960-1279), Liao (916-1125), Jin (1115-1234), Yuan (1271-1368), Ming (1368-1644), and Qing (1644-1911) are all ancient dynasties of China. For nearly 4,000 years, China had been in a period of dynastic rule, and the situation lasted until in the early 20th century when a modern State was founded in China.

Though China suffered from divisions, the end result was unification which features the flourishing of the culture of the Central Plains. The change in dynasties did not result in the change in the social system but, instead, led to continued tradition of inheritance and maintained the integrity of Chinese culture. In the long historical development of Chinese culture it was inherited and carried forward continuously. In spite of foreign invasion, it was never replaced by other cultures. The ancient history of China is mainly different from the histories of other countries in its length, continuity and unification.

(I) Continuity of Chinese History

"Since Pan Gu separated heaven and earth....Since the Three Sovereigns (Fuxi, Suiren and Shennong) and Five Emperors (Huangdi, Zhuangxu, Di Ku, Tang Rao and Yu Shun)" is a phrase much heard in China not only in the past but also today. It shows the continuity of Chinese history from antiquity to the present.

Pan Gu's story is a Chinese version of Genesis from China's remote antiquity. It indicates ancient people's imagination and understanding of the origin of heaven and earth. Legend has it that in ancient times, the universe remained in chaos until one day, a god named Pan Gu, cracked the darkness with a big ax. Light and clear things rose to become heaven and heavy and turbid things fell down to become the earth. Thereafter, the sky rose higher and higher and the earth became denser. To prevent them from combining again, Pan Gu held up the sky with his hands and stood on the earth. This condition lasted for 18,000 years until the sky and earth eventually came into being. Unfortunately, Pan Gu exhausted all his energy and died.

As recorded in the *Bible*, it is God who created Adam and Eve. China's legend says Nu Wa is the mother of all Chinese. After Pan Gu separated the sky and the earth, the earth was desolate and lifeless. Nu Wa, a goddess with a woman's head and serpent's body, made a clay baby beside a clear pool. Finally, the clay baby turned into a lively human being. She continued to make many men and women. In order to maintain the proliferation of the human species, Nu Wa created marriage between men and women to give birth to new generations.

The Three Sovereigns (Fuxi, Suiren and Shennong) and Five Emperors (Huangdi, Zhuangxu, Di Ku, Tang Rao and Yu Shun) were deemed as the ancestors of the Chinese people and also the creators of Chinese civilization. The legend of the ancient times is thought to have originated in the clan tribe period. It is said that about 10,000 years ago, a tribe, which originated in the Kunlunshan Mountains in west China, called Suiren-shi, moved to the Hexi Corridor of the Qilianshan Mountians (present-day Gansu Province). There they invented a method of making

fire by drilling dry wood. Their invention enabled human beings to cook foods, which contributed to disease reduction, and the enhanced ability to stand coldness. A new era, called the era of the Suiren, began, and Suiren-shi was respectfully addressed as the Heavenly Emperor by later generations.

The Suiren-shi era was replaced by the Fuxi-shi era about 10,000 to 7,000 years ago. Fuxi issued an improved calendar and began to raise the livestock and cultivate crops; he also invented written characters. Fuxi was thus widely respected by all the clans and became their leader. He was

Nu Wa and Fuxi

addressed as the Human Sovereign. Legend says, in this period, a hole was torn in Heaven, resulting in disasters such as floods, fires and so forth, which threatened the existence of human beings. To save the people, Nu Wa melted five colored stones to patch the sky. People lived peacefully afterwards. This is the story of *Nu Wa Patching Heaven,* which is so well known in China's history.

In the mythology of ancient China, after the Fuxi era, some influential tribal unions came into being 7,000 to 6,000 years ago, including the tribes of Emperor Yandi, Emperor Huangdi, and the Chiyou tribe. Emperor Yandi's tribe, surnamed Jiang, lived in the Jiangshui River Valley (the eastern part of present Shaanxi Province). According to historical record, Emperor Yandi was Shennong, who invented farming and created medicine. He taught the people how to use farm tools. Legend has it that he tasted all kinds of herbs to identify medical herbs and taught people how to cure diseases. He was regarded as the Emperor of Farming for his familiarity with the productive use of land and farming skills. As land is the base of

Ceremony held on the ninth day of the ninth lunar month to pay sacrifices to Emperor Huangdi.

farming, he was also regarded as the Emperor of Land, and the creator of the agricultural culture of China. Emperor Huangdi's tribe lived in the Jishui River Valley. Surnamed Ji, they were also called Xuanyuan-shi and Youxiong-shi. Many talented people were in Emperor Huangdi's tribe. They invented many things, including sericiculture, vessels and vehicles, texts,temperament, medical science, mathematics. The Chiyou tribe, also called Jiuli tribe, lived in area between the Yangtze River and the Huaishui River. Of all the tribal unions, the tribes of Emperor Yandi and Emperor Huangdi held the leading position. Their inventions exerted great impact on

Sculpture of Da Yu the Great Subdued the Flood in the Yuexiu Park in Guangzhou of Guangdong Province.

later generations; they were both regarded as joint ancestors of the Han Chinese, who called themselves "descendants of Emperor Yandi and Emperor Huangdi". Even now, the Chinese people pay homage to the Emperor Huangdi Mausoleum in Shaanx Province every spring.

About 4,000 years ago, floods happened frequently and endangered the existence of human beings. A story titled *Yu the Great Subdued the Flood*, which spread among the Chinese, occurred in this historical period. It is said that, at that time, rain poured down and floods occurred everywhere. People suffered greatly from the disasters and many of them died of starvation. A leader of a tribe from the middle reaches of the Yellow River, whose name was Gun, was ordered by the emperor to control the flood. Unfortunately, he failed in this task and was killed by Emperor Shundi. His son, called Yu, was ordered by the emperor to complete the task. Having learned from his father's lessons and experiences, Yu led people to dig ditches and dredge rivers before diverting the floodwater into the sea, other than blocking them up. He succeeded in harnessing the flood, and created advantages for farming. Yu was highly praised by later generations because during his more than 10 years of struggle with the floods, he didn't visit to his home even when he passed his house.

According to historical documents, the demise of the era of Yao, Shun and Yu happened in this period. When he was old, Yao, as the leader of the tribal union, chose Shun as his successor and transferred his power to Shun, with the permission of a meeting of all tribe leaders. Later, Shun handed over leadership to Yu. However, when Yu came to power he was actually a monarch of a dynasty, which was titled Xia.

(II) The Formation of the Ancient Country

The Xia (2070 BC-1600 BC), Shang (1600 BC-1046 BC) and Zhou Dynasties (1046 BC-256 BC) were the early regimes of ancient China.

The Xia Dynasty (2070 BC-1600 BC) is very important in Chinese history because its establishment marks the formal beginning of Chinese civilization. From then on, the ensuing dynasties followed the Xia practice of all emperors coming from the same family.

The Xia was an ancient tribe that inhabited the middle and lower reaches of the Yellow River. They expanded their territory after Da Yu (Yu the Great) came to power. The central area of the Xia kingdom was the modern-day western part of Henan Province and the southern part of Shanxi Province. The Xia conquered other clans and tribes and made them slaves. After the death of Da Yu (Yu the Great), his son came to power and created the system of hereditary rule which replaced the original abdication system. This would greatly influence China's history. Jie, the last emperor of Xia, led a licentious life. He once compared himself to the sun, claiming that as the sun never dies he and his kingdom would never die. Later, Tang, the leader of an eastern Shang tribe led his troops to defeat Jie, ending the Xia Dynasty.

The Shang Dynasty (1600 BC-1046 BC) was the second regime in China's history. The Shang tribe had long inhabited the lower reaches of the Yellow River. When Xia established its state, Shang created a powerful alliance with other tribes. Tang,

Four-Goat Zun bronze container of the Shang Dynasty (1600 BC-1046 BC).

Inscriptions unearthed from Anyang, totalling some 15,000 pieces of bones and tortoise shells, are the earliest test found in China.

the leader of the Shang, defeated the Xia and established the Shang Dynasty. The Shang Dynasty continued to expand its territory, and the central area stretched from the modern-day areas of northeast Henan Province to southwest Shandong Province and south Hebei Province. Compared to the Xia Dynasty, the Shang Dynasty had more well-developed administrative organs, military forces, criminal laws and prisons, which combined to ensure a brutal system of slavery. The emperor of the Shang had total power.

During the Shang Dynasty, much headway was made in bronze smelting techniques. This made it possible for bronze wares to be widely used in common people's daily life. Bronze tripods, callad Ding in Chinese, include round ones with three legs and square ones with four legs. They wrer symbol of power and wealthy. The Shang capital moved several times until eventually Shang Emperor Pan'gen moved it to Yin (area close to present-day Anyang, Henan Province). Thus, "Yinshang" was widely used in ancient documents to refer to the Shang Dynasty. In the latter period of the Shang Dynasty, several years of war decreased the power of the Shang, and the Zhou tribe which had prepared for many years took advantage and conquered the Shang.

The great progress made during the Shang Dynasty was the vast quantities of inscriptions on bones or tortoise shells. These inscriptions on bones or tortoise shells are among China's oldest written characters. This is of incomparable sig-

Dayuding Tripod and inscriptions on it of the Western Zhou Dynasty (1040 BC-771 BC).

nificance because it marks the beginning of written records of China's history. This was a great achievement of one of mankind's major civilizations. It is still the common fortune enjoyed by the culture circle of Han-character in Eastern Asia at large.

The Zhou tribes, who had been in existence as long as the Xia and Shang tribes, established a new regime called Zhou after defeating the Shang, and set up a feudal lord system. In China's history, Zhou is divided into two periods: the Western Zhou Dynasty (1046 BC -771 BC) and Eastern Zhou Dynasty (770 BC -221 BC). The Western Zhou

Jade "cong" with a round hole in the center of the Western zhou Dynasty (1046 BC-771 BC).

established its capital in Haojing (present-day Xi'an, Shannxi Province). The emperor of the Zhou was not only the leader of the central government but also the governor of dukes and princes. Zhou adopted the system of "Granting Lands to Officials". The area around the capital was given to "Wangji", meaning land governed directly by royal family members. Besides the Wangji, vast areas of land were granted to royal family members, officials and tribal leaders. Based on these lands, various kingdoms were established. At the beginning, these kingdoms maintained a close relationship with the central government. In the Zhou Dynasty, the State possessed all the land and all land transactions were prohibited. Following the "System of the Jing Land", land was separated into several squares by irrigation ditches and roads, resembling the Han Chinese character "井" (Jing). It can still be seen in the plains of China today. Progress was made in agriculture, the handicraft industry, and business during the Western Zhou Dynasty. Its territory stretched to the eastern part of today's Gansu Province in the west, seashore in the east, the Huaishui River Valley in the south and northern Hebei Province and southwest Liaoning Province in the north.

In 770 BC, the imperial court of the Zhou Dynasty was divided by internal conflict, and the capital was moved to Luoyi (today's Luoyang, Henan Province). This marked the end of the Western Zhou Dynasty and the establishment of the Eastern Zhou Dynasty. As Luoyi was located to the east of Haojing, the former capital of Zhou, the dynasty was called Eastern Zhou, and the former dynasty with its capital in Haojing was called Western Zhou. The Eastern Zhou Dynasty is divided into two parts: the Spring and Autumn Period (770 BC-476 BC) and the Warring States Period (475 BC-221 BC). Since the events which happened from 770 BC-476 BC were all recorded in the *Spring and Autumn*, an historical book, it is called the Spring and Autumn Period. The following years saw continuous battles between kingdoms, so people called it the Warring States Period. At that time, various kings were estranged from the royal family and the Zhou Dynasty's power began to decline. These kings ruled over their respective lands and savage conflict was commonplace. Kings rose to hegemony including "Five Hegemonies in the Spring and Autumn Period" and "Seven Powerful States in the Warring States Period". This was a period of turmoil in China's history but also a period witnessing the emergence of various thoughts and culture. Numerous ideologists, politicians, litterateurs and militarists, including Confucius, Lao Tzu, Mozi, Mencius, Xun Zi, Zhuangzi, Sun Tzu and Qu Yuan, all emerged at that time. Various schools of thoughts such as Confucianism, Taoism and Legalists were all shaped at that time. All these theories exerted great influence on the nation.

The situation of separate States did not end until the State of Qin united the whole country and established the Qin Dynasty (221 BC-206 BC).

(III) The First Unification and Separation of China

The Qin and Han Dynasties (221 BC - 220 AD) witnessed the first unification and prosperity in China's history, exerting great and deep influence on later generations.

After the Han Dynasty (206 BC-220 AD), the formerly centralized and unified country split into many states in a period of close to 400 years.

The Qin Dynasty (221 BC-207 BC) was the first dynasty to establish the emperor as the ruler of the entire country. The first emperor Ying Zheng took the throne at the age of 13 years old. He adopted the policy of "making the nation affluent and strengthening military forces" and implemented the strategy of preventing alliances between different states in order to defeat them one by one. In 221 BC or the 26th year of his reign, he unified China and established Xianyang (in Shannxi Province today) as the capital.

The Qin Dynasty established a relatively complete central government. It replaced the system of "granting titles to various dukes" with the "prefecture-county system". China was then administratively divided into 41 prefectures governed by prefects, each exercizing jurisdiction over counties, During this period, the currency, weights and measurements, vehicle tracks and written characters were all standardized. The Qin Dynasty lasted only

Sculpture of Emperor Qin Shihuang of the Qin Dynasty (221 BC-207 BC) and the Mausoleum of Emperor Qin Shihuang in Lingtong of Shaanxi Province.

15 years, but laid a solid foundation for the unification of China's politics, economy and culture. The Qin's tyranny destined it to a short reign. The Qin's rule came to the end shortly after the first emperor's death. His son ascended the throne but was quickly overthrown by a peasants' uprising, leading to the founding of the Han Dynasty (206 BC- 220AD).

Qin Emperor Ying Zheng is regarded as the greatest emperor in China's history for his contribution to China. He lifted China out of the "Warring States Period" and unified all the ethnic groups to form a unified country. However, he was an arrogant and violent emperor who granted himself the title of "Huangdi (meaning emperor)" implying his virtue and merit had surpassed "the three Huang (emperors) and five Di (kings) in ancient China". He hoped his offspring would govern China forever. During his 12-year reign, he levied heavy taxes, imposed serious punishment, and built many extremely luxurious palaces. He also engaged in wars for several years. He placed a heavy burden on people and life was harsh. He burnt books which were opposed to the Qin and buried scholars alive who spoke against the Qin. This was the famous event knows as "burning books and burying Confucian scholars alive" in China's history. He recruited tens of thousands people to build the 5,000-km-long Great Wall and built the marvelous Mausoleum of Emperor Qin Shihuang. The famous Terracotta Warriors and Horses are part of it.

Emperor Wudi Liu Xiu of the Eastern Han Dynasty (25-220).

The Han Dynasty was the next monarchy after the Qin Dynasty. It was controlled by the Liu family throughout its history. The Han Dynasty was divided into the Western Han Dynasty (206 BC-25 AD) and Eastern Han Dynasty (25-220). Liu Bang, the founder of the Western Han Dynasty, reestablished the regime and moved its capital to Chang'an (Xi'an, Shannxi Province today) in 25. The Western Han Dynasty followed the Qin policy of strengthening centralized power. Drawing lessons from the failure of the Qin Dynasty, it introduced the policy of "developing economy and increasing population". At the beginning of the Han Dynasty, many soldiers were allowed to return home, and their taxes were reduced or abolished. Efforts were also made to support agriculture and discourage businesses. This period saw a stable society and fast economic development. Peace and prosperity appeared for the first time in China's history.

In the later period of the Western Han Dynasty, social conflicts intensified, and the peasants revolted repeatedly. Other royal family members coveted the imperial power and tried to usurp the throne, which resulted in a war. Finally Liu Xiu, a member of the royal family, reestablished the regime of the Family Liu as the Eastern Han Dynasty with its capital in Luoyang (present-day Luoyang of Henan Province). At the end of the Eastern Han Dynasty, the famous Huangjin (Yellow Turbans) Uprising broke out. Taking advantage of this, various warlords set up separatist regimes and the Eastern Han Dynasty only existed in name. Much headway was made in foreign relations during the Eastern Han Dynasty. In 57, Japan sent an envoy to China, marking the beginning of the Sino-Japanese relationship. Ban Chao, a famous general of the Han Dynasty, visited the Western Regions (area west of Yumenguan of Gansu Province, including Xinjiang and Central Asia).

Liu Bang, the first emperor of the Han Dynasty, was born to a common family and used to be a low official of the Qin Dynasty. He had great talent and bold vision and employed all kinds of talents despite their family or educational backgrounds. The Han Dynasty was totally different from the previous dynasties in that the emperor came from the ordinary family and his generals and ministers also rose up from the grass-roots level. The ensuing dynasties followed suit.

In the latter period of the Eastern Han Dynasty, various warlords were locked in infighting. In the end, there were three kingdoms left: Wei, Shu and Wu. Cao Cao, a famous politician who had built a solid foundation for the Kingdom of Wei, unified north China. In 220, Cao Pi, son of Cao Cao, forced the last emperor of the Eastern Han Dynasty (Emperor Han Xiandi) to abdicate. He came to power, named the Kingdom Wei and established a capital in Luoyang (present-day Luoyang of Henan Province). Liu Bei, espousing the slogan of "Restoration of Han Dynasty" established the Han Kingdom in 221 in Chengdu of Sichuan Province. As Sichuan is called "Shu"for short, Liu Bei's Han Kingdom is often referred to as Shu-han in history. Zhuge Liang, the famous militarist, was the Primer Minister of the Kingdom of Shu. In 229, Sun Quan, the representative of southeast China, established the Kingdom of Wu with its capital in Jianye (present-day Nanjing of Jiangsu Province).

After the Three Kingdoms, there were the Western Jin Dynasty (280-316) and Eastern Jin Dynasty (317-420). They are called "Jin" because their emperors had the same family name — Sima. The difference is their choice of capital: the Western Jin's capital was in Luoyang, and the Eastern Jin's capital was in Jiankang. The Western Jin won a war against the Wu in 280, ending 90 years of turbulence since the end of the Eastern Han Dynasty, and China was unified. Before long, howeverr, China was plunged into separation once again during the Eastern Jin Dynasty.

(IV) The Chinese Empire Reunified and Split Again

The period of the Sui and Tang Dynasties (581-907) saw the second reunification in ancient Chinese history. China experienced prosperity again and unprecedented power.

The Sui Dynasty (581-618) ended centuries of division, and achieved the reunification and the establishment of the centralized state. The first Emperor of the Sui, Yang Jian, had been an important court minister of the last regime of the Northern Zhou Dynasty (557-581), In 581, Yang Jian replaced the Northern Zhou with the Sui. Thus the Sui Dynasty was founded, with Chang'an (present-day Xi'an of Shaanxi Province) as the capital. After the north was well consolidated, the Sui Court defeated the last of the Southern Dynasties, Chen.

The Sui Dynasty lasted less than 30 years, only some 10 years longer than the Qin Dynasty (221 BC-207 BC). The Sui Dynasty was often compared to the Qin Dynasty, which had a far reaching influence to the Han Dynasty (206 BC-220 AD), there would be no the Tang Dynasty (618-907) without the Sui. The Sui ended a long period of

Hanzhou Section of the Beijing-Hanzhou Grand Canal.

division, laying an important foundation for the future development of the Tang Dynasty. The Sui period saw great pioneering undertakings unparalleled in history: the imperial civil examination system, which made it possible for ordinary scholars to become officials; the digging of the Grand Canal, which has always been the main artery in the nation's transportation between southern and northern areas. The decline of the Sui Dynasty started from the second monarch, Emperor Sui Yangdi, who was a typical tyrant. Emperor Sui Yangdi led a luxurious and corrupt life. He employed over

Sketch Map of Territory of the Tang Dynasty (618-907).

1 million laborers to build irrigation ditches; some half of them died within 10 days. As a result, the regime of the Sui Dynasty became rather unstable, rebellions broke out frequently, and the national power declined, and finally collapsed.

Li Yuan, a vassal in the Sui Court, seized the opportunity to take control during the rebellions at the end of the Sui, proclaimed himself emperor and changed the state title into Tang, still with Chang'an as the capital city. The nation thus was unified. As one of the longest dynasties, the Tang Dynasty (618-907) lasted 289 years. The Tang Dynasty was an unparalleled powerful and prosperous period in China's history. This historic period is divided into the early Tang, having a powerful national strength and cultural prosperity, and the later Tang, featuring social unrest and people's declining livelihood.

During the Tang Dynasty, Buddhism, Taoism and Islam coexisted. Many great poets and writers emerged, such as Li Bai, Du Fu and Bai Juyi. There were new developments in the aspects of astronomy, calendar, medical treatment and construction. During the period, the business road was restored, and envoys from over 40 countries came to paid visit to the capital city of Chang'an. China was the most powerful and prosperous country in the world. Such a prosperous scene lasted until in 755 when two military generals of the Tang Dynasty, An Lushan and Shi Siming, launched a rebellion. Although it was put down the central authority weakened increasingly from then on. A new local separatism emerged. The internal struggle for power grew. The national control was gradually lost. In the later Tang Dynasty, most parts of China saw raging peasants rebellion. The peasants seized the opportunity to fight. In 907, the Tang was replaced by the Later Liang Dynasty (907-923).

Emperor Taizong, Li Shimin, was the second son of Emperor Gaozu, Li Yuan. He is considered to be one of the greatest Chinese emperors. Li Shimin assisted his father in unifying China in about four years. Li Shimin wasn't the Crown Prince. He launched a palace coup and killed his brother to seize the Crown Prince position. The emperor was forced to abdicate, and Li Shimin became Emperor Taizong. He rethought the lessons of Sui's decline, listened to opinions and proposals from all sides, used talented people, reduced the tax burden on people and encouraged and developed production. He successfully strengthened the relationship between the Han and minority ethnic groups. This era of peace and prosperity is called the Prosperity of Zhenguan in history. This peaceful time reached a summit during the reign of Emperor Xuanzong, who was Taizong's successor. That period is called the Heyday of Kaiyuan in history. Emperor Taizong's capacity for recognizing a man's ability, regardless of his background, was demonstrated by appointments he made. People who had been opposed to him even got positions. Taizong practiced the art of control. He looked at the people as water and the government a vessel, saying the water can both float and capsize a vessel.

After the Tang Dynasty came to an end, China stepped again into more than 50 years of division. The Five Dynasties of the Latter Liang, the Latter Tang, the Latter Jin, the Latter Han and the Latter Zhou emerged in the north. The Five Dynasties lasted for only 53 years, from 907 to 960. At the same time, 10 states were built in the south and some places in the north. They were called the Ten States, which lasted for 88 years, from 891 to 979. Thus the Period of the Five Dynasties and Ten States

Life in Bianjing (present-day Kaifeng of Henan Province), then the national capital, as described in the "Riverside Scene at Qingming Festival", masterpiece of Zhang Zeduan of the Northern Song Dynasty (960-1127).

was named by China's historians.

The Song Dynasty (960-1279) succeeded the Five Dynasties and Ten Kingdoms. Zhao Kuangyin, through a mutiny, seized imperial power in 960. He changed the state title into Song, and named Bianjing (today Kaifeng of Henan Province) as the capital. This period was known as the Northern Song Dynasty (960-1127) in history. In 1127, as the regime established in Bianjing was destroyed by the Jin Dynasty (1115 - 1234), they had to re-establish political power in Lin'an (now Hangzhou of Zhejiang Province) in the south. This period was known as the Southern Song Dynasty (1127-1279) in history. In the early period of the Northern Song Dynasty, southern China had been basically reunified, and most parts of the country were under the control of the Song.

Emperor Taizu of the Song Dynasty, Zhao Kuangyin, was originally senior officer of the imperial guards in the Later Zhou Dynasty (951-960). He seized political power by launching a mutiny. To avoid the recurrence of his story, he decided to weaken the power of the generals. At a banquet he hosted to entertain the generals who had followed him for many years, and had contributed a lot to the establishment of his reign, he lamented: "I will never forget that it is you who brought me today. But do you know that the emperor is not happier than a military governor?" The generals felt surprised and asked why. He replied: "Who does not want to be the emperor?" The generals said: "Your Majesty, why did you say so?

Now who will do that?" The emperor calmly said: "May it be right. Even if you don't think so, there is no guarantee that your subordinates will not covet the wealth." The generals were scared and said quickly: "In our ignorance we implore the guidance of Your Majesty to give us a way out." He said, "You'd better relinquish the leadership of the military, and buy more fertile farmland and big houses to enjoy yourselves. There isn't any problem between us. Let's live in peace. Is it all right?" The next day, the generals handed in letters saying they decided to resign because of illness. He immediately agreed, and rewarded them large amounts of money. This is the famous story in China's history.

With a prosperous economy, radiant arts, education and culture, developed science and technology and liberal governing, the Song Dynasty was one of the best periods in Chinese history, and also considered as another period of Renaissance and economic revolution by Western scholars. There were more than 50 countries with trade relations with China in the Song Dynasty.

(V) The Third Reunification of the Chinese Nation

When the Yuan Dynasty (1271-1368) succeeded the Song Dynasty, China entered its third reunification period. During the Yuan, Ming (1368-1644) and Qing (1644-1911) Dynasties, China enjoyed prosperity, but it went into its decline in the late 18th and early 19th centuries.

The Yuan Dynasty is the first Central Government in Chinese history established nationwide by an ethnic minority. In the 11th century, the Mongolian tribes emerged and grew in strength in the Mongolia steppes in north China. In 1204, Temuchin, born into an aristocratic family, reunified the Mongolian steppes. In 1206 he was formally made ruler of Greater Mongolia, and he adopted the name of Genghis Khan, and established the Mongol Khanate. In the early stage of the Mongol Khanate, Genghis Khan attacked Central Asia and Europe many times. Its territory constantly expanded, the Western Xia (1038-1227), Jin (1115-1234) and Tubo (ancient Tibetan government in China) were defeated consequently. In 1271, Kublai, a grandson of Genghis Khan, adopted a dynastic title of Da Yuan in place of the Mongol, and made Dadu (today's Beijing) the capital. He respected Genghis Khan as Emperor Taizu, and named himself Emperor Shizu. Since that time Beijing would become the capital of the Yuan, Ming and Qing Dynasties. China's political center was transferred from south to north. In 1279, the Southern Song Dynasty was destroyed by the Yuan. China

Ruins of the Dadu, capital of Yuan.

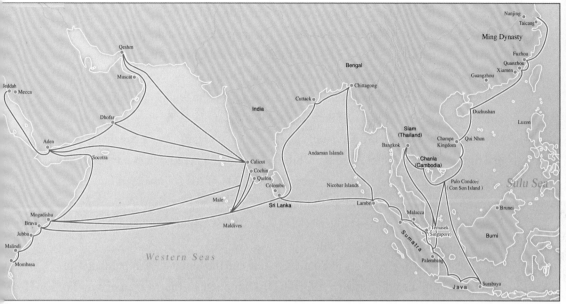

Route Map of Zheng He's Voyages to the Western Seas.

also achieved the third unification.

The Mandate of Heaven now shifted to Zhu Yuanzhang, historically known as Emperor Taizu of the Ming Dynasty (1368-1644). He was a peasant leader who became eminent during the rebellions. After eliminating his rivals, Zhu Yuanzhang became the emperor in 1367, and established the state title Ming in 1368. The capital city first was in Yingtianfu (present-day present-day Nanjing in Jiangsu Province) and later in Beiping (now Beijing), which was renamed from Dadu. In 1421, Ming Dynasty Emperor Chengzu, Zhu Di, moved the capital from Nanjing to Beijing, in order to facilitate the consolidation of the northern border, and further control the northeastern region. During the Ming, the Great Wall in the north was built, repaired and consolidated, and became a major barrier for foreign invasion. Since the Yuan Dynasty, Beijing had experienced repeated expansion. The Palace museum was built in this period. Meanwhile, emperors who did not forget to build his palaces used after death. The Ming Tombs located in the northern part of Beijing were built in this period.

Emperor Taizu of the Ming Dynasty, Zhu Yuanzhang, was born poor. He used to be a beggar and a Buddhist monk when he was young. He was courageous, resourceful and was able to get followers to fight the Mongols. So he soon became a peasant rebel leader. He proposed "to construct high walls, to store grain everywhere, and to be the king gradually". He managed to found a powerful army, by which he removed all obstacles and finally reunited China. After becoming the emperor of Ming, he formulated new laws, adopted a new system of government, and reformed the administrative agencies to strengthen the feudal centralization. In order to strengthen the supervision and control of his subjects, he also set up special officials, such as the Patrol Division and the Imperial Guard. Zhu Yuanzhang was one of the cruelest emperors in the Chinese history. To avoid others coveting the reign of his family Zhu, he killed more than 30,000 of his followers at one time, including the veteran generals who had made great contribution. According to historical records, he looked ugly. Because some honest painters could not paint him as a male beauty, they were killed.

Zheng He's long voyages to Southeast Asia and the Indian Ocean produced an important impact on world navigation. It happened in the Ming period. To strengthen the friendly ties with overseas countries, Emperor Chengzu sent Muslim Zheng He (1371-1433) as a Chinese ambassador to the West Seas. From 1405 to 1433, Zheng He made seven navigations, visited over 30 countries and regions in Asia and Africa, with the farthest having reached the coast of the Red Sea and

Qing Emperor Kangxi.

Africa. Zheng He's magnificent voyages occurred half a century earlier than European navigators.

During the Ming Dynasty, China's economy and culture became more developed. It also was the period of the Western Renaissance, geographic discovery and religious reformation. With some Western missionaries coming to China, the exchange of Eastern and Western cultures was in initial stage.

In the later years of the Ming, an ethnic minority living in northeast China, known as Manchu, was rapidly expanding. The Jin was established in 1616. In 1636, the minority leader of the

Emperor Qianglong Reviewing His Troops by Italian painter Giuseppe Castiglione (part).

local government proclaimed himself Emperor Huangtaiji, renamed the Later Jing as Qing, In 1644, a Ming commander stationed in Shanhaiguan Pass surrendered and the Qing troops seized the pass, quickly securing rule of the whole country. The Qing was the last feudal dynasty in Chinese history and ruled the country for 267 years. In the early and middle period of the Qing Dynasty, the unified multi-ethnic country was consolidated and developed. Emperors Kangxi, Yongzheng and Qianlong were the greatest ones in the Qing history. They put down rebellions and exercised strong rule over Taiwan, Outer Mongolia, and Xinjiang. They also set up the Tibet Minister, to defend against invasion, and basically laid a territory the size of China today.

Emperor Kangxi was a great emperor in China. His rule began at almost the same time as King Louis XIV ascended the throne of France, and they had many similarities: both being the emperor or the king very young, being gifted, being of the same talented and very high caliber, and firmly controlling the power under autocratic monarchy rule for half a century, and bringing their own country into a new historical peak of prosperity. Kangxi came to the throne at eight years old. He ruled the country for 61 years. He was the longest reigning monarch since there were written records in Chinese history. As well as rare in history, he loved reading books and studying. He is the first Chinese emperor to come into contact with Western modern scientific knowledge and was most interested in Western technology.

Qianlong was the last great emperor in feudal China. As Emperor Kangxi's grandson, he came to the throne at age 25, reigning for 60 years. He was the overlord for four years after an abdication, and died at the age of 89 as the oldest emperor in Chinese history. He ruled the country for over 63 years, and was the longest reigning monarch in Chinese history. Emperor Qianlong commissioned his officials to compile the well-known *"Si Ku Quan Shu" (Complete Collection in Four Treasuries),* which is a major contribution for the preservation of Chinese culture. This project took 20 years and 4,186 people worked on it. Many of the royal palaces and gardens of the Qing Dynasty found in Beijing today were built or repaired in the period of Qianlong They in Clude the Summer Palace, Yuanmingyuan and the Hall of Prayer for Good Harvest at the Temple of Heaven, now mostly listed as world cultural heritages. Emperor Qianlong was diligent, gifted and productive. He loved writing poems, essays, calligraphy and painting. Whenever he was free, he never forgot to do three things: writing articles, painting and writing poems. He left behind more than 42,600 poems in his life.

In the middle and later period of Qing Dynasty, China's agricultural civilization came to an end while the Western countries started to accumulate primitive capital and to grow their colonial expansion. China and Western countries collided for more than one century. However, the agricultural empire was unable to resist the powerful capital empires, and autocratic monarchy was forced to step off the stage of history.

(VI) A Multi-Ethnic Country

China has 56 ethnic groups. It is this cultural diversity that distinguishes it from other countries in the world.

All the ethnic groups have made their own contribution to China's present territory. The ancient Cathay people first settled in Shaanxi and Gansu in the basin of the Yellow River and the Central Plains. The Dongyi people were the first to exploit the coastal areas. The ancestors of Miao and Yao were the pioneers who developed the basins of the Yangtze, Pearl and Minjiang Rivers. The Tibetan and Qiang ethnic peoples cultivated present-day Qinghai Province and the Tibetan Autonomous Region. The Yi and Bai ethnic peoples fought to make a sustainable life for themselves in the remote and unforgiving mountainous areas of southwest China. The Manchu, Xibe, Ewenki and Oroqen ethnic peoples were the first to occupy northeastern China. The Huns, Turks and Mongolian peoples first made the vast Mongolian Grassland their home. The Li people first settled what we know today as Hainan Island, and the Gaoshan ethnic people first built their homes on the island of Taiwan.

In the Chinese history, people of the Han ethnic group, which always constituted the major part of China's population, lived mainly in the Central Plains on the middle and lower reaches of the Yangtze and Yellow Rivers. This part of the world boasts a temperate climate and vast and fertile land, the combination of which makes this a prime farming area. However, other, minority ethnic groups were mostly found in the surrounding areas, where geographic conditions are more varied. Thus, instead of farming, they had to develop excellent skills of herding, hunting and fishing, based on the unique local conditions of grassland, desert, forest, plateau, mountains, hilly areas and lakes. Over time, the Central Plains, fabled as a land of milk and honey, became well developed in culture and economy. The economic development of most minority people living in the border regions, however, lagged behind. Thus they tended to engage in trade with the people of other regions, especially those of the Central Plains, resulting in economic and cultural ties, and a limited migration of some of the minority people to those Plains. As our history progressed, many ethnic groups which originated on the Mongolian grasslands moved southward in search of economic and cultural development, and subsequently dropped their nomadic way of life and took up farming. So successful were some that they even established dynasties of great historical significance, such as the Northern Wei Dynasty (386-534) established by the Sienpi people and the Yuan Dynasty (1271-1368) by the people of Mongolian origin. This would indicate that

A Brief Chinese Chronology

Xia Dynasty	2070 BC - 1600 BC
Shang Dynasty	1600 BC - 1046 BC
Western Zhou Dynasty	1046 BC - 771 BC
Eastern Zhou Dynasty	770 BC - 256 BC
Qin Dynasty	221 BC - 206 BC
Western Han Dynasty	206 BC - 25 AD
Eastern Han Dynasty	25 - 220
Three Kingdoms (Wei, Shu, Wu)	220-280
Western Jin Dynasty	265 - 317
Eastern Jin Dynasty	317 - 420
Northern and Southern Dynasty	420 - 589
Sui Dynasty	581 - 618
Tang Dynasty	618 - 907
Five Dynasties	907 - 960
Northern Song Dynasty	960 - 1127
Southern Song Dynasty	1127 - 1279
Yuan Dynasty	1271 - 1368
Ming Dynasty	1368 - 1644
Qing Dynasty	1644 - 1911
Republic of China	1912 - 1949
People's Republic of China	Founded on October 1, 1949

they became assimilated into the culture and lifestyle of the Han people.

Throughout the years, the Central Plains had always been the center of China's territory, and their original settlers—the Han ethnic people—has still dominated the cultural and ethnic makeup of the Chinese population. Ancestors of the Han ethnic people lived on the Central Plains some 4,000 to 5,000 years ago. From the Xia (2070 BC-1600 BC) to Zhou (1046 BC-256 BC) Dynasties, they incorporated some minority peoples such as the Yi, Qiang, Di and Miao and evolved into a new ethnic tribe, the Cathay. Then, during the Qin (221 BC-206 BC) and Han (206 BC-220 AD) Dynasties, the incorporation of smaller tribes with the majority Cathay people eventually led to the rise of the Han ethnic group. During the Sui (581-618) and Tang (618-907) Dynasties, some nomadic tribes, such as the Sienpi, Jiesi, Qiang and Huns, migrated from their northern homelands and came south to settle on the Central Plains where, with time, they became assimilated into the local Han people. There were mutual benefits to be gained: while those minority groups adopted the language, costumes, customs and ideologies of the Han people, the Han, for their part, also learned from their cooking, music, dance forms, and the style of their clothes. A good case in point is Emperor Xiaowen of the Northern Wei Dynasty (386-534), who carried out reforms in the Sienpi regime. He not only encouraged his people to learn the Han language and wear Han clothes but also advocated the adoption of Han family names and intermarriage with members of Han society. Hundreds of years later, the Manchu rulers also followed the same idea when they established the Qing Dynasty (1644-1911). In 300 years following establishment of the Qing Dynasty, the Manchurians moved into the Central Plains in large numbers, and the period saw they wholly adapt to the local culture and their complete assimilation with the local people.

Feudal regimes followed from centralization. History shows that every regime must have a set of policies to deal with the relationship between the Central Administration and regional powers. Here in China these policies and methods helped to safeguard the unification of the country. Among them, two major systems featuring either regional or semi-regional autonomy were commonly adopted by feudal rulers as the basic political systems by which they would unite their fiefdoms. One of them was characterized by conferring an official title on the regional ruler. The other involved the establishment of a system for the Central Government to deal with local authorities in the border areas. Irrespective of the political methods

Portrait drawn by Yan Liben, noted painter of the Tang Dynasty (618-907), which shows how Tang Emperor Taizong met with Gar Tongtsan, envoy sent by Tubo King Songtsan Gambo for marriage with Tang Princess Wencheng in 641.

employed, however, the Central Government tended to take a softly-softly approach when dealing with the alliances between different ethnic groups. Based on the actual situation of the minority tribes involved, the Central Government adopted a variety of measures. In some cases, they would send envoys to the local region, or even a member from the imperial family to marry the local ruler. In other cases, it would confer official titles on the most influential local figures or otherwise establish stronger and stronger economic links. Over the course of 2,000 years, these methods promoted significant ties between regional powers and the Central Government and unquestionably promoted the national solidarity of China.

III. THE TRADITIONAL IDEOLOGY, CULTURE AND SOCIETY

When we speak of traditional Chinese ideology and culture, we are in fact referring to the value, ideology and cultural form of China before establishment of the modern country. The traditional Chinese ideology and culture are unique in style. Throughout history, although they have drawn from other cultures, they have still preserved many distinct Oriental characteristics, which have been powerful enough to have a far-reaching influence on the culture of China's neighbors. The traditional Chinese ideology and culture are the foundation of the spirit and character of the Chinese nation and lie behind all the achievements of China's historical development.

(I) Confucianism and the Orthodox

A variety of schools of thought and their exponents emerged during the period from the pre-Qin period to the early Han (202 BC-220 AD) Dynasty, including Confucianism, Taoism, Legalism and Mohism. Prominent figures emerging during that span of time include Confucius, Mencius, Lao Tzu and Zhuang Zi.

The three major schools of thought dominating the traditional Chinese ideology and culture are Confucianism, Taoism and Buddhism. Among them, Confucianism is the most influential. That influence can be found in many major concepts concerning the life of ancient Chinese people, such as the idea of how to be a successful ruler, the moral value of society, and the way one conducts oneself in that society. It has also greatly influenced schools of thought in other parts of East Asia, perhaps most significantly those of the Korean Peninsula and Japan.

The honorific adjective "Confucian" at first referred to people who presided over specific rites, but subsequently took on a broader application as it became an honorific title for scholars.

Portrait of Confucius.

Confucius was the founder of Confucianism. Born in the state of Lu (present-day Qufu of Shandong Province), he is still revered as a thinker, politician and educator. Legend has it that he himself compiled six ancient classics, namely *The Spring and Autumn, The Classics of Music, The Classics of Poetry, The Classic Rites, The Classic Changes* and *The Classics of History.* Confucius coined many wise phrases and expounded theories about the law, life and government. Our main access to his thinking is through *The Analects*, a work compiled by his disciples and considered the most reliable source of information about his life and teachings.

Confucius heavily emphasized what he called "benevolence and rites" in his ideological system. In his opinion, benevolence, concentrating on "loving people", represents a variety of moral standards. He once said, "The humane man, wishing himself to be established, sees that others are established, and, wishing himself to be successful, sees that others are successful." And, on another memorable occasion, "Do not do to others what you do not want done to yourself". He lived in a

Portrait of Mencius.

period when the Zhou King was weak and the real power rested with other local state rulers. Seeing rampant intrigue and vice, he deplored the contemporary disorder and lack of moral standards. He came to believe that the only remedy was to convert people once more to the principles and precepts of the sages of antiquity. He therefore lectured to his disciples on the principles of the "rites and music". He believed that rites give public display to social hierarchies and music unifies hearts in shared enjoyment. Both of them act as a form of communication between the citizen's humanity and his social context, and strengthen social relationships. To these ends he urged people from all walks of life to voluntarily follow social conventions, and to effect a balance between order and harmony.

In China's history, Confucius was the first to establish private schools and this

Book on Xun zi.

make it possible for common people to get access to education. He was worshipped by the Chinese people as Master Kong and the "great educator". Legend has it that he had some 3,000 students, including 72 who turned out to be very successful. Many of his most famous ideas were expressed when he answered questions of his students and it is these ideas, often contained in wise sayings, that were subsequently compiled by his followers and gained wide acceptance in China. Today, these sayings are still part of everyday speech, and it is quite common to hear people quote such lines as "To study and not think is a waste; to think and not study is dangerous," "Isn't it a pleasure to study and practice what you have learned?" and "When three men are walking together, there is one who can be my teacher."

Another prominent figure who has made a great contribution to the Confucian ideal is Mencius (385 BC-304 BC). Also a great thinker, politician and educator, he is regarded as the true transmitter of Confucius' teachings. Chinese scholars worship him as the greatest Confucian thinker after Confucius himself. He developed Confucius' ideals and put forward a series of concepts expressing the principle that a ruler should govern his country with benevolence. He pointed out that only if the ruler were to adopt policies of benevolence, would he get real support from his people, this being a development of his belief that the people's support is more important than anything else for good governance. He was passionately opposed to oppression or misuse of force. He also believed that human nature is fundamentally good, a concept which deeply influenced ancient Chinese society. A statement of this belief is to be found in *The Three-Character Scripture*, which begins with the words: "Men, at their birth, are naturally good."

But this view was challenged by another Confucian thinker, Xun Zi (318 BC-238 BC), who held the opposite opinion, proclaiming that "human nature is fundamentally bad". Xun Zi greatly emphasized the importance of rites and made a significant contribution to the development of Confucianism in this regard. In his opinion, rites represent social regulation and the estate system, which are essential for a well-ordered life, society and country. He described the relationship between the king and his people as that between a boat and water, once being quoted as saying "while the water can carry a boat, it can also overturn it."

Confucianism dates back to the pre-Qin period. However, it did not gain its prominence over other schools of thought until the Han Dynasty (221 BC-220 AD), when Emperor Wudi designated it as Orthodox. Later, during the Song (960-1279) and Ming (1368-1644) Dynasties, Confucianism further developed into two schools, which respectively emphasize heavenly principles and consciousness. The rise of these two schools led to the formulation of what is known as Neo-Confucianism. Neo-Confucianism, the innovative reinterpretation of the traditional Confucian core, associates the moral standards put forward by Confucius and Mencius with the heavenly principles. It demonstrates human nature, the status of human beings in the universe, and the relationship between the two. It attaches importance to the pursuit of cultural and ideological promotion. Thanks to it, the moral principles of Confucianism have been much enriched.

(II) Taoist Thought and Taoism

Among traditional Chinese thoughts and culture, Taoist thought holds a position only second to that of Confucian thought. "Taoist" thought emerged before the pre-Qin (before 221 BC) period in Chinese history while the "Taoist school" emerged in the early period of the Western Han Dynasty (206 BC-25 AD). Originally it was called the "moral" school or "moral school of thought", and later "Taoist school" for short. The Taoist school got its name for its focus on "Tao" as the core thought. In the history of Chinese philosophy, the Taoist school was the first to discuss the issue of the origin of all things in the world through the concept of "Tao".

The founder of Taoist thought was Lao Tzu (about 600 BC-500 BC) who was a contemporary of Confucius. He wrote the book *Lao Tzu*, i.e. *Dao De Jing*, called the *Classic of the Way* and the *Natural Virtue by the Old Master* by later generations, to clarify his philosophy. "Tao" is the most important concept among Lao Tzu's thoughts. He held that "Tao" evolved from but was different from the "divine order of things" and that the essence of everything on earth was generated from "Tao". Auording to Lao Tzu, "Tao" is a blend of two aspects, the unity of "not-being" and "being" which can mutually transform each other. Lao Tzu viewed "no-action" as the quality of "Tao" and "no-action" means complying with the original situation of all existing things.

Sculpture of Lao Tzu in Quanzhou, Fujian Province.

Lao Tzu also put forth the famous proposition that "all existing things are bound together in a universal context that is founded upon a principle called 'Tao' " and held that "Tao" is "nature" complying with all things existing on earth. Lao Tzu believed that "no-action" had a close relationship with "nature", and if rulers did "no-action" people would be "natural."

The Huang Lao School was a major sect of the Taoist school during the Warring States Period (475 BC - 221 BC). "Huang" refers to the forefather of the Chinese race, the Yellow Emperor (Emperor Huangdi), and "Lao" refers to Lao Tzu. The Huang Lao School explains Lao Tzu's thoughts with dependence on the Yellow Emperor. Literature left by the Huang Lao School mainly include the *Medical Classic of the Yellow Emperor* and *Guan Zi*, which mostly discuss social political issues and self-cultivation. The Huang Lao School called Tao "the great void" and explained Tao as "qi", holding that the generation of all existing things relied on "vitality" which was the source of man's life and wisdom. The Huang Lao School attached importance to the idea of "temporization", stressing that "Tao" temporized the nature of all existing things. Regarding politics, monarchs should temporize the nature of officials and common people subject to them and remain tranquil and empathize with the role of officials and common people when managing State

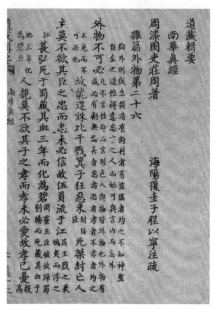

Book on Zhuang Zi.

affairs. This school of thought was adopted and accepted by rulers of the early Western Han Dynasty (206 BC-25 AD) and served as the source of policies such as "managing State affairs by no-action" and recuperating and multiplying the State.

Zhuang Zi (about 369 BC-286 BC) was the most influential ideologist of the Taoist school in the pre-Qin period (before 221 BC). As Mencius inherited and developed the thought of Confucius, Zhuang Zi inherited and developed the thought of Lao Tzu. Later generations often juxtaposed Zhuang Zi and Lao Tzu and called them together as Lao Zhuang. Zhuang Zi's thought is mainly manifested in his book

Baiyunguan, a noted Taoist monastery in Beijing.

Zhuang Zi. Zhuang Zi's thought focuses on seeking man's spiritual freedom. He held that the most difficult position for men was the loss of spiritual freedom. Man created wealth and culture and yet man was dominated by wealth and culture and became the slave of substance. In the view of Zhuang Zi, the fundamental way to break free of such a difficult position was to reach "no-self", meaning surpassing self and reaching the realm in which the "heart wanders about in Tao", i.e. the extremely beautiful and joyful realm of "unity of heaven and man."

During the Wei (220-265) and Jin (265-420) Dynasties Taoist thought experienced a renaissance and the Wei Jin Metaphysics Sect (Xuan Xue) came into being, and held the works such as *Lao Tzu, Zhuang Zi* and *Zhou Yi* as its major classics. The system of a "new Taoist school of thought" was established by re-explaining these classics with a focus on "the fundamental and the incidental, and being and not-being". The Lao Tzu philosophy is the knowledge of universal profoundness and abstruseness, while the word "Xuan" (metaphysical) means profoundness and abstruseness and can be used to describe "Tao", the universal origin, so people at that time called the Taoist school adhering to the theories of Lao Tzu the"Xuan Sect". The Wei Jin Xuan Sect discussed many issues. Fundamentally it was to solve the relationship between the cosmology philosophy of the Taoist

School and the idea of administration by the feudal ethical code of Confucianism, i.e. the relationship between Confucian thought and Taoist thought.

Under the influence of Taoist thought, Taoism came into being in the 3rd century. Taoism views Lao Tzu as the fundamental classic expressing its religious creed and Lao Tzu as its founder. Taoism, seeks longevity and integrates its beliefs and arts of necromancy, astrology and medicine to preserve man's health. It makes use of Taoist thoughts, especially the thought of "qi" (which is used to show the existence of all living things on earth) to form a vast system of religious thought absorbing some thoughts of Buddhism and Confucianism. The earliest Taoist organizations were Taoping Tao and Wudoumi Tao at the end of the Eastern Han Dynasty (25-220). Taoism was supported by governments for more than 1,000 years after the Eastern Jin Dynasty (317-420) and spread and developed very quickly. By the time of the Song Dynasty (960-1279) many schools and sects had formed across China, with Zhengyi and Quanzhen as the two most influential sects. In the middle of the Ming Dynasty (1368-1644), the government discontinued the policy of worshipping Taoism and the influence of Taoism began to decline.

Taoist thought had great impact on the development of aesthetics, literature and arts of China, such as imagist theory and the theory of artistic conception. The Taoist theory on "unity of falsehood and reality" became an important principle of classic aesthetics in China and had great impact on poetry and painting in ancient China.

(III) Introduction of Buddhism

Buddhism was born along the Ganges River in Indian in the 6th century BC. At the end of the Western Han Dynasty (206 BC-25 AD), it was introduced into China via Central Asia and gradually penetrated into Chinese society, becoming an important part of Chinese culture.

Standing image of a Boddhistava.

During the Eastern Han Dynasty (25-220), one evening Emperor Mingdi (reigning 58-76) dreamt of a golden man in the west. The next morning he asked his ministers to explain the dream. A minister told him, "You must have dreamt of Buddha in the west." Emperor Mingdi immediately sent envoys to invite Buddha to China. Later his envoys brought back two monks and a number of Buddhist books and records. Emperor Mingdi had a temple built in his capital Luoyang for the two monks.

Translation of Buddhist sutras in China was mainly done by monks from Central Asian and South Asian countries, but their translation was not satisfactory. Then Chinese monks began to go to Central Asian and South Asian countries for Buddhist scriptures. The most outstanding representative of them was Xuanzang (602-664) of the Tang Dynasty (618-907). Born in a poor family, Xuanzang became a monk at 13. In the course of research and religious discussion over many years, he came to understand it was difficult to have a good command of Buddhist sutras due to different opinions from various Schools. So he made a decision to go to India for Buddhist scriptures. After experiencing innumerable hardships he reached India, and devoted himself to studying Buddhist sutras. His knowledge was respected and praised highly by Buddhist community. When he completed his study in India and returned to Luoyang, Emperor Taizong of the Tang Dynasty (618-907) told him to leave the Buddhist circle and take a political position. Xuanzang declined with thanks and focused his attention on the translation of a great number of Buddhist sutras he had brought back from India, making great contribution to the development of Buddhism.

Tang Dynasty (618-907) Monk Xuanzang who went to India for Buddhist sutras.

The Buddhist thoughts accepted by Chinese people were mainly Mahayana which, created in the 1st century in India, upholds the idea of giving lenity to all living things. During the Sui (581-618) and Tang (618-907) Dynasties, owing to the prosperity of social economy, Buddhism achieved unprecedented development in China and gradually several large Buddhist sects such as Sanlun, Tiantai, Faxiang, Huayan, Lu, Chan and Jingtu formed.

Although it was an exotic culture at the beginning, Buddhism had a very wide impact on the development of Chinese culture after its localization. Buddhism had great impact on the development of Chinese phonology, linguistics and philology. The use of Chinese *pinyin* was enlightened first by Sanskrit, a phonetic language. Many Buddhist words became Chinese words, such as "freedom","equality", "world", "all living things" and "realm", which enriched the vocabulary of the Chinese. Buddhism also created temple culture in China. Buddhist thoughts about void, realm and soul, and theories of the Chan sect in particular, had great impact on Chinese culture, arts and architecture. Buddhism also played a role in accelerated development of Confucianism and Taoism. Buddhist ideas such as leniency, being a Samaritan, getting rid of evil and accepting goodness influence the behavior of Chinese people.

(IV) Traditional Thought and Culture

American scholar Philip Lee Ralph and others set forth their thoughts in their book *World Civilizations* (first published in 1998 by the Commercial Press): When the ancient Greek philosophers were discussing the quality of the substantial world and Indian ideologists were thinking about the relations between soul and god, China's sages were trying to find the basis of human life and the fundamental principles of wise and able government.

The traditional thought and culture of China has a long and rich history. It has added enormously to the spiritual wealth of succeeding generations, and is in many ways unique in the overall history of human thought and spiritual endeavor. Its findings can be summarized as follows:

Fundamental is the principle of putting people first. China is the country where what we might describe as humanistic thoughts made their earliest appearance. The ancient ideologists in China mostly advocated the building up of a moral and orderly cultural society by means of a humanistic view of civilization. According to this philosophy, if heaven and earth are the father and mother of all existing things, human beings are the most intelligent and important among all existing things. As the ancient scholar Xun Zi put it, "Water and fire have *qi* but no life, grass and trees have life but no awareness, animals have awareness, and human beings have *qi*, life, awareness, and also friendly sentiments. Thus we can plainly infer that human beings are the most precious inhabitants of this earth." "Benevolence" is the core of Confucian thought. Confucius himself maintained that "benevolence means loving others." When one of his disciples asked how to define those all-important attributes of wisdom and knowledge, Confucius replied that a wise person gave preeminence to other people's affairs. In ancient China there was popular saying, "People are the root of a country, and, when the root is firm, the country is tranquil." Mencius put forward the thought that "people are most precious, the nation comes next, and monarchs are not important", which developed the Confucian philosophy of

Huashan Mountain is more than a tourist attraction in China. As a famous Taoist mountain, it shows the idea of "Man and Nature Being United as One".

"putting the people first."

Another important strand of thought is the concept of the unity of heaven and man. "Heaven" holds a special position in China's traditional culture; it refers to both the heaven in nature and the heaven of God's will. The former views sky and earth as the root of all existing things; the latter is subjective, imagined and irresistible.

According to the proposition of "unity of heaven and man" in traditional Chinese culture, heaven and man have necessarily contradictory aspects. Heaven is of the supreme, the most sacred and inviolable; heaven's force is far greater than that of man, and heaven's will determines man's will. Man must comply with heaven in order to realize and coordinate the unity of heaven and man. A distinctive character of Taoist thought is its emphasis on the idea that man should do things in compliance with nature, should develop alongside the development of all existing things, and should neither act in isolation nor seek to change nature in a random manner. This compliance with nature is also most strongly advocated in Confucian thought.

The concept of harmony is valued highly in Chinese thought. Harmony is the inner spirit of Chinese culture and its importance is manifested mainly by the concepts "harmony is valuable", "be harmonious but individual" and "benevolence". Confucius said, "Anything, no matter how big or how small, must have harmony, as its starting point and harmony as its end-result." Why is "harmony" so important? According to ancient philosophers in China, all things on earth are produced and developed from "harmony", and it is perfectly possible for the world itself to be continuously peaceful and prosperous. Meanwhile, the traditional Chinese philosophers were also laying stress on "being harmonious but individual." On the one hand they viewed "harmony" as the supreme value for which one should seek, and on the other maintained that difference and diversity should be acknowledged, that each of us should respect and understand others and mutually forgive any wrongs arising out of that diversity. Thus "harmony" can only be realized gradually by mutual and equal consultation, dialogue and cooperation. Traditional Chinese thought holds that "people must be divided according to stipulated regulations and laws" to prevent them from starting wars due to unsatisfied desires and unworthy ambitions. Hence, "benevolence and charity" should be followed by everyone, the ideal being a kind of universal benevolence to be attained by an education based on the precepts of kindheartedness, justice and morality. The resulting "benevolent people" are unassailable and will continue on the path that leads from "benevolence" to "peace."

"Seeking for the world of great harmony" is the Chinese pursuit. What is this "world of great harmony"? Confucius thought that the world of great harmony was a world where correct reasoning was universally adopted. Lao Tzu also postulated an ideal society in which everyone could "enjoy sweet food, wear beautiful dresses, live in peace and maintain joyous customs." The so-called world of great harmony is in fact what modern commentators would refer to as a Utopian social ideal; a world without differences between classes, with neither oppression nor exploitation where people live equally and harmoniously and can enjoy the fruits of their labors. The direct result of this idealistic view of society was that in the history of China various peasants' uprisings were inspired by an ambition to establish a society in which there would be no distinction between the nobleman and the peasant, and where wealth would be equally shared. Kang Youwei (1858-1927), a revolutionary

Portrait of Kang Youwei.

leader far closer to our own time, wrote a book, *On Great Harmony*, in which he put forward a society "featuring the whole world as a community where there is no class distinction, all things are equal, and there is neither despot nor elected president above the people" as his personal vision of a "world of great harmony." Sun Yat-sen (1866-1925), a forerunner of China's democratic revolution, also took the view that "the whole world as a community" as his political credo. In traditional Chinese culture, the idea of great harmony has its restrictions, both historical and political, but the simplicity of its message, its advocacy of public ownership, personal freedom, equality and philanthropy in fact reflect the longings of many people throughout the ages for a fairer and happier future society.

The spirit of going into society is emphasized. The Confucian philosophy, which holds the leading position in traditional Chinese culture, required people to care about reality, and appreciate the internal moral cultivation which would lead to the benefit of real society. When one of his disciples enquired of him how he could discover more about the issues related to ghosts and deities, Confucius rebuked him sharply, "If you cannot act properly in the world of men, how can you be in a position to talk of the things related to ghosts." So it was that Confucius himself only talked about things in this life, did not speak of ghosts, deities, or an afterlife, and firmly stated that although he "respected ghosts and deities", he was "very far off from them." Going into society, he stressed, one must continuously enhance oneself by moral cultivation and become useful in the administration of public affairs. Everyone can accomplish great things if they do so from their innermost beings, basing their courses of action on the things around them and the simple realities of daily life. This method of achievement has as its starting point a just and sincere heart, and proceeds through studying the phenomena of nature, the acquisition of knowledge, the cultivation of personal morality, the good governance of one's family, and finally results in the ability to govern a state—and why not ultimately the whole world?

It is true to say that much of great value has been accumulated in the traditional Chinese culture, with an agricultural ideology as its base, but also that there exist within it a number of limits, some defects, and even aspects that are completely wrong. The principle errors inherent in this traditional Chinese culture include: a lack of democratic spirit and excessive praise for rulers and the concept of rule; advocating hierarchy; making men more important than women; giving too great a prominence to collectivism and in consequence overlooking the value of the individual; and pursuing egalitarianism at the expense of creativity.

(V) Society against the Background of Traditional Thoughts and Culture

Formed against a background of agricultural society, traditional Chinese culture took the form of a patriarchal clan system with families as its basic units. The concept of "the country" was rarely seen, in its place were usually such concepts as "under heaven" or "the god of the land and the god of the grain". In traditional Chinese culture, no family meant no country; family was both a group of living breathing beings as well as a unit of production. It is important to note, however, that the term "family" in this context does not simply refer to the family who live together under one roof but rather a whole extended family of multiple blood relations on both the male and the female sides, including uncles, aunts, cousins, grandparents, great uncles, great aunts, etc. It was customary to refer to the paternal side of this extended family as "internal" members, whereas on the female side they were "external". It does not take a mathematician to calculate that after only a few generations this could result in a very large "family" indeed.

A happy family of four generations, with 41 members.

At grass-roots level in ancient Chinese village communities, families and clans were organized according to the above-mentioned principles of distinction between men and women and the hierarchy of older and younger. Such families and clans often lived in the same region, used the same ancestral temple, and could trace their lineage back to a common forefather. Within a clan there would usually be men of superior knowledge, perhaps even one who had passed the imperial exams in old China, or who were simply older, or who held a higher position in the family hierarchy, or who would be accorded greater prestige. In a clan, a person of noble character and high prestige took the position of clan chief; he would be charged with administering the clan, making decisions that affected the clan as a whole, organizing the offering of sacrifices to their ancestors, and punishing those who violated the clan's own laws and regulations. These grass-root social organizations with clans as the principle units played a vital role in establishing order and stabilizing the entire fabric of ancient Chinese society. It is the greatest single difference between ancient oriental society and that of the west.

Chinese society against the background of traditional culture founded a country based on morality instead of laws. Moral criteria became the rules of this society and everyone was constrained by morality. Confucian thoughts became the core values of traditional Chinese culture and formed the basis of the aforesaid moral criteria, perhaps the most famous being represented by the expression "three main-stays and five constant virtues", where the three main-stays are the king (main-stay of officials), the father (main-stay of sons) and the husband (main-stay of wives), and the five constant virtues refer to the relationships between the five principle pairings in that society, i.e. the monarch and his officials, fathers and sons, husbands and wives, the old and the young, and bonds between friends. Thus, according to these precepts, there is "loyalty between the king and his officials, blood relation between fathers and sons, distinction between husbands and wives, order between older and younger, and trust between friends." Those betraying these moral criteria were considered, respectively, traitorous, disloyal, unfaithful, dis-obedient or unfriendly, and were rejected as such by their society. This ancient Chinese society viewed the above-mentioned Confucian morality and ideals as its most basic foundation by which the social order could best be regulated and maintained.

In order to found a country on the basis of morality, it is absolutely necessary to ensure that every member of society is himself a moral person, which involves the issue of enhancing the inner morality and cultivation of all the people. According to traditional Chinese culture, a man of good virtue should at first cultivate his own moral character, then seek to influence others by his speeches, and at last contribute personally to the general good of society. A virtuous man should gain knowledge, learn from direct inspection, think cautiously, distinguish clearly between right and wrong, and carry things out with boldness and vigor.

Under the influence of traditional culture, religion was not developed in ancient Chinese society. In fact, throughout the history of China religion has never held a prominent position in society, and so, during the ancient period under discussion, there was no dispute between religious and imperial power, nor was there conflict or outright war between different religious factions — another significant difference between ancient Chinese society and that of the west. In China there were not such books as the *Bible* and the *Koran*, or such propagators and preachers as Jesus or Mohammed.

The Confucian culture, the principle foundation of traditional Chinese culture, puts forward the virtues of going into society and living among mankind. It mainly discusses human and ethical relations, and does not involve the issues surrounding religious belief. Confucian thoughts were much respected as orthodox thoughts by rulers of past dynasties, thus severely restricting the development of religious thought in China. Another important part of traditional Chinese culture is Taoism. Although it later developed religious overtones, original Taoism focused on the discussion of natural rules and the cultivation of temperaments, which is greatly different from, say, the Christian belief in God. Classical Buddhism, quite contrary to all we have said about traditional Confucian thought, says that we should stand aloof from worldly affairs, but in ancient China it experienced a sort of make-over and eventually evolved into the Chan sect with its religious elements much weakened and its adherents given a great deal of liberty. In China there is a saying which goes, "one dies for a righteous cause and one stands to become a Buddhist," which vividly makes the point that it is not difficult to become a Buddhist disciple. Even today, if you go into any of China's temples you will still see many people burning joss sticks and kneeling in worship. In fact, the majority of them are not genuine Buddhist disciples, but are only praying for peace or an end to some personal misfortune. In traditional Chinese culture Heaven is the greatest

God, but people worship instead of believing in Heaven. At the very dawn of Chinese history the people performed totem worship activities, in which the dragon was often the object of worship, but these were more an expression of their awe and lack of understanding of the power of nature, not a religious belief. Today Chinese people maintain the tradition of offering sacrifice to ancestors, and each year there are several festivals at which ancestors are remembered in this way, but equally these are not religious activities and are simply a way for people to preserve their memories of, and pay their respects to, the departed.

Against the backdrop of this traditional cultural background, there were many other unique phe-

Worshipping Buddha at the Zhanshansi Temple in Qingdao of Shandong Province at the beginning of the new year.

nomena in old Chinese society still worthy of our continued attention today. Traditional Chinese society was one in which "men are noble and women are inferior," and it was customary for people to undervalue women's role in society. This was the age of high-born women having their feet bound, also the period when a man would have both a wife and concubines. In fact, men could marry a concubine, and those men holding positions of wealth and power could even marry several. Take, for another example of how traditional society worked, the system of grass-root country gentlemen. Country gentlemen were not themselves government officials but they had special relations with the government. They were greatly influenced by Confucian schools of thought and made use of their cultural knowledge and social influence to serve the government in a disguised form and obtain benefits, it being the actual case that the government effectively implemented its administration over the grass roots population via them. And finally, let us not forget the system of eunuchs in royal palaces where the affairs in those royal palaces were managed by the eunuchs, some of whom achieved positions of great power and influence.

(VI) National Character Shaped by Traditional Thoughts and Culture

In the long course of historical development, the traditional Chinese thoughts and culture, as an ideology, were injected into the blood of Chinese nation and had a profound impact on the shaping of the Chinese national character.

Constantly striving to become stronger! "Heaven goes soundly, and man should constantly strive to become stronger." This famous exhortation to men of accomplishment encouraged them to follow the natural spirit of marching forward, working hard, contributing to society, and never ceasing, however hard the task. The sage Mencius viewed these precepts, combined with the ability to bear hardships and difficulties, as the only route to success. He said, "So, if God were to give an important task to a certain person, the first thing that person must do is to temper his will power, and thus be prepared to strain his muscles and bones, starve his stomach and lay waste his body..." Thousands of years of history have proved that the Chinese nation is full of toughness, that its population will never yield to the sufferings of natural disasters, will overcome domestic troubles and foreign invasion, and will persevere constantly until the task at hand is complete.

Tolerance and harmony. The Chinese national character has a very strong degree of tolerance. Traditional Chinese culture makes great play of "harmony and peace" and "neutralization." It also recommends solving conflicts and differences by cooperation, does not advocate attacking or invading others, and is opposed to the idea of war. Such tolerance is manifested in the acceptance of other nationalities and the absorption of cultural achievements of other peoples. The Central Plains were invaded, but on each occasion the cultures of these invaders were absorbed into the culture of the Central Plains and became an important part of the Chinese national culture. Regarding the issue of morality, Chinese people pay attention to being "even-tempered and good-humored;" regarding governing a family, they believe that "a harmonious family makes everything prosperous;" regarding governing a country, they hold to the dictum that it is "peace and harmony which can make a country prosper;" and regarding foreign relations, they expound the ideal of "harmonizing millions of people." When dealing with the relations between men, families and country respectively, they attach importance to the pursuit of common interests, but while seeking them still preserve respect for other points of view, mutual tolerance and a continuance of common development.

Diligence and frugality. This has long been an essential aspect of the Chinese character. In fact there is an ancient maxim which tells us that "a country should be diligent and a family should be frugal." Here, "being diligent" means that a man should pursue his course with concentrated attention, with the utmost effort, and not allow remissness or weariness to deflect him from his task. This is because in Chinese culture the word "diligence" actually means a combination of the two concepts of "diligence" and "being hard-working." "Being frugal," on the other hand, means that a man should use his wealth reasonably, eschew extravagance and waste, persevere, and see things through to the end. Here we in fact have a combination of the ideas of "diligence" and "acting vigorously," often referred together as "frugality." In ancient times, due to primitive laboring methods, the fruits of such labor were hard-earned and people could only live by diligence and frugality. So it was that very early on these ancient farming peoples learned to equate frugality with the public good and extravagance with the bad. There have been many popular apothegms throughout the long history of China, a number of which are still relevant today: "When we look back we can see

Two university students in Xuzhou of Jiangsu Province soliciting donations for one suffering from leucocythemia.

that the successful ones depended on diligence and frugality and the unsuccessful on extravagance and waste;" "the way to have a family is by being frugal and diligent". Praising highly diligence and frugality and accumulating social wealth by honest hard work has always been regarded as the simplest but greatest virtue with which to make a state or a family prosperous.

Be kindhearted and tolerant. Chinese culture emphasizes "the accumulation of good deeds in order to make virtue," advocating doing good deeds and holding that many such good deeds can make people capable of reaching a higher plain. In China Buddhism expounds the doctrine of standing aloof from worldly affairs, but it also contains a positive spirit of going out into society. The feelings of leniency and assistance advocated by Buddhism not only help people to be freed from the various sufferings of the real world but also strive to harmonize the relations between man and his fellow man, man and all other living things, and man and the very fabric of nature itself. It further attempts to mitigate various forms of conflict and encourages people to improve themselves and their lives by study. Many of China's popular folk sayings are concerned with the contrast between good and bad, the need to pursue the one and repudiate the other. Examples include, "Goodness necessitates a sharing of itself," "Sow the wind and reap the whirlwind," "We must do good rather than evil, on however humble a scale," "Those families doing many good deeds have endless luck and happiness, but the families doing many bad deeds have endless disasters." Consistent with being kindhearted, Chinese culture also stresses "tolerance, " advocates "being lenient with an offender," believes in the "abandoning of former enmity," and opposes the "accumulation of rancor and mutual hostility." In traditional Chinese culture there are various ways in which one can follow the path of a good and virtuous life, such as "loving to do philanthropic work" and "showing sympathy towards the weak." There is one particular phrase which Chinese people like to repeat: "When one is in trouble, others will offer aid." Such aid will usually take the traditional form of solidarity, friendship and mutual assistance. Thus is kindheartedness and tolerance expressed in a typically Chinese way.

Be optimistic and practical. The Confucian culture believes that it is proper to take one's place in day-to-day society. It advocates active participation in social activities and administrative affairs. Mencius, the previously quoted ancient philosopher, once said, "No wise gentleman will stand at the foot of a dangerous wall." The Confucian culture respects, confirms and faces reality, holds a positive and optimistic attitude toward life, and opposes pessimism and disheartenment. Under the influence of this Confucianism, the Chinese people have always paid attention to reality and practicality, pursued merit and opposed mere empty show, and scorned idle talk and empty thoughts. In the minds of the ordinary Chinese people, man should live to pursue reality, neither evading real issues nor embracing chimera, and most of all should keep actively pushing forward. Confucian culture stresses the value of self-study, not just for the simple accumulation of knowledge but as a way of enhancing one's self-cultivation and better enabling one to make contributions to social life. Another ancient saying makes a similar point: "Research both natural phenomena and human relations in society; thoroughly understand the changes from ancient times to today; ultimately form the theory of a school."

Now let's take a look at what is meant by moderation and "the golden mean." Due to the impact of traditional culture, Chinese people give great consideration to "the golden mean" when considering a course of action. This advocates not doing things excessively, but rather aiming for an appropriate moderation. For a simple illustration one can take eating. If one eats too much, one will feel unwell due to excessive fullness; if one eats too little, one will be hungry and undernourished. Or, again, consider the wearing of shoes. Shoes that are either too big or too small are uncomfortable and make walking difficult; shoes of the correct size are an analogy of "the golden mean." In traditional Chinese business culture there is the thought that attempting to make more and more profit will eventually result in loss and in fact all things, when developed to extremes, will tend to produce the opposite of what is intended. Nothing should be done excessively; to do so is to develop in the opposite direction.

The ideology of worry and disaster. Chinese people have a very optimistic attitude towards life, but at the same time are full of the ideology of worry and disaster. Mencius said, "Live in

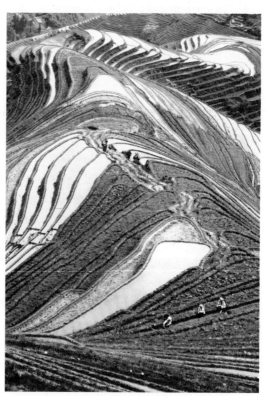

Fruit of labor of farmers throughout the history in Longji of the Guangxi Zhuang Autonomous Region.

worry and disaster and die at ease." In different historical times, people with lofty ideals had different worries and disasters; some worried about the decline of monarch and the country, some worried about the nation being in peril, and some worried about the sufferings of the common people, all of which meant that the ideology of worry and disaster became part of the essential character of the Chinese people. As a result we have been left a number of well-known sayings, handed down to us from antiquity, representing this facet of the national character.

"Worry about the common people in a year of poor harvest;"

"Be the first to worry about the people's woes, the last to share the weal of the people;"

"Although the age has not exceeded a hundred years, yet our minds contain the worry of ten-thousand;"

"Every common man has his obligation to the rise and fall of the nation;"

"I must care about my home, my country and even the whole world;"

"Disregarding my humble position, I will not forget to worry about the nation;"

"Without worry, a man is not wise;"

"He does not have a penny in his pocket, yet must always have worry about the nation in mind."

All of these are intended to encourage the people to attain a profound and lofty realm of "being both happy and worried in accordance with the whole nation."

Traditional culture has also had some negative impact on the shaping of the Chinese character. Due to an excessive emphasis on reality, there is a comparative lack of idealism; the ideology of the "golden mean" encourages the self-sufficient mind and makes people satisfied with the present situation, and has the tendency of producing people who lack the will to explore and take risks; there is arrogance, and people, not believing that others might in some ways be superior to themselves, become inward-looking and conservative; others stick to conventions, excessively believe in the doctrines of their predecessors, and are unwilling to attempt to exceed those who came before them. These are just some of the negative traits of the traditional culture as it has shaped the Chinese character.

(VII) Exchanges between Ancient Chinese and Foreign Cultures

Influenced by such geographic features as high mountains, broad deserts, high plateaus and vast oceans, ancient China experienced a difficult exchange with the outside world, but that does not mean that there was no communication at all. The highly-developed ancient Chinese culture once had a profound impact on the cultural process of the outside world, and in the long course of its historical development absorbed other exotic cultures, especially those of Central and South Asia.

The Silk Road was the main passage by which ancient China was able to make exchanges with the outside world. Originally used to unite the Central Asian states in resistance to the Hun powers on the northern grasslands, the Silk Road was opened during the Han Dynasty (220 BC-206 BC). Owing to the Silk Road, China opened up communications with the Central Asian and West Asian states in regard to politics, economies, and cultural and military affairs. In the long period of more than 1,500 years from the Han Dynasty to the Ming Dynasty (1368-1644), i.e. from the 3rd century BC to the 17th century, the Silk Road carried the responsibility of developing relations with other states in Europe and

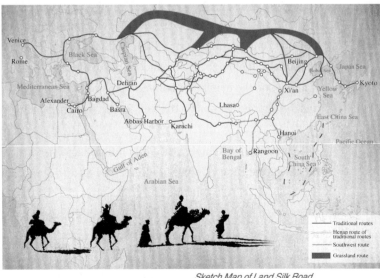

Sketch Map of Land Silk Road.

Foreign envoys in Chang'an during the Tang Dynasty (618-907).

Asia. It was the precious link between ancient eastern and western cultures and had a significant influence on the development of both.

In the long years of the Silk Road it was usually merchants carrying bales of silk who trudged along its seemingly endless miles of often difficult terrain, thus giving a name to one of the most important thoroughfares in history. At that time the silk of China was well known in Central Asia, South Asia and Europe. The Roman writer Pali Ahatis said, "The precious colorful silk made in China looks like the beautiful blooming flowers in the fields and its fineness can bear comparison with the gossamer spun by spiders." The tea, perfume, porcelain, lacquer work, ironware and medicines of China, plus the knowledge in various fields such as astronomy, medicine, music and architecture, and most especially paper-making, printing and the making of colored inks, were transported or spread to Central Asia and the regions beyond by the Silk Road, thus influencing the cultural development of all the known world. Meanwhile, the Silk Road also introduced the culture west of Central Asia to China, especially religion and the arts, which greatly influenced the development of Chinese culture. Thus, for instance, Islam was introduced to northwestern China, which had a profound impact on the local social development. Acrobatics, operas, music and dancing from the regions to the west of Central Asia were also introduced via the Silk Road, and these were all catalysts for a great surge in the development of traditional Chinese art. The Silk Road's prosperity reached its summit during the Tang Dynasty (618-907), when the exchanges between China and foreign countries were most frequent and many envoys of countries from behind the western mountains came to the Tang Dynasty's ancient capital, Chang'an.

Regarding the exchanges between ancient eastern and western cultures, it is necessary to mention the introduction of Christianity and its subsequent influence on the future of East-West communications.

As early as the Tang Dynasty (618-907), Nestorianism (from the Nestorian sect of Christianity) was introduced to China by means of the Silk Road. It had a limited popularity and never achieved wide-scale recognition. Of far greater significance was Monte Corvino, who became the first person to propagandize Roman Catholicism in China. He landed on Quanzhou, Fujian in 1293, reached the capital of the Yuan Dynasty (1271-1368), Dadu (Beijing) in 1294 and began to preach the Catholic faith. Later he moved to Peking where he spread the word on the Roman version of Christianity for more than thirty years. During the Ming (1368-1644) and Qing (1644-1911) Dynasties, Jesus Penitent came to China by sea and tried to spread religion to the hinterland of China. In 1557 Portugal occupied Macao by force and turned it into an important base for the promulgation of Catholicism in the east. In 1583 an Italian Jesus Penitent Matteo Ricci (1552-1610) arrived in Guangdong in South

Statue of Matteo Ricci

Statue of Johann Adam Schall von Bell.

China. A remarkable man, he harmonized Catholicism and Chinese culture, and persuaded the Chinese people to accept the faith of Rome. In return he accepted the costume of a Chinese Buddhist disciple granted to him by local officials of the Ming Dynasty (1368-1644), believing that by so doing he could integrate both himself and his religion into the mainstream of Chinese culture. Trading western sciences for Confucianism, he studied hard and wrote works in Chinese in order to preach Western philosophy and Christian doctrines. In 1600 Matteo Ricci presented a mechanical chiming clock as a tribute to the Chinese emperor and was granted approval to live in Peking (Beijing). While there he made a wide circle of friends among the city's scholar-bureaucrats and strove to gain their sympathy. By the time he died of illness in 1610 there were over 2,500 Catholic disciples across China. Early missionaries, under the influence of Matteo, played a very great role in spreading western knowledge in China. They translated many books on Western science and technology in collaboration with the same class of Chinese scholar-bureaucrats who had aided Matteo.

It was a German, Johann Adam Schall von Bell (1592-1666), an academician of Roman Academy of Apostolic Sciences, who was the next most influential missionary in China after Matteo Ricci. Having accurately forecasted a solar eclipse, he was appointed as an astronomic official to the Chinese court. He and a fellow scientist, the Belgian Ferdinand Verbiest (1623-1688), made great efforts to promote the western calendar in China. Although stoutly opposed by some Chinese scholar-bureaucrats, they obtained support from Emperor Kangxi of the Qing Dynasty (1644-1911). According to statistics, by 1701 there were 130 Catholic missionaries and nearly 300,000 Catholic disciples in China.

Later, however, there occurred what became known as the "Argument on Rites." This concerned the questions of whether Catholicism should become part of Chinese culture, how to translate the concept of "Creator," and whether Chinese Catholics could still participate in such traditional ritual activities as offering sacrifice to ancestors and Confucius. The missionaries representing Matteo Ricci thought that "Heaven" in the Confucian classics had a meaning equal to that of "the Lord in" Catholicism; furthermore, that the activities of offering sacrifice to ancestors and Confucius by the traditional Chinese were only a kind of worship and were not contrary to the tenets of Catholicism. The opposition held an opinion exactly to the contrary. Both sides put forward vehement arguments, and at last the Vatican ordered that Chinese Catholics were henceforth banned from offering sacrifice to ancestors and Confucius. Not to be outdone, and in a classic case of tit for tat, Chinese Emperor Kangxi immediately imposed a ban on Christian preaching. This argument developed from within China to outside and from east to west, lasting for more than a hundred years, until at last Catholicism was banished once again from China. But the Argument on Rites achieved a rather unforeseen result: it aroused Europeans' enthusiasm for Chinese culture. Soon books on Chinese history, philosophy, geography, arts and customs were popular in Europe, and all of these branches of Chinese culture became topics of urgent debate among western scholars. Matteo Ricci himself had already introduced China's Confucianism, Buddhism and Taoism to a Western audience in his book *A History of Christianity in China*, and had said, "The greatest philosopher in China is Confucius. He lived into his seventies and, throughout his life, was tireless in teaching through speech, action and writing. People respect him as the greatest sage the world has ever known. In fact, both by virtue of what he said and how he lived, he is never inferior to even the most revered of our ancient philosophers. Indeed, the majority of western philosophers cannot be compared with him."

Traditional Chinese thoughts and culture had their greatest influence on some of the countries in its neighboring regions, particularly the ancient Korean Peninsula and the many separate islands forming Japan. At the time of the Tang Dynasty (618-907), Chinese culture was particularly highly developed and during this period Japan sent thirteen

Statue of Monk Jian Zhen (688-763) who went to Japan.

separate envoys to review the culture and system of the Tang court. They also sent their brightest students to study at the Tang Imperial College. After returning to their homeland, these students were appointed by the Japanese court to various departments of education, medicine, criminal law and arts according to their studies. In the 6th century, Buddhism was introduced to Japan by China and soon became the largest and the most influential religion in that country. Japan also sent its own monks to study at the Tang court, where they learned Buddhist knowledge from China's acknowledged masters. In 753 an accomplished Tang Dynasty monk named

Jian Zhen was invited to Japan by Japanese monks and eventually completed the journey after eleven years of hardship and a perilous sea voyage. Jian Zhen passed the last ten years of his life in Japan where, by dint of his great wisdom garnered over many long years of patient study, he made great contributions to their religion, architecture and medicine and became the symbol of friendship between China and Japan. In the middle of the 7th Century Japan witnessed the famous Taika Reform of 646 following the political and economic systems of the Sui (581-618) and Tang (618-907) Dynasties, which led to an all-around reform of Japanese society, as a result of which Japan entered a whole new period of social, political and economic development.

No less important was the influence of traditional Chinese thoughts and culture on ancient Korea. In the Sui (581-618) and Tang (618-907) Dynasties from the end of the 6th century to the beginning of the 10th, the Silla regime on the Korean Peninsula also sent students to study abroad in China just as they sent monks to study among the learned at the Tang court. Regarding its political system, Silla followed the system of three ministries and six departments adopted by the Sui and Tang Dynasties to establish its central administrative organ and followed the local system of those same Dynasties when establishing their system of prefectures and counties. Silla also based its educational system on Sui and Tang models, opened the subject of Chinese national study with the teaching of such Confucian classics as *Analects of Confucius*, the *Spring and Autumn Annals* and *The Book on Filial Piety* and adopted the Chinese system of imperial examinations in order to determine which scholars were worthy to become government officials.

IV. DEVELOPED COUNTRY OF THE AGRICULTURAL CIVILIZATION ERA

China is written into the annals of history as a developed country in the era of agricultural civilizations. Both domestic and foreign historians are in consensus that ancient China represented the agricultural civilization, whose productivity and social development led the world for a fairly long time. For more than 2,000 years the Chinese ancestors worked hard and were creative, hence enriching and developing the civilization of human beings.

(I) Progress in Agriculture and Development of the Handicraft Industry

In Sichuan Province in southwest China, a flood control and irrigation project designed and built in the Qin Dynasty (221 BC-206 BC) is still in service, which is the famous Dujiangyan Irrigation Project.

Ancient China took agriculture as the main economic model. The alluvial plains formed by major water systems such as the Yellow River, the Yangtze River, the Pearl River and the Liaohe River provide favorable natural conditions for developing agriculture. All previous dynasties of China regarded agriculture as the foundation of the country and encouraged agricultural production with effective policy measures. For a rather long period of history, the agricultural technology level of China was at the forefront of the world.

Dujiangyan Water Works in Sichuan.

As early as the Shang (1600 BC-1100 BC) and Zhou (1100 BC-221 BC) Dynasties, Chinese people began to engage in farming. The main crops at that time included millet, barley, wheat, beans and rice. In the Spring and Autumn Period (770 BC-476 BC), ironware was adopted for farming tools. In addition, people began to plow using cows and agricultural production gained further development. In the Qin (221 BC-206 BC) and Han (206 BC-220 AD) Dynasties, with the improvement of tools and techniques of production, especially the adoption of irrigation systems and reclamation movement organized by the government enlarged the area suitable for farming. During the 70 years from the foundation of the Han Dynasty (206 BC-220 AD) to the enthronement of the Emperor Wudi of the Han Dynasty, because there were no severe wars and turbulences in the country and the weather was favorable without great natural disasters, people harvested adequate crops and barns in both rural and urban areas were full. Meanwhile, the finances of the State enjoyed a surplus. Some literature records that due to such good harvests of crops at that time, the accumulation of grains stored in the barns of the State was so great that they had to be stored outdoors, resulting in putrescence. However, people competed with each other for fortune. It was popular to raise horses, rich or poor. Groups of horses were commonly seen running in the lanes in the countryside. After the Eastern Han Dynasty (25-220), the agricultural economy in the Yangtse River areas began to develop quickly and in the vast southern areas of China rice was harvested twice a year and the level of agricultural production was further improved.

In the early Tang (618-907) Dynasty, the development of China's agricultural economy reached a new record high. With developed production and abundant

Rough Estimate on the Population of China, Europe, Indian Subcontinent and the World From 50 to 1820

(Unit: 1 million)

Year	China	Europe	Indian Subcontinent	World
50	40	34	70	250
960	55	40	—	300
1280	100	68	—	380
1500	103	72	110	425
1700	138	96	153	592
1820	381	167	209	1049

Source: *China: Renaissance of a World Power* by Konrad Seitz (Germany), first edition by the International Culture Company in April 2007.

grains, population increased and people became rich. The cultivated area spread from north to south China, with all the flat ground being utilized. In 732, China had a population of 45.43 million, doubling that of the early Tang Dynasty. In the Song

Dynasty (960-1279), the country vigorously started using irrigation systems, making use of most rivers and lakes. The old channels were repaired and irrigated areas increased. Meanwhile, efforts were made to strengthen intensive cultivation, bringing about an increase in grain output. During the reign of Emperors Kangxi and Qianlong of the Qing Dynasty (1644-1911), the policy of giving the people peace and security was put into practice, reducing the burden on farmers and encouraging agricultural production. As a result, the history of China saw a period with unprecedented development in agricultural production and rapid increase in population.

Rough Estimate on the Per-Capita Income in China, Europe, and the World From 50 to 1820
(According to the Price of 1990 US Dollar in the International Market)

Year	China	Europe	World
50	450	450	—
960	450	400	—
1280	600	500	—
1700	600	870	359
1820	600	1129	706

Source: *China: Renaissance of a World Power* by Konrad Seitz (Germany), first edition by the International Culture Company in April 2007.

Ancient China set great store by agricultural production and summarizing the farming experience so as to popularize it and put it application. Before the Qin Dynasty (221 BC-206 BC), articles on agriculture appeared, not only studying agricultural technology but also discussing agricultural policies. The important literature of the Qin Dynasty (221 BC-206 BC), *Lu's Spring and Autumn Annals*, puts forth four thesis on agriculture. The *Book of Master Si Shengzhi* was an important agricultural work of the Western Han (206 BC-25 AD), taking the central Shanxi Plain as experimental base. In the Eastern Han Dynasty (25-220), *Si Min Yue Ling* recorded farm life in the present day Luoyang area of Henan Province. Another book *Qi Min Yao Shu (Essential Techniques for the Peasantry)* written by Jia Sixie in the Northern Wei Dynasty (386-534) is a key agricultural literature of ancient China, introducing agricultural production technology in the middle and lower reaches of the Yellow River. Statistics show that there are more than 300 literatures studying agriculture in the history of ancient China, which, in one aspect, reflects the advanced development of the agricultural civilization.

The handicraft industry was an important supplement to the agricultural economy, which gave impetus to the development of agricultural production and, at the same time, enriched the style and content of the agricultural civilization. In the period of the origin of Chinese civilization, the level of ceramic art, weaving and manufacture of jade articles was fairly high. In the Shang (1600 BC-1100 BC) and Zhou (1100 BC-221 BC) Dynasties, the handicraft industry became mature, and was called as "all sorts of crafts". The jade articles and bronze vessels were of a high level. In the Spring and Autumn Period (770 BC-476 BC) and Warring States Period (475 BC-221 BC), the ironware foundry became a key handicraft sector, with various kinds of ironware being used in war, social production and life. The Han Dynasty (206 BC-220 AD) saw iron making and casting, steel making, textiles, lacquer manufacturing and paper making upgraded. In the Sui (581-618) and Tang (618-907) Dynas-

Square bottle with flower-bird patterns of the Ming Dynasty (1368-1644).

ties the castings industry developed quickly, the level of metalwork was greatly improved and the technology of manufacturing porcelain became more mature. The porcelain produced in the Tang Dynasty (618-907) featured pure and exact color. In the Song Dynasty (960-1279), the handicraft industry was enlarged in scale, with further compartmentalizing of division of labor. Meanwhile, technology and quality grew at an unprecedented rate. The famous Jingdezhen Kilns entered the golden period. The Ming Dynasty (1368-1644) witnessed fast progress in cotton weaving and metal smelting. The largest iron furnace had a capacity of more than 1,000 kg of ores, with a daily output of 500-plus kg. In the Qing Dynasty (1644-1911), the scale of the handicraft industry was constantly enlarged, with even more distinct division of labor. Jingdezhen Imperial Kilns had an annual output of more than 100,000 articles.

The handicraft industry of the ancient China was mainly managed by governments. After the Song Dynasty (960-1279), especially in the Ming Dynasty (1368-1644), the private handicraft industry gradually developed. From the mid Ming Dynasty (1368-1644), due to blooming consumer demand, the private textile industry greatly exceeded the one controlled by the government. In addition, wage labour and handicraft shops came into being.

(II) Top-Ranking Technologies

China "maintained a scientific knowledge level too far ahead for the Western world to catch up with from the third century to the 13th century" is a comment of Dr. Joseph Needham (1900-1995), a famous expert on the history of Chinese science and technology, on ancient China in this regard. Ancient China's science and technology ranked at the forefront of the world for a long time, not only contributing the "four great inventions" for the human beings, but also leading the world in the fields of astronomy, aerography, medicine, agriculture, botany, zoology, irrigation, transportation, construction, garden design, metal smelting, watercraft manufacture, ceramic making, textiles and printing and dyeing.

The "four great inventions" of ancient China refer to paper making, printing, gunpowder and the compass, which changed the course of human civilization.

Ts'ai Lun of the Eastern Han Dynasty (25-220).

The adoption of paper as writing materials is undoubtedly revolutionary. The paper making technique was invented in the Han Dynasty (206 BC-220 AD), before which, people wrote on tortoise shells, bamboo and thin silk. However, those materials are heavy, expensive and hard to use. In the Eastern Han Dynasty (25-220), a eunuch named Ts'ai Lun summarized experiences of predecessors and improved the paper making technique. Finally, he invented the plant-fiber paper making technique, which greatly increased the output of paper. Through a long period of development, especially in the Song Dynasty (960-1279), paper making techniques grew more mature, widely adopting bamboo paper and grass paper. Furthermore, there appeared *Zhi Pu*, a book specially summing up paper making techniques. China's paper making techniques were first introduced to neighboring countries such as Viet Nam, Korea and Japan in the 3rd-4th centuries and then to the Central Asian areas around the 8th century and to North Africa and Europe in the period from the 11th century to 13th century.

The invention of paper facilitates writing; and that of printing provides access to knowledge for people, which is also revolutionary and promotes social development. In the early 6th century, several centuries after the invention of paper making techniques, China invented block carving printing, which carved characters on a wood block and then added ink to it to print. The Five Dynasties (907-960) saw the appearance of copper plate printing, and the printing of a large number of sutra books, historical records, medical books and Buddhist and Taoist books. In addition, chro-

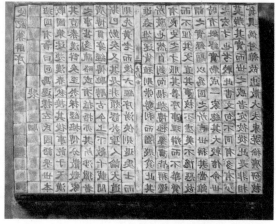

Bi Sheng's movable type (mould).

matic printing was invented. However, moveable-type printing is no doubt a major revolution in printing history. In the Northern Song Dynasty (960-1127), a civilian called Bi Sheng invented the mud movable type technique. Therefore, people no longer used the whole block. In the Yuan (1279-1368) and Ming (1368-1644) Dynasties, wood and metals such as tin, copper and lead movable types were invented. The printing technique was introduced to foreign countries from the Tang Dynasty (618-907), first to Japan, Korea and then to the states of East Asia, South Asia and West Asia and to North Africa and Europe via Persia. In 1456, Gutenberg of Germany printed the *Bible* in movable type. After it was introduced to Europe, it played an important role in promoting the Renaissance and religious reformation of Europe.

The ancient world suffered frequent wars. Hence, the adoption of gunpowder in wars was a major upgrade in the means of warfare, with far-reaching ramifications. The invention of gunpowder is related to the alchemy of China's Taoism. Alchemy is to abstract various medicinal and mineral substances so as to make a drug good for healthcare, with a purpose to make people live forever and never grew old. The Taoists gradually learned the chemical properties of sulfur and saltpeter, which are the materials of gunpowder. Gunpowder was invented in the Jin (265-420) and Southern and Northern (420-589) Dynasties and adopted in the military field in the Tang Dynasty (618-907). In the Northern Song Dynasty (960-1127), gunpowder was produced on a large scale and firearms such as bows with exploding arrows, crossbows with exploding arrows, jet exploding arrow and pipe-typed exploding arrow appeared. The technique of making gunpowder was introduced to Arabian states via India. European people learned to make gunpowder and firearms during their wars with Arabian people.

The invention of the compass informed people as to directions. As early as the Warring States Period, Chinese people discovered the polarity pointing property of magnets and invented the magnetic directional instrument called "Sinan". In the Song Dynasty (960-1279), people discovered the method of artificial magnetization and further developed the compass and made it a tool for navigation. Hence, the celestial navigation method of "watching stars at night and watching the sun in the daytime" was gradually eliminated. Extensive adoption of the compass in navigation opened an epoch in this regard. Thanks to the mature technique of the compass, in the early Ming Dynasty (1368-1644), Zheng He made seven ocean voyages to the west, a feat in the history of navigation. Around the 12th and 13th centuries, the compass was introduced to the Arabian states and then to Europe. It played an important role in the opening-up of European navigation and the discovery of the new continent.

In many aspects of the astronomy such as astronomical observation, calendrical calculation and astrological instruments, ancient China also made

Magnetic needle lying on rush on water-a compass.

world-recognized achievements. The earliest *Spring and Autumn Annuals of China* records 37 solar eclipses, 33 of which were correct, and a lot of records in astronomical phenomenon such as eclipses of the moon, star showers, Halley's Comet, macula and polar lights. Ancient China attached great importance to the formulation of a calendar. As early as the Qin Dynasty (221 BC-206 BC), China confirmed the year of to have 365.25 days, which was the most exact calendar in the world at that time. Most dynasties subsequent had their own calendar, of which the most famous one was the *Shoushi Calendar*, compiled by Guo Shoujing, an astronomer of the Yuan Dynasty (1279-1368), fixing the length of the year at 365.2425 days, exactly the same as the present-day calendar. There were numerous sorts of astrological instruments in ancient China. In the Han Dynasty (206 BC-220 AD), a scientist named Zhang Heng invented an armillary sphere, which adopts water drops from clepsydra to drive the gear equipment inside so as to make it rotate once at a uniform rate every day. The appearance of the stars is completely in accordance with the star images of observatories.

Ancient China is the earliest State which established a mathematics system. In the Eastern Han Dynasty (25-220), thanks to compilation, preparation and supplement by numerous people, *Nine Chapters on the Mathematical Art* which

Statue of Guo Shoujing, noted astronomer.

collected all the achievements on mathematics since the Qin Dynasty (221 BC-206 BC) came out, setting up the mathematics system of ancient China. It mainly served the daily life, involving arithmetic, algebra and geometry and so on. Its concept and calculation of fractions, calculation of proportion, introduction of negative, algorithm for plus and negative and solution of setting up a linear equation group were all 800-odd years earlier than those of India and 1,000-odd years earlier than those of Europe. In the Southern and Northern Dynasties (420-589), mathematician Zu Chongzhi calculated a pi (π), exact with seven significant figures, which was 1,000-

plus years earlier than the world computing method.

Before the appearance of Western medicines in modern times, the development of Chinese medicines was at the forefront of the world, with a system of traditional Chinese medicines coming into being. The *Medical Classic of the Yellow Emperor*, or *Huang Di Nei Jing*, began to discuss Chinese medicine theories systematically. This is the earliest existing book of its kind, guiding the clinical practice of herbalist doctors for thousands of years. In the late East Han Dynasty (25-220), a medical scientist called Zhang Zhongjing completed the *Treatise on Febrile Diseases Caused by Cold and Miscellaneous Diseases*, laying the foundation of therapeutics of Chinese medicines. Another medical scientist named Li Shizhen spent his whole life writing the *Compendium of Chinese Materia Medica*, systematically summing up the theories of traditional Chinese medicines before the 16th century.

Theories of the traditional Chinese medicines base on "Qi", which is divided into Yin and Yang. It was believed that the relative balance of Yin and Yang served as the basis to maintain the normal activities of the human body. If such a balance was disturbed, diseases occurred, thus affecting people's health. Another thought of the theories is the theory of the five elements. It tries to generalize the attribute of various things in the objective world by using the five philosophical categories — wood, fire, earth, metal and water, and explains the interrelationships and transformation rule by using the dynamic mode of the promoting and restriction relation in the five elements. The promoting relation is wood promoting fire, fire promoting earth, earth promoting metal, metal promoting water and water promoting wood; the restriction relation is wood restricting earth, fire restricting metal, earth restricting water, metal restricting wood and water restricting fire. Hence, only grasping the interrelationships of the whole could the doctor know the pathogeny and pathology and then make a prescription to cure diseases.

(III) Complete Political, Legal and Official-Selecting System

China had a set of complete political, legal and official-selecting systems in conformity with an economic system with agriculture as the main part. Different from those of Western countries, these systems have ancient oriental characteristics.

Political System. Beginning from the Qin (221 BC-206 BC) and Han (206 BC-220 AD) Dynasties, the centralized system and the autocratic monarchy system were established, consolidated and developed.

The Qin and Han Dynasties established the Yamens in the Central Government, namely the Three Excellencies and Nine Ministers to implement policies and administer affairs. Three Excellencies refers to the Prime Minister (Chengxiang), the Great Commander (Taiwei), and the Censor-in-chief (Yushi Dafu). Nine Ministers are the Keeper of the Rites, Chief of Retainers, Keeper of the Imperial Chariot, Chief of Honor Guards, Grand Diplomat, Chief Justice, Grand Agriculturalist, Censure of the Imperial Bloodline, and Keeper of the Imperial

Emperor's throne in the Palace Museum in Beijing.

Wealth. The system of the Three Excellencies and Nine Ministers made the division of power among organs systemically and enforced the imperial power, and this system was used by following dynasties. The whole country was divided into two tiers, namely the commanderies and counties, and later changed to three tiers, i.e. prefectures, the commanderies and counties.

China's autocratic monarchy which began in the Qin Dynasty is the core of China's ancient political system. The emperor was regarded as the Son of Heaven, with special status and unbounded power. The emperor differed from the common people even in his title. Beginning from the Han Dynasty, each emperor had his special temple name, posthumous title and reign title. In general, the temple name of the founding emperor of a dynasty was called ancestor (zu in Chinese), such as Emperor Gaozu of the Han, and Emperor Gaozu of the Tang. The Chinese character which most expresses the achievements of an emperor was used as his posthumous title, such as Wen, Wu, Yuan, and Jing. A phrase with a special meaning was used to outline the title of an emperor's reign, such as Jianyuan, Zhenguan, Tianbao, Kangxi, and Qianlong.

In order to ensure the smooth inheritance of the imperial throne, the crown prince system was established during the Han Dynasty. The crown prince may be the son of the emperor or the younger brother of the emperor. If the emperor could not handle the State affairs by virtue of his youth, his mother would do so for him. This is the system of the empress' holding court. This system caused an unforeseen problem in that the empress and her trusted followers contended for imperial power with the emperor and his trusted followers. The empress' trusted followers who have consanguinity with the empress are called the Waiqi (relatives of a king or an emperor on the side of his mother or wife). The emperor's trusted followers who were castrated and lived in the imperial house were called eunuchs. In Chinese history, incidents in which the Waiqi or eunuchs seized power often took place, and competition between crown princes also happened. Qing Emperor Yongzheng drew lessons from the history and set up the system of "secretly choosing the crown prince". The secretly chosen crown prince's name would be written on duplicate documents and one copy would be hidden in a box behind a plaque. The other copy would be kept with the emperor. If the designated name on the two copies were the same, the designated prince could ascend to the throne.

China's autocratic monarchy was perfected in the Sui (581-618) and Tang

(618-907) Dynasties. The prime minister system also was improved in those dynasties. In ancient China, the prime minister was the highest-ranking chief executive who assisted the emperor in handling government affairs and led other officials of all ranks and descriptions. The position of the prime minister was thought to be "below one person, above 10,000 people" among the common people. The prime minister differed in the way to address in different dynasties. When the prime minister assisted a ruler in governing the country, there was sometimes a contradiction between him and the emperor in power. The Sui and Tang Dynasties reformed this system. They let the officials discuss official business collectively, thus weakening the power of the prime minister. This also eliminated the contradiction between imperial power and the power of the prime minister and forced the latter to submit to the former. The central organs serving the emperor were also improved, namely the "three departments and six ministries". Three departments refers to the Department of State Affairs (Shangshusheng), the Imperial Secretariat (Zhongshusheng) and the Imperial Chancellery (Menxiasheng). The Department of State Affairs was the highest administrative organ with its Six Ministries (Liubu) for Personnel (Libu), Population (Hubu), Rites (Libu), War (Bingbu), Justice (Xingbu) and Works (Gongbu). The Imperial Secretariat was the highest decision-making organ and the Imperial Chancellery was the highest deliberative organ.

During the Ming (1368-1644) and Qing (1644-1911) Dynasties, the autocratic monarchy was further strengthened and redeveloped. In order to prevent powerful and imperious officials from seizing power, Emperor Taizu of the Ming Dynasty abolished the position of prime minister and directly controlled the six ministries of government affairs, thus intensifying imperial power. The Ming Court also set up the Eastern Depot (a secret police organization), Western Deport, imperial guards and other secret agent organs run by the eunuchs to protect imperial power and to strengthen supervision over officials of all ranks and descriptions, thus taking the autocratic system to the extreme. The Ming and Qing Dynasties followed the provincial administration systems of the Yuan Dynasty. The Ming Court divided the whole country into 13 provinces and two Zhili (meaning "directly ruled by the Imperial Court"), namely south Zhili and north Zhili. The Qing Court divided the whole country into 18 provinces and directly ruled five regions—northeast China, Inner Mongolia, Outer Mongolia, Hui area and Tibet. In the late Qing Dynasty, the Court also set up Xinjiang Province, Taiwan Province, northeastern China's

Fengtian Province, Jilin Province and Heilongjiang Province.

Legal System. The purpose of the ancient Chinese legal system was to guarantee the imperial power. Its basic frame was the combination of courtesy and punishment, with no division between justice and administration.

The Qin Dynasty put rule by law at a premium. It formulated the *Law of the Qin Dynasty*, which in content covers 29 aspects, such as politics, military affairs, agriculture, market administration, currency flows, traffic, administrative management, case trying and judicial proceedings. The Qin Dynasty adhered to severe punishment for people committing misdemeanors as well as serious crimes. There were a dozen kinds of death penalty. The strict laws did not help the Qin Dynasty last long, but triggered the dissatisfaction of the people, thus accelerating the subversion of the Qin Dynasty. At the beginning, the Han Dynasty drew the lessons from the downfall of the Qin Dyansty due to cruel and complicated laws and made lenient and simple laws. It formulated the *Nine Basic Laws of the Han*. After the rule by the Han Dynasty became stable, the articles of law became increasingly complicated and numerous. The law of the Han Dynasty was grouped into four varieties— the legal articles, imperial decree, application of law, and case analogy. The law of the Han Dynasty puts more emphases upon imperial power, takes Confucian classics as the basis for legal principle, adheres to the principle of combination of courtesy and law, turning courtesy into law, primary virtue and accessory punishment, and virtue being prior to punishment, thus laying solid foundation for the later legal system of "combination of courtesy and punishment".

The building of the legal system witnessed new developments during the Sui and Tang Dynasties. The Sui Court formulated the *Kaihuang Codex*, while the Tang Court, on the basis of it, enacted the *Law of Wude*, the *Law of Zhenguan*, and the *Code of Yonghui* and compiled the *Interpretation of the Laws of the Tang Dynasty* and China's first administrative corpus juris — the Six Corpus Juris of the Tang Dynasty, all of which together formed a perfect legal system. The law of the Tang Dynasty followed the principle of "turning courtesy into the law", and definitely stipulated, "virtue and courtesy are the root of ruling a country while punishment is the way of ruling a country". The punishment was divided into five categories. In the aspect of law enforcement, the death penalty review procedure in particular was improved. Legal supervision was enforced and the system of "three interdependent judicial departments", i.e. first trial, review, and supervision was implemented.

The Ming and Qing Dynasties followed similar legal systems. The Ming Court formulated the *Collected Statues of the Ming Dynasty*, while the Qing Court the *Criminal Laws of the Qing Dynasty*. The two dynasties both made up for the insufficiency of the law by enacting regulations. By the late Qing Dynasty, about 2,000 regulations had been added to the *Criminal Laws of the Qing Dynasty*. In the Qing Dynasty, juridical practice was carried out in light of regulations prior to the laws. The Ming and Qing Dynasties were different in governing the country. The Ming Dynasty was strict while the Qing Dynasty lenient.

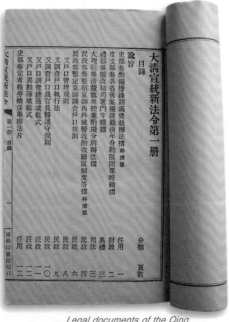

Legal documents of the Qing Dynasty (1644-1911).

Official-Selecting System. The perfect official-selecting system which met the requirement of the autocratic monarchy system was set up in ancient China. It experienced many stages of development, such as recommendation, an official's previous experience in feudal time and examination.

The Han Dynasty formed a complete official-selecting system. Departments of the Central Government and main local governments might recommend the talents to the emperor. Whenever there was the need, the emperor might directly appoint the special talent to an official position. And an official was able to directly appoint his subordinate to a position. Children of high-ranking officials would enjoy preference in promotion. But officials were restricted in terms of assets they owned.

The Nine Rank System became the only official-selecting system in the period from the Wei and Jin Dynasties to the early Sui Dynasty. Under this system, the Court appointed the Talent Rater called Zhongzheng in Chinese in various prefectures and counties, who was responsible for judging the talents. The Talent Rater classified the talents into upper-upper, upper middle, upper-lower, middle-upper, middle-middle, middle-lower, lower-upper, lower-middle, and lower-lower ranks, in light of the judging standard and his perception of the talents, in order for their future selection. With the right to judge but no right to appoint, the Talent Rater

Drawing on the imperial examination during the Song Dynasty (960-1279).

needed to submit his opinion to the government agency, and this was regarded as the basis for the government agency choosing someone for a job. Although having the right to appoint, the government agency had to do so in accordance with the judgment by the Talent Rater (zhongzheng) and could not make bold decisions. This formed the separation between the Talent Rater and government agency. Apparently this system was reasonable, but it met the needs of the High Family Politics. In fact, the position of the Talent Rater was mostly controlled by the families of officials for generations.

The Imperial Examination System was instituted to select officials in ancient China. This system began in the Sui Dynasty, developed in the Tang Dynasty, was standardized in the Song Dynasty, and was improved in the Ming and Qing Dynasties. The Sui Dynasty abolished the old method of selecting talented people, and gradually set up the system of examination in three subjects—Xiucai, Mingjing, and Jinshi. The Tang Dynasty developed the imperial examinations set up by the Sui Dynasty, especially the ones in Jinshi and Mingjing subjects. The examination was held annually with dozens of talents being selected each time. The examination covered knowledge and theory on Confucian classics, political comment and literary talent and grace. The Song Dynasty made adjustment to the imperial examination system and set forth strict provisions regarding the examination procedure and methods, so that the imperial examination tended toward standardization. More than 50,000 scholars were recruited. The imperial examinations in the Ming and Qing Dynasties were more standardized and complete. Compared with the Song and Yuan Dynasties, the new imperial examinations adopted the eight-part essay to choose scholars as officials. The eight-part essay is a type of writing, which assigns a topic focusing on the *Four Books (The Great Learning, The Doctrine of the Mean, The Confucian Analects,* and *The Works of Mencius)* and the *Five Classics (The Book of Songs, The Book of History, The Book of Rite, The Book of Changes* and *The Book of Spring and Autumn)* annotated by the Confucians of the Song Dynasty. The candidates needed to model after the manner of speaking and expound their ideas for the sage in a special style in writing.

An imperial examination was held every three years during the Ming and Qing Dynasties, which was divided three levels—the imperial exam at the provincial level, the metropolitan examination, and final imperial examination. The successful candidates in the imperial examinations at the provincial level were called Juren. The successful candidates in metropolitan exams were called Huiyuan. The successful candidates in the highest imperial examinations were called Jinshi, and were divided into three ranks. The first rank includes three persons—Zhuangyuan (title conferred on the one who came first in the highest imperial examination), Bangyan (second place in the palace examination), and Tanhua (number three in the palace examination), on whom the title Jinshi would be conferred. There were no restrictions on the origin of the candidate in the imperial examination. One could be "a common farmer in the morning and ascending in the emperor's hall in the evening." In feudal Chinese society, imperial examinations were almost the only opportunities for intellectuals from all walks of life to realize their political ambitions.

The political, legal and official-selecting systems set up in Chinese ancient times are the outcome of an agricultural civilization. Historically, these systems helped the court stabilize the ruling order, admit outstanding persons, enhance the quality of officials, and still be in conformity with the imperial autocracy.

(IV) Language and Character

China is one of the countries in which language and written characters appeared earliest forming the Chinese language and alphabet.

In the Spring and Autumn Period (770 BC-476 BC) before the Qin Dynasty, the common Chinese language appeared. Since the 12th century, the Beijing dialect has become the representative of northern dialects. The modern standard language used by the Han people is called Putonghua (Mandarin) in the inland area, Hong Kong and Macao, the Chinese national language in Taiwan and Chinese among the overseas Chinese. It takes the pronunciation of the Beijing dialect as standard pronunciation, the northern dialect as the basic dialect, and the model for modern vernacular Chinese. Chinese language underwent three development stages, namely Chinese ancient language, modern Chinese and contemporary Chinese language. Chinese ancient language is the wording used in ancient times with the written language being the classical style of writing. Contemporary Chinese language is the one formed in the past 100 years, including the spoken and written language. Compared with the Chinese ancient language, contemporary Chinese language is easier to understand and use. Chinese language, belonging to the Sino-Tibetan family, is the language with the most native speakers in the world. It is one of the official languages in Singapore. It is also one of the official and working languages of the United Nations.

The Chinese language has its own features. As far as the syllable structure, the Chinese syllable structure is regular. A Chinese syllable is composed of the initial

Syllable	Initial Consonant	Simple or Compound Vowel
dong (east)	d	ong
xi (west)	x	i
nan (south)	n	an
bei (north)	b	ei

consonant, and simple or compound vowel. For example:

The same Chinese syllables are differentiated from each other by the tones. In Chinese Mandarin, the syllables of the four characters "酣 (han), 韩 (han), 喊 (han), 汗 (han)" are the same, but different in tones, so each expresses a different meaning.

The Chinese word is composed of the morpheme, which is the smallest linguistic unit that has semantic meaning. For example, the word "国 (nation)" is composed of a morpheme, the word "宇宙(universe)" two morphemes, and the word "人民币 (RMB)" three morphemes, while the word "窈窕(gentle and graceful)" consisting of two Chinese characters is a morpheme and word, and the word "巧克力 (chocolate)", composed of three Chinese characters, is also a morpheme.

Quite different from many Western languages such as the English language, the Chinese language does not pay attention to the morphological change of a sentence, but instead the word order, namely the order of the words in a sentence. It shows the grammatical relation and expresses different meaning through changing word order. For example, the sentence "我要学 (I want to learn)" differs from the one "要我学 (let me learn)".

Just as from Chinese ancient language to contemporary Chinese language, Chinese language is constantly developing. As a whole, its development trend is simplification. Words and phrases of the Chinese language obviously develop from more monosyllabic words to more polysyllabic words and disyllabic words are in the majority. For example, "曾"—"曾经" (ever)、"可"—"可以" (OK)、"但"—"但是" (but)、"宾"—"宾客" (guest)、"目"—"眼睛" (eye) and "日"—"太阳" (the sun).

Any foreigner who has been to China will find that in north, south, east or west China, Chinese people always communicate in different accents. These spoken languages are different from each other in sound, words and phrases and expression. They are called the Chinese dialects. Due to historical and geographical reasons, they can be roughly classified into

Inscriptions at the bottom of Maogongding Tripod of the early Zhou Dynasty (1100 BC-221 BC)

one of the seven large groups — Northern dialects (Putonghua, Mandarin), Wu dialect (Jiangsu-Zhejian dialect), Gan dialect (Jiangxi dialect), Xiang dialect (Hunan dialect), Kejia dialect (Hakka), Min dialect (Fujian dialect), and Yue dialect (Cantonese). The speakers of the northern dialect live in most areas of China to the north of the Yangtze River. The speakers of the Wu dialect are generally distributed in southern Jiangsu Province and Zhejiang Province. The speakers of the Gan dialect live in most areas of Jiangxi Province and parts of Hubei Province. The speakers of the Xiang dialect are distributed in Hunan Province. The speakers of the Kejia dialect are scattered in Guangdong, Guangxi, Fujian, Jiangxi and Sichuang. The speakers of the Min dialect are found in Fujian, Taiwan and Hainan and parts of Guangdong Province. The speakers of the Yue dialect live in most areas of the Guangdong Province and part of the the Guangxi Zhuang Autonomous Region.

Chinese characters have more than 3,000 years of history, which makes it the oldest writing system still in use in the world.

The most sophisticated and earliest Chinese characters are Jiaguwen or inscriptions on bones or tortoise shells of the Shang Dynasty (16th-11th century BC). To date, China has unearthed more than 100,000 pieces of animal bone and tortoise shells bearing over 3,500 distinctive Chinese characters, among which one-third have been identified. Jiaguwen is a kind of Chinese characters that resemble drawings very much. Another kind of Chinese characters which appeared after the Jiaguwen is the Jinwen, inscriptions on ancient bronze objects. After Emperor Qin Shihuang unified China, he also unified Chinese language and introduced Xiaozhuan (lesser seal script). Since the Xiaozhuan script was very time consuming, people of the Qin further improved the characters and created a new style, Lishu (official script). During the stages of Xiaozhuan and Lishu, the character font and structure underwent great changes with little hieroglyph color. Kaishu came into being in the Eastern Jin Dynasty (317-420) and was based on Lishu. After Kaishu appeared, the block-shaped Chinese characters were finalized and Kaishu has been used ever since. Kaishu is the standard calligraphy that has been used for the longest period of time.

Chinese characters differ from English words. The basic units of English are letters, which have tone but no meaning. However, those of Chinese are separate characters, with both tone and meaning. Hence, the Chinese character is an ideogram. English has only 26 letters, and the words are comprised of various

Examples of Evolution of Chinese Character Font

Inscriptions on bones or tortoise shells			
Inscriptions on ancient bronze objects			
Xiaozhuan — the lesser seal style Chinese character			
Official script, an ancient style of calligraphy current in the Han Dynasty			
Regular script	魚 (fish)	鳥 (bird)	羊 (sheep)

combinations of the letters, while Chinese characters are comprised of strokes, some having scores of strokes.

Though the structure of a Chinese character is complicated and difficult to grasp, there are mainly four types. The first one is a hieroglyph, made by depicting the shape of the object. For example, the Chinese character "Yu (referring to fish)" is in the shape of a fish and "Shui (referring to water)" is in the shape of water. The second is a self-explanatory character, made by adding abstract symbols to the hieroglyph. For example, the Chinese character "Mu (referring to mother)" is made by adding two points to the character "Nu (referring to woman)", which indicates the character of a nursing woman. Another Chinese character "Zu (soldier)" is made by adding a left-falling stroke to the character "Yi (clothes)", meaning that soldiers wear clothes with symbols. The third is an associative compound, made by combining several ideographs. For example, the Chinese character "Yi (spill)" looks like water spilling from a vessel. Another character "Jian (reflect)" looks like one is looking into a vessel of water, with a meaning of looking into a mirror. The fourth is a pictophonetic character, with one element indicating meaning and the other sound, such as the Chinese characters "Ling", referring to bell, and "Jiang", referring to river.

The number of Chinese characters is one of the largest in the world. It is hard to accurately count the number of Chinese characters, which is estimated to add up to over 60,000. However, only 3,500 of them are commonly used and only 2,500 are the most common ones. This figure is generally equal to the number of common English words. In this regard, it is not an extremely difficult thing to learn Chinese.

(V) Incomparable Achievements in Literature

Ancient Chinese literature is of long standing and boasts brilliant achievements. With its unique style it has enriched the civilization of human beings and elevated it to new heights. Ancient Chinese people committed themselves to creating literature, resulting in various styles of literary works, including *ci* (lyric poetry), *qu* (a type of verse for singing), *fu* (prose-poetry), prose, rhythmical prose characterized by parallelism and complexity, fiction and drama. Numerous excellent works were produced.

The Book of Songs **and** *The Songs of Chu.* Poem is an important style of ancient Chinese literature, and possesses a prominent place among the ancient literary works. The oldest extant literature is the *Book of Songs*, the first collection of poems in the history of Chinese literature. It includes 305 poems collected over a span of 500 years, from the early years of Western Zhou (1100 BC-771 BC) to the middle of the Spring and Autumn Period (the 11th and 6th centuries BC). The works were originally sung with music, but the music book was lost, and only the lyrics remain. There are three sections, namely Feng, Ya, and Song. Feng contains local ballads; the contents of Ya include praying for a good harvest and nobles praising the monumental contri-

Poetry painting drawn by Ma Hezhi, an artist of the Song Dynasty (960-1279), according to the artistic conception of The Book of Songs.

bution of the forefathers; Song is comprised of songs of sacrifice. The book mainly consists of four-character poems, with rich contents and diverse artistic approaches. Many poems especially those in the section of Feng provide true and vivid depictions on people's lifestyles such as working, every-day life, wars and feasts. There is a passage describing a soldier who was on expedition for a long time, which tells about army life, the grief of leaving home and his return home. It reads like this, *"When I left here, willows shed tears. Now I come back on a snowy track. Long, long is the way, hard, hard the day. My grief overflows, who knows? Who knows?"* Moreover, there are a large number of poems with the theme of love and marriage. One which depicts a young man missing his sweetheart reads like this, *"By riverside are cooing a pair of turtledoves. A good young man is wooing a maiden fair he loves. Water flows left and right of cresses here and there. The youth yearns day and night for the good maiden fair. His yearning grows so strong, he cannot fall asleep. He tosses all night long, so deep in love, so deep!"* The realistic writing and awareness of unexpected development expressed in The Book of Songs exerted great influence on the creation of subsequent literature.

Another style of poetry originated in the State of Chu in south China in the late Warring States Period (475 BC-221 BC), namely the songs of Chu. Qu Yuan, a great ancient patriot and poet, is a representative writer of the literature of this style. His magnum opus, *The Sorrow of Separation*, which is the longest lyric among the Chinese classical literatures, depicts his grief and wrath because there was no way to save the nation and realize his ideal during the period when he was exiled. The Sorrow of Separation adopted the artistic approach of romanticism, *"In the morning I drank dew drops on the lily magnolia, and in the evening I ate fallen flowers of the autumn chrysanthemums....I used waternut leaves to make my coat, and used lotus flowers to make my skirt."* Those became the direct source of the romanticism of Chinese literatures. Some enterprising verses are still recited by people today, *"The road ahead is long and long, I will seek truth in the heaven and on the earth."*

Tang Poems. After experiencing *fu* (prose-poetry) of the Han Dynasty (206 BC-220 AD) and rhythmical prose characterized by parallelism and complexity prevailing in the Jin Dynasty (265-420) and the Southern and Northern Dynasties (420-589), Chinese literature saw the Tang (618-907) become the dynasty of poems. During those 300 years, poets came forth in great number, creating a vast quantity of poems. *The Complete Poetry of the Tang* compiled in the Qing Dynasty

(1644-1911) contains more than 48,900 poems by more than 2,300 poets. The authors were of different statuses, including emperors, nobles, officials and men of letters as well as monks, nuns and geishas. It is obvious that poetry became a common literary style in the Tang Dynasty (618-907).

The poems of the Tang Dynasty (618-907) feature the maturity of "modern style" poetry, which is categorized into Lushi (poem of eight lines), Long Lushi and Jueju (poem of four lines). The eight-line poem with five characters to a line and a strict tonal pattern and rhyme scheme and eight-line poem with seven characters to a line and a strict tonal pattern and rhyme scheme are two common types among Lushi, the former totaling 40 Chinese characters and the latter 56. The Lushi which have more than eight lines are called as long Lushi. The Jueju only have half the number of characters as Lushi, the one with five characters to a line totaling 20 characters and the one with seven characters to a line totaling 28.

Lushi stresses rhyme and having a level tone, namely the first and second tones in modern Chinese. The first, third, fifth and seventh lines do not rhyme, but the second, fourth, sixth and eighth lines do rhyme. Moreover, Lushi also attaches great importance to antithesis, matching both sound and sense in two poetic lines. For example, "heaven matches to earth, cloud to wind and land to sky". The middle couplets are required to have neat antithesis. In addition, Lushi stresses tonal patterns, which are divided tones of Chinese characters. In the Southern and Northern Dynasties (420-589), the four tones of Chinese came into being, of which, the first tone was designated as the level tone, and the other three as oblique tones. They are used in line with a certain scheme, making the poem suitable for reading aloud and fluently.

Farewell to Vice-Prefect Du Setting out for His Official Post in Shu

A five-character regular verse of the Tang Dynasty by Wang Bo

By this wall that surrounds the three Qin districts, through a mist that makes five rivers one.

We bid each other a sad farewell, we two officials going opposite ways.

And yet, while the world holds our friendship and heaven remains our neighborhood.

Why should you linger at the fork of the road, wiping your eyes like a heart-broken child?

The Yellow Crane Terrace

A seven-character-regular-verse of the Tang Dynasty by Cui Hao

Where long ago a yellow crane bore a sage to heaven, nothing is left now but the Yellow Crane Terrace.

The yellow crane never revisited earth, and white clouds are flying without him forever.

Every tree in Hanyang becomes clear in the water, and Parrot Island is a nest of sweet grasses;

But I look toward home, and twilight grows dark with a mist of grief on the river waves.

On the Stork Tower

A jueju with five characters to a line of the Tang Dynasty by Wang Zhihuan

The sun beyond the mountains glows,

the yellow river seawards flows

You can enjoy a grander sight,

by climbing to a greater height.

Leaving White Emperor Town at Dawn

A jueju with seven characters to a line of the Tang Dynasty by Li Bai

Leaving at dawn the White Emperor crowned with clouds, I've sailed a thousand li through canyons in a day.

Yellow Crane Pavilion in Wuhan of Hubei Province.

With monkeys' sad adieus the riverbanks are loud; my skiff has left ten thousand mountains far away.

As literary works, Chinese ancient poems have strict standards for creation, being required to not only follow strictly the composing rules of rhyming and having neat antithesis and tonal patterns, but also stress the artistic conception of poems. Chinese ancient poets set great store by dealing with the relation between the connotation and description, the former lying in explaining the truth of matters and the latter depicting phenomenon of matters. Only by unifying the two organically could the poem be excellent. It is "a successful blend of scenery and sentiment". In this process of seeking the best poetic conception and background, it is hard to image how hard the ancient Chinese people worked on composing poems. "Unless my words are shocking I'll not let it rest till death" and "Only by revising a poem thousand times do I feel comfortable" were the determinations of the ancient poets. One poet of the Tang Dynasty (618-907) expressed his painstaking work in composing poems, "Two lines at last! It's been three years; reciting them, I let fall tears. If for you, still, they don't ring true, I'll go back to my autumn hills".

Of the Tang poets, Li Bai, Du Fu and Bai Juyi are the most outstanding ones. Li Bai, reputed as the "fairy poet", lived in the most prosperous time of the Tang Dynasty (618-907). His poems are of both grand and elegant flavors, which find full expression in his poem depicting the fall of Lushan Mountain in Jiangxi Province, *"The sunlit Censer Peak exhales a wreath of cloud; like an upended stream the cataract sounds loud. Its torrent dashes down three thousand feet from high, as if the Milky Way fell from azure sky."* Du Fu is equally famous to Li Bai, enjoying the title of "poet of high attainments". He lived in the declining period of the Tang Dynasty (618-907); hence most of his poems were concerned about the country, with rich social contents and full of humanism. For example, *"Behind the vermillion gates meat and wine go to waste while out on the road lie the bones of those frozen to death". "In the boundless forest, falling leaves swirl and twirl all around; On the endless Yangtze, rolling waves crash and splash all along". "Oh, for a great mansion with ten thousand rooms where all the poor on earth could find welcome shelter".* His poems unified art and thought highly. Bai Juyi is a great poet in the Tang Dynasty (618-907). His poems bravely face reality and reveal and criticize the abuses of society, representing a genre. His two famous long poems *Song of*

Enduring Sorrow and *Song of the Pipa* harmoniously combine narrating and expressing sentiment, and are time-honored masterpieces. Verses like *"The boundless sky and endless earth may pass away, but this vow unfulfilled will be regretted for aye,"* and *"Both of us in misfortune go from shore to shore. Meeting now, need we have known each other before?"* are deeply loved by later generations.

Ci Poem of the Song Dynasty (960-1279). In the middle of the Tang Dynasty (618-907), another literature style namely *ci,* equally famous to the Tang poems, sprung up and entered into its golden age in the Song Dynasty (960-1279). It is a kind of lyric adding words in line with a musical score, with a fixed number of Chinese characters and a stress on rhythm. Meanwhile, it has a fixed tune, also called tonal pattern, such as *Sunset on the River, Reminiscing Princess Tender* and *Buddhist Dancers.* Like poems, *ci* also stresses structure and rhythm. The Song Dynasty (960-1279) saw large numbers of outstanding *ci* poets, with masterpieces emerging continuously. Different styles and genres were also formed. *The Complete Ci-Poetry of the Song* is a collection of some 20,000 *ci* poems from more than 1,330 *ci* poets.

Before the mid-Song Dynasty (960-1279), the *ci* poems sought to be graceful and exquisite as well as connotative. *The Beautiful Lady Yu*, written by King Li Yu of the Southern Tang Dynasty (937-975) expressed missing his homeland and the past like this:

When will there be no more moon and spring flowers, for me who had so many memorable hours? My attic which last night in vernal wind did stand reminds cruelly of the lost moonlit land. Carved balustrades and marble steps must still be there, but rosy faces cannot be as fair. If you ask me how much my sorrow has increased, just see the over-brimming river flowing east!

Ci poet Liu Yong introduced it to the ordinary citizens. He expressed a scene that a pair of young lovers parted in *the Bells Ringing in the Rain*, reading sad and restrained:

Cicadas chill and drearily shrill, we stand face to face at an evening hour before the pavilion, after a sudden shower. Can I care for drinking before we part? At the city gate where we're lingering late, but the boat is waiting for me to depart. Hand in hand, we gaze at each other's tearful eyes and burst into sobs with words congealed on our lips. I'll go my way far, far away on miles and miles of misty waves where sail the ships, evening clouds hang low in boundless Southern skies. Parting lovers would grieve as of old, how could I stand this clear autumn day so cold!

The mid-Song Dynasty (960-1279) saw a turn in *ci* poetry's development, which was brought about by Su Shi, a great poet. He changed the gorgeous, graceful and restrained flavor of *ci*, introducing materials, sentiment, interest, artistic conception and techniques of poems into *ci* so as to diversify its styles. His *ci* poems are both graceful and inspiring. He established a school of heroic abandon for *ci*, new and fresh both in content and form. All of those can be found in his Reminiscing the *Ancient Times at Chibi Cliff* in the tune of *Reminiscing Princess Tender*.

Eastward the Yangtse River flows, its waves washing away traces of giant people of all times old. West of the ancient stronghold is said to be Chibi of Three Kingdoms, glory of Yu Zhou's. The disorderly peaks piercing the sky and splashing waves splattering the bank produce foams like piles of snows. What a great quantity of heroes came to the picturesque land. How splendid and heroic, imagine I, Zhou was at the time when Little Qiao became his wife. When Zhuge and Zhou talked and laughed, Cao Cao's warships and masts were burnt and sank. Touring the old land is my mind; how sentimental and laughable you may find me, on whose head early

Yangtze River

gray hair grows. Human lives are dreamlike; back to the moon my respectful cup of wine goes.

Another *ci* poet of the school of heroic abandon is Xin Qiji. He lived in the Southern Song Dynasty (1127-1279), a hero with great talent but having no room to maneuver. Hence, he used *ci* poems to express his thoughts, overwhelming and inspiring. In the history of *ci* poetry, he was paid equal attention to Su Shi. His famous sentences include *"Young I was, and ignorant of the taste of care, alone I loved to mount the stairs"*. *"The rice fields' sweet smell promises a harvest good; I listen to the frogs croak in the neighborhood"*. *"For, everywhere, no trace of her can be seen, when, all of a sudden, I turned about, that's her, where lanterns are few and far between"* and *"Blue hills can't stop water flowing, eastward the river keeps on going"*.

The Tang (618-907) and Song (960-1127) Dynasties saw not only the brilliant development of poems and *ci* poetry but also plentiful results in the creation of prose. Litterateurs, represented by Han Yu and Liu Zongyuan, launched the Classical Prose Movement, renovating the rhythmical prose characterized by parallelism and complexity and advocating to learn the prose of the Qin (221 BC-206 BC) and Han (206 BC-220 AD) with odd numbers of lines. They created a large number of excellent literary works, leading prose to a new realm. In the Song Dynasty (960-1279), Ouyang Xiu, Su Shi, Su Xun, Su Zhe, Wang Anshi, Zeng Gong and others further developed prose. They are the well-known "eight great men of letters" of the Tang (618-907) and Song (960-1127) Dynasties in the history of Chinese literature.

Yuan verse. Yuan verse is comprised of Sanqu (a type of verse popular in the Yuan (1279-1368), Ming (1368-1644) and Qing (1644-1911) Dynasties, with tonal patterns modeled on tunes drawn from folk music) and Yuan-Dynasty Zaju plays. The former originates from the folk people, mostly from ethnic minorities of north China; the latter is also a kind of Chinese classical poetry, freer than *ci* poetry. A Yuan-Dynasty Zaju play is a kind of drama sung according to Northern Opera. Famous playwrights of the Yuan Dynasty include Guan Hanqing, Ma Zhiyuan and Wang Shifu, with their magnum opuses being *The Injustice Done to Dou E, Sorrow in the Han Palace* and *The Western Chamber* respectively. *The Injustice Done to Dou E* reveals the seamy side of the officialdom and injustice of society. Guan Hanqing criticized the society with expressive techniques in a simple and natural way. The following is the melody sung by Dou E when she was taken to the execution ground, full of grief and indignation:

[Rolling Embroidered Ball] The sun and moon give light by day and by night; mountains and rivers watch over the world of men. Yet Heaven cannot tell the innocent from the guilty, and confuses the wicked with the good! The good are poor, and die before their time; the wicked are rich, and live to a great old age. The gods are afraid of the mighty and bully the weak; they let evil take its course. Ah, Earth, you will not distinguish good from bad, and, heaven, you let me suffer this injustice! Tears pour down my cheeks in vain!

Novels of the Ming (1368-1644) and Qing (1644-1911) Dynasties. The late period of ancient Chinese society namely the Ming (1368-1644) and Qing (1644-1911) Dynasties saw continued development of various styles of literatures, represented by fiction and plays. Fiction is divided into novel and short stories. All the novels are comprised of many chapters, each headed by a couplet giving the list of its content and telling a story of certain length. The story has a beginning, middle and end. It is derived from the folk story-telling. Hence, all of them were vernacular, easy to understand and spread quickly. The Ming (1368-1644) and Qing (1644-1911) Dynasties boast large numbers of novels, including the famous *Romance of Three Kingdoms* by Luo Guanzhong, *The Outlaws of the Marsh* by Shi Nai'an, *The Golden Lotus, Records of a Journey to the West* by Wu Cheng'en, *Unofficial History of Officialdom* by Wu Jingzi and *A Dream of Red Mansions* by Cao Xueqin. *Romance of Three Kingdoms* is a historical novel about the Wei, Shu and Wu States fighting for dominion of the country in the late Eastern Han (25-220). It creates a large num-

Picture edition of A Dream of Red Mansions.

ber of characters such as Zhuge Liang, Guan Yu and Cao Cao. *The Outlaws of the Marsh* is a hero-legend novel, portraying a number of insurrectionists fighting against the wicked, getting rid of the cruel, helping others and doing chivalrous things, and the novel succeeds in creating a large number of vivid heroic characters. *Records of a Journey to the West* is a supernatural novel of evil spirit characteristics. It is created on the base of the story that Xuanzang, a monk of the Tang Dynasty (618-907), went to India to obtain sutras. With magnificent images, it successfully portrays Sun Wukong, a reincarnation of justice. *The Golden Lotus* is a novel revealing the ways of people and the world. It tells the story of Ximen Qing's family, from their becoming rich to their decline. It marked a transition in the development of Chinese novels. From then on, humanism and realism began to appear in novels. *Unofficial History of Officialdom* is a satiric novel, profoundly portraying the face and ugly deeds of a number of men of letters, business people, officials and country gentlemen under the system of imperial examinations and the cannibalistic feudal ethics.

A *Dream of Red Mansions* is a collective work and the crest of ancient Chinese literature. Cao Xueqin, with his experience as background, is the story of a feudal family from being flourishing to being in decline to eventual ruin. It is a masterpiece full of humanism and realism, reflecting the social visage and human relationships in the early Qing Dynasty (1644-1911) in an unprecedented extent and depth. It creates numerous characters each with a special meaning such as Baoyu, Daiyu, Baochai, Xiangyun, Tanchun, Xiren, Wang Xifeng and Jia Zheng. Cao Xueqin collects all the traditional cultures of China in the novel, establishing a literary monument with extensive and profound wisdom and culture. It enjoys a title of encyclopedia of Chinese traditional culture. Hence, it will help you know more about Chinese traditional culture if you read it carefully.

Compared with the Western novels, Chinese traditional novels stress story and plot and feature fast rhythm, but are comparatively weak in mental description of characters.

(VI) Unique Artistic Style

Compared with arts in other countries, Chinese traditional arts, including calligraphy, painting, music, dance, architecture and gardening, have a unique style, featuring colorful Chinese culture.

Calligraphy. Calligraphy is a traditional artistic form with Chinese characteristics, displaying oriental aesthetic value.

Calligraphy may be understood as the method or rule of writing Chinese characters. Calligraphy, as an art, refers to the art of writing Chinese characters. Chinese calligraphy serves the purpose of conveying thought and aesthetic tastes but also shows the "abstract" beauty of the line. Calligraphy takes the Chinese character as the vessel. And the Chinese characters, which feature the complex combination of lines and spots, may be written in many different forms. This makes it possible to create art through calligraphy. At the same time, Chinese characters still remain the main feature of hieroglyphic, symbolic and ideographic writing, which provides the conditions for the calligraphers to create aesthetic imagery. The tools are the brush pen, ink, paper and ink stone, which are commonly referred to as the four treasures of calligraphy. The brush pen made of animal hair is soft for soaking up ink, but also has strong retractility. Using it to write Chinese characters consisting of dots and lines makes Chinese characters appear complicated and changeable, thus forming different styles. When practicing calligraphy, one should pay attention to three basic elements, i.e. the technique of writing calligraphy (the written lines need to have an aesthetic feeling), the form of Chinese characters (strokes collocation need to be reasonable), and layout (many characters are arranged in one through artistic conception).

Chinese calligraphy dates back to the early ages of China. When Chinese characters were created, people took note of the variation of their lines and graphs. The inscriptions on bones or tortoise shells, and inscriptions on ancient bronze

Zhongqiu Tie (book containing models of calligraphy) by Wang Xianzhi.

objects, seal script and lishu (official script) all take on their different features in the form of a Chinese character, application of technique of writing and layout, displaying different aesthetic feelings. Starting from the Western Han Dynasty (206 BC-24 AD), people pursued the art of calligraphy. The Zhangcao (an early form of cursive script) of the Han Dynasty (206 BC-220 AD), a great contribution to calligraphy, is an elegant cursive script integrating cursive script and the official script. In the Wei and Jin period, Chinese calligraphy entered into a new age in which Kaishu (regular script) and xingshu (running script) came into being and there were two calligraphist masters Zhong Yao and Wang Xizhi. Zhong Yao was the originator of Kaishu (regular script). Most calligraphists came from the Wang family which made great achievements in the history of Chinese calligraphy. Wang Xizhi and his son Wang Xianzhi, known as the "Two Wangs" in Chinese calligraphy history, pushed the art of Xingshu (running script) to a new phase. Of the Xingshu (running script) works by Wang Xizhi, the *Preface to the Poems Composed at the Orchid Pavilion*, which is known as the "First Xingshu Work Under Heaven", is the most famous. During the same period, there was a kind of Kaishu (regular script) called "Wei Monumental style" in north China, which was inscribed on steles.

In the Tang Dynasty (618-907), there appeared famous calligraphists such as Ouyang Xun, Zhu Suiliang, Yan Zhenqing and Liu Gongquan, and the Kaishu (regular script) reached its peak. In the Tang Dynasty, Caoshu (cursive script) experienced development to some extent, and Kuangcao (highly cursive script) appeared. In the Song Dynasty, calligraphy began to convey the feelings and interests of calligraphers, instead of pursuing the esthetic values which ideally featured moral standards, so that calligraphy began to embody artistic quality. Su

Shi, Huang Tingjian, Mi Fu and Cai Xiang were the most famous calligraphists of the Song Dynasty (960-1279), known as the "Four Calligraphist Masters of the Song Dynasty". Their calligraphy works, vivid and natural, do not follow the set rule, but instead develop a school of their own. Zhao Mengfu is the most well-known calligrapher of the Yuan Dynasty (1271-1368), whose Kaishu (regular script), well-knit and graceful, is known as the "Zhao Style". Calligraphy continued to undergo development in the Ming (1368-1644) and Qing (1644-1911) Dynasties. Dong Qichang is the most influential calligraphist of the Ming Dynasty. He learned from his predecessors and took nature as method and he made great achievements in Kaishu (regular script), Xingshu (running script) and Caoshu (cursive script), which were praised highly by the later generations. In the early Qing and late Ming period, there appeared a number of calligraphers preferring a style featuring romanticism, which broke the rules of traditional calligraphy and created peculiar romantic works.

Chinese calligraphy was introduced into the Korean Peninsula in the 2nd-3rd century. In the 7th century, Korean calligraphy entered into a period of great prosperity, in which a great number of calligraphists and calligraphy works appeared. Of them, many still exist today. In the 7th century, Chinese calligraphy was introduced into Japan from the Korean Peninsula. In the 8th century, the Tang Dynasty conducted frequent cultural exchanges with Japan, and Chinese calligraphy became prominent throughout Japan.

Painting. Painting and calligraphy are the twin arts of Chinese traditional culture. Like calligraphy, Chinese traditional painting has unique and bright artistic features, giving it a style different from that of other countries.

Chinese painting pays attention to both painting realistically and freehand brushwork, and more attention to catching the spirit rather than shape. The basic method of Chinese painting is the application of lines and ink color. Pen and ink are the core tools for Chinese painting. Chinese painting substitutes ink for color, which is the big difference from western paintings. Traditional Chinese paintings are mainly ink-wash paintings. Ink-wash paintings mainly include landscape paintings, flower-bird paintings and figure paintings.

Chinese painting has a long history. Before the Qin Dynasty, many kinds of painting such as painting on silk, mural painting and lacquer painting were common. In the Wei, Jin, Southern and Northern Dynasties, painting began to pursue independent aesthetic value, a number of figure paintings and landscape paintings appeared, and systemic painting theories began to form. Chinese traditional painting blossomed in the Sui (581-618) and Tang (618-907) dynasties. Zhan Ziqian, the outstanding painter of the Sui Dynasty, was good at painting horses and landscapes. Yan Liben and Wu Daozi were painters of the Tang Dynasty excelled in figure painting, Li Sixun and Wang Wei were good at

Children Playing in an Autumn Garden, by Su Hanchen, a painter of the Song Dynasty (960-1279).

landscape painting, and Xue Su was good at painting flowers and birds. Starting from the Tang Dynasty, the technique of washing with water colors replaced painting with dark green. It is the method of ink-wash painting, which gradually developed into the mainstream of Chinese painting from the late-Tang period.

From the Five Dynasties (907-960) to the Song Dynasty (960-1279), figure painting, flower-bird painting, and landscape painting underwent great development. Jing Hao, Guan Tong, and Ju Ran were famous landscape painters during this

Coloured Parrot, by Emperor Huizong of the Northern Song Dynasty (960-1127).

Dead Tree and Strange Rock, by Su Shi (1037-1101), noted painter and calligrapher of the Northern Song Dynasty (960-1127).

period. Li Gonglin, a painter of the Song Dynasty, created the line drawing method, pushing figure painting to new heights. It was said that the *Vimalakirti Figure* was painted by Li Gonglin, which is an elaborate work of line drawing of a figure. Zhao Ji, Emperor Hui of the Song Dynasty, was good at painting flowers and birds, and the *Peach and Cooer Painting* is his most famous work. The ink-wash paintings of plum blossoms and bamboo attained perfection in the Song Dynasty. *The Ink Bamboo Painting* by Wen Tong and the *Dead Tree and Strange Rock* by Su Shi are from this period. The ink-wash landscape painting also witnessed great development, with the father and son painters, Mi Fu and Mi Youren, as the representatives. They adopted techniques such as the ink work including splash-ink, thus enriching the technique of washing with water colors. During the Yuan Dynasty, many changes took place in painting. The literati paintings held the dominant position. Most literati painters were also poets and calligraphers, thus integrating the paintings with the poems and calligraphy. Huang Gongwang, Wang Meng, Ni Zan and Wu Zhen were the most famous painters from the Yuan Dynasty, known as the "Four Masters of the Yuan Dynasty."

In the Ming and Qing Dynasties, Chinese paintings, especially the ink-wash paintings paid more attention to the general expressive force. Dong Qichang, a great calligrapher and painter of the late-Ming period, learned from his predecessors' strong points and formed his clean, elegant painting style which exerted important influence upon painting during the Qing Dynasty. Among the paintings of the Qing

Dynasty, paintings by the Four Wangs (including Wang Shimin, Wang Jian, Wang Hui, and Wang Yuanqi), the Four Monks (including Shi Tao, Badashanren, Hong Ren and Shi Xi), and the Eight Eccentrics of Yangzhou (a group of painters in Yangzhou during the years of Qing Emperor Yongzhen's and Emperor Qianlong's Reign, and Zheng Banqiao was one of the members) made the greatest accomplishments. The Four Wangs represented the so-called "orthodox school" of ink-wash painting with deep force and skill and their works are elegant and graceful. The Four Monks refused to follow the orthodoxy, stressed original creation, and argued against the bigoted beliefs of the ancients. The Eight Eccentrics of Yangzhou not only inherited the tradition, but also set store by life experiences, making their personality widely known. Their ink-wash paintings, the perfect combinations of poem, calligraphy, painting and stamp, exerted great effect upon modern Chinese painting.

Music and Dance. Chinese traditional music and dance, with a long history featuring the culture of the orient, obviously differs from those of Western countries.

According to historical documents, there were as many as 70 varieties of musical instruments in the Western Zhou Dynasty (1100 BC-771 BC). The Bayin system used in those days classified Chinese musical instruments into eight categories by their materials (i.e. metal, stone, skin, gourd, bamboo, wood, silk and earth). In 1978, some 124 musical instruments were unearthed from the Tomb of Marquis Yi of the Zeng State of the Warring States Period (475 BC-221 BC) in what is now Hubei Province in central China, showing the world China's splendid musical heritage. The unearthed bell set, exquisite, covers approximately five octaves, which means it can produce melodies in seven musical scales. In the Han and Tang Dynasties, the musical instruments underwent constant development. Some instruments such as Pipa (four-stringed lute with 30 frets and pear-shaped body), Sanxian (a long necked lute with three strings without frets), Erhu (a two-stringed fiddle), Yue Qin (a moon-shaped lute with shorter neck and four strings), which are still popular today, were the main ones introduced from Central Asia into the Central Plains and experienced renovation during that period. Music in the ancient Chinese court was very developed with numerous persons were involved. There were tens of thousands of persons involved in making music in the court, and there was a special music institution in charge of the management of the performers and organizing, researching and creation of the music.

Chinese traditional dance originated from the performances in the totem,

Part of Han Xizai's Evening Banquet, by Gu Hongzhong, a painter of
the State of Southern Tang (937-975).

sorcery and sacrifice offering activities and later evolved into the dance with musical accompaniment. In the Western Zhou Dynasty, the musical dance performed by the female performers especially engaging in song and dance appeared. This kind of dance reached a fairly high level in the Han Dynasty and played an important role in ancient Chinese dance for a long period. Performers of this kind of dance received special training, so that the artistic level of ancient Chinese dance was enhanced constantly. Feast music and dance performed by the musical dancers represented the highest level of dance in the Tang Dynasty. Musical dance is a kind of large scale performance combining instrumental music, dance and song. In the Song Dynasty, another unique dance performance form known as the Team Dance appeared. This dance required numerous performers, each with one's own specific role. With regular procedure, it integrated song, dance, recitation, dialog and other artistic techniques that alternate, being a comprehensive artistic form.

Sculpture. The art of sculpture holds an important position among Chinese traditional arts. Featuring oriental culture it is very different from that of other countries with ancient civilizations such as Greece, Egypt and Rome.

The origin of Chinese civilization has close links with sculpture. After the Neolithic Age, China produced rich and brilliant sculpture art. Pottery Sculpture appeared first. The bronzes of the Shang (1600 BC-1100 BC) and Zhou (1100 BC-256 BC) Dynasties show excellent sculpture technique. After the Qin and Han Dynasties, Chinese sculpture art experienced continuous development and a large number of sculptures were left in mausoleums, grottoes and temples. Chinese traditional sculpture absorbed and integrated foreign techniques in its development, thus forming its own characteristics. The Terra-cotta Warriors and Horses discovered in Lintong of Shaanxi Province in 1974 are affiliated with the Mausoleum of Emperor Qin Shihuang, the first emperor of the Qin Dynasty (221 BC-206 BC) who unified China. They became recognized universally as the Eighth Wonder in the World.

After Buddhism was introduced into China, the Buddhist statues gradually became popular. Most of the Buddhist statues are distributed in the grottoes, including the Yungang Grottoes near Datong City of Shanxi Province, the Longmen Grottoes near Luoyang of Henan Province, the Mogao Grottoes in Dunhuang of western Gansu Province, and the Maijishan Grottoes near Tianshui City of Gansu Province. These Buddhist statues reached the peak of perfection, and are of high artistic value. Chinese temples and monasteries still

The terracotta warriors and horses arrayed in battle formation in Pit 1 of the Terracotta Army in Xi'an, Shaanxi Province.

Panoramic view of the Front Hill of the Longevity Hill of the Summer Palace in Beijing.

house many statues of Buddha, Bodhisattva and Arhats.

Garden. Ancient Chinese gardens express the humanistic spirit through pursuing the beauty of the natural landscape and are in harmony with the thought "a perfect integration of man and nature".

The Chinese garden is divided into two categories: The royal garden and the private garden. Through long development, the two categories of garden building reached a peak in the Ming and Qing Dynasties (1368-1911). After the Ming Dynasty moved its capital to Beijing, it increased input into the building of the royal gardens. Besides the Imperial Garden (Yuhuayuan) inside the Forbidden City, there were the Beihai, Zhonghai and Nanhai Seas, together known as Sanhai (Three Seas), to the north of the Imperial Palace. With long and narrow waterways and natural and comfortable layout the Sanhai contrasts finely with the grand and majestic Imperial Palace architectures. Looking around on the Jade Flowery Islet in the center of the Sanhai, the Sanhai, Imperial Palace, Jingshan (Coal) Hill, and hills in the distance present a splendid sight and show the royal strength and grace. The Qing Dynasty rebuilt the Sanhai on the basis of that of the Ming Dynasty and constructed several royal gardens in the west of Beijing. The largest of these was

Yuanmingyuan, which tried to include all the beautiful sceneries under the heaven. In addition, the Qing Dynasty also built the Summer Resort in Chengde of Hebei Province, which covers an area of 560 hectares. The Summer Resort creates a quiet atmosphere by maintaining the natural features of a mountain forest, and constructing some small buildings.

While the royal gardens were built, some officials, rich merchants, celebrities and gentries set about building their private gardens. Chinese private gardens date back to the Han Dynasty and in the Wei, Jin, and Northern and Southern Dynasties, focused on natural landscapes. There were some 1,000 private gardens with the natural landscapes as the theme in Luoyang during the Tang Dynasty, which had an elegant and secretive style. In the Song Dynasty, the view borrowing, view in opposite place and other techniques were adopted in building the private gardens and ornamental stones were also applied. In the Ming and Qing Dynasties, Chinese private gardens reached their zenith. They are mainly distributed in Beijing, Nanjing, Suzhou, Yangzhou, Hangzhou, Wuxi and other places. There were as many as over 150 private gardens in Beijing, with the Banmu Garden, Yimu Garden,

The Humble Administrator's Garden of Suzhou, Jiangsu Province, a famous private garden in China.

Cuijin Garden and Tsinghua Garden as representatives. A great number of private gardens were built in Suzhou, and at one time there were as many as 270. Of them, the Humble Administrator's Garden, the Lingering Garden, the Lion Forest Garden and the Canglang Pavilion are most well-known. These gardens are characterized by the combination of dwelling house and garden, making them perfect for habitation. And they were constantly enhanced culturally to be a synthesis including various hills and pools, flowers and trees, architecture, engravings, calligraphy, paintings, and handcrafts. Private gardens in Suzhou, as the representative of Chinese classical private gardens, are the cream, featuring the combination of culture and life. The gardens follow the principle of adaptation to nature and tactically encapsulate diverse natural views through limited spaces so that people can see big things through small ones and a quiet place in a noisy environment.

(VII) Colorful Social Life

Clothing, food, housing, travel, birth, aging, sickness and death, not to mention various customs and habits, are all essential parts of social life reflecting the level of civilization of a specific society. Influenced by the teachings of Confucianism, ancient Chinese people strove to improve the quality of their life filled with interest and happiness.

Marital Culture. The concept of marital life developed from the inherent reproductive need of humankind to multiply and develop. In China, this began with a group marriage system practiced by primitive society. In the Xia (2070 BC-1600 BC) and Shang (1600 BC-1046 BC) Dynasties, monogamy commonly prevailed, although polygamy was widely practiced among nobles. In the Qin (221 BC-206 BC) and Han (206 BC-220 AD) dynasties, the traditional marriage pattern of China was established, strictly adhering to the principle of "non-marriage between persons with the same family name". Apart from mem-

Hoffman, an American groom in a traditional Chinese wedding.

bers of the imperial family, some aristocrats and persons holding high positions who engaged in polygamy, monogamy was the rule among ordinary families. Traditional Chinese culture regarded marriage for both boy and girl as proper upon coming of age. Chinese people usually regard a happy marriage and successful career as the two major goals in life, and that, once married, a couple should love each other and remain in harmony throughout their lives by assuming various obligations and responsibilities. The traditional Chinese wedding is extremely complicated with much stress on formality. It is divided into six stages known as the "six etiquettes". The first stage is the proposal. The boy's family asks a matchmaker to propose a marriage and then, if the other side agrees to negotiate, they will visit the girl's family with prepared gifts to make a formal proposal. Originally, the gift was a wild goose, but a domestically-raised goose, or even a wooden carved wild goose, was substituted in modern times. The second stage is then the "birthday matching" to ensure the couple's compatibility. If the couple's birthdays and birth hours do not conflict according to astrology, the marriage formalities can then proceed to the third stage, which is the presentation of betrothal gifts. The boy's family should send such gifts as a ring, various other pieces of jewelry and colored silk as a keepsake of the engagement. The fourth stage is the presentation of wedding gifts. These should be sent to the girl's family accompanied by a band of drummers, and it is an important part of pre-nuptial etiquette. The fifth stage requires the two families to select a suitable wedding date, which strictly speaking, requires the boy's side to fix the month and the girl's family the day [especially to avoid the bride's menstrual period]. The last step is for the bridegroom to set out to receive his bride.

Catering Culture. Chinese catering culture has a long history and rich content well-known to the world. The developed agriculture of ancient China provided the natural conditions for the development of the profound catering culture. In the Xia

Attractive Beijing cuisines

and Shang Dynasties, catering ware was categorized into cooking, drinking and table ware. Most were ceramic in the Xia Dynasty and bronze in the Shang Dynasty. Chinese catering culture came into being in the Western Zhou Dynasty (1046 BC-771 BC), featuring a profound etiquette. In the Spring and Autumn Period (770 BC-476 BC) and the Warring States Period (475 BC-221 BC), exquisite and convenient lacquer ware replaced bronze and became widely used in daily life. The nine major tastes of Chinese cuisine, namely sour, sweet, bitter, spicy, salt, fresh, fragrant, tongue-numbing and light, were completed by the time of the Jin (265-420) and Southern and Northern (420-589) Dynasties. The Sui (581-618) and Tang (618-907) Dynasties saw the creation of numerous edible vegetables in people's daily life with a stress on daintiness. The Song Dynasty (960-1179) witnessed great development in catering culture. The national capital was the center for the exchange of southern and northern culinary techniques in numerous varieties. Ceramic table ware was also widely used. In the Ming (1368-1644) and Qing (1644-1911) Dynasties, people in southern China began to eat mostly rice, while wheat predominated in northern China. In addition, corn and tomato were introduced from America. The Qing Dynasty witnessed the peak of Chinese catering culture, forming Jiangsu, Shandong, Sichuan and Guangdong cuisines. The representative of the Qing catering culture is the Feast of Complete Manchu-Han Courses, comprising a vast array of refined Manchu and Han dishes including delicacies of every kind. In ancient China, the daily dietary habits of the ordinary people were two meals in autumn and three meals in summer. They ate porridge in slack seasons and cooked rice during busy times.

Wine Culture. Wine is widely enjoyed around the world and China has its own great drinking culture. The earliest wine in China made from fruits can be traced back to the Stone Age. As the most developed country in agricultural civilization, China was able to brew liquor from corn more than 5,000 years ago. After the Western Han Dynasty (206 BC-25 AD), wine came into being. Among the liquor made from corn, "yellow wine" prevailed before the Tang Dynasty with a rather low alcoholic content. Potent distilled spirits made their debut in the Song Dynasty. There was also "medicinal liquor" containing herbal medicines used to cure disease. Beer was introduced into China from the West in modern times. In the Xia and Shang and Western Zhou Dynasties, wine was mainly used for worship but gradually began to be enjoyed by the people, thus enriching Chinese culture. After

Sipping tea in China.

drinking, one becomes braver and more high-spirited and vigorous, and there are many stories related to drinking in Chinese history. On the occasion of festivals, lucky days, gatherings and departure, or just to ward off the winter chill, people turned to wine. A lot of wonderful verses have been left by great poets, such as *"wait till we empty one more cup"; "if you drink with a bosom friend, a thousand cups are not enough";* and *"never tip an empty golden cup towards the moon".*

Tea Culture. Differing from wine culture, the tea culture of China stresses weak instead of strong. Tea originated in China and was first grown on the Yunnan-Guizhou Plateau in the southwest China before spreading east along the Yangtze River via the Sichuan Basin during the Western Han Dynasty. The Yangtze River Valley has soil and climate suitable for growing tea. In the Wei and Jin Dynasties, the prevailing culture stressed mildness, if not insipidity. Hence, the custom of drinking tea emerged. A family with position would offer a guest with tea. Certain literati, people of elegance, as well as hermits and monks, with much time for leisure and contemplation, developed the tea-drinking habit. In the Tang Dynasty, the work *Tea Classics* was published, spreading the culture further afield. People at this time cherished clarity and sense and this was considered to be fully embodied in the art of making and drinking tea. In the Song Dynasty, tea became popular both in the imperial court and among ordinary people, and the tea culture was continuously enriched in the following dynasties. Scholars of the Ming Dynasty attached great importance to personal integrity and they saw drinking tea as epitomizing moral refinement. The bitterness of the tea also reminded them of the harsh life experienced by the masses. Many people of letters in the Qing Dynasty sought mental liberation and balance and felt that slowly sipping tea induced great calmness. But, in traditional Chinese culture, there is a great difference between "tasting" and "drinking" tea, with the former becoming strongly associated with mental behavior. 'Tasting' is the act of appreciating, enjoying, meditating and commenting on such aspects as color, fragrance and taste. It is favorable for the tea to be green in color, light in fragrance and moderate in taste. Famous teas such as Dragon Well Green Tea, Biluochun Tea, Dahongpao Tea and Junshan Silver Needle are highly prized. In regard to water, that drawn from a mountain stream is best, that of the river of moderate value and that drawn from a well decidedly inferior in making tea. With regard to tea ware, this should be worthy of appreciation and collection. Finally, the environment in which one savors the tea should be elegant, quiet and clean.

Housing Culture. Housing in ancient China was categorized into four types, including fence style, crypt style, house and tent style. Fence-style architecture was a kind of dwelling common in southern China in ancient times. It was raised from the ground and hence was most defensible and sanitary. Crypt-style architecture existed in northern China in primitive times and involved digging holes in the loess soil to create a dwelling. The soil layer in the north is deep and straight with low water content of water favorable for digging. Cave dwellings of this kind are

A tourist hotel in Beijing, featuring the style of the old siheyuan (rectangular courtyard with rooms on four sides).

economical and simple, warm in winter and cool in summer. Houses replaced the crypt-style dwelling as the ancient people of northern China emerged to live on the surface. They featured a distinct culture of agricultural cultivation. The hard walls of houses were built by stamping earth between board frames to create a structure that was warm in winter and cool in summer, with good ventilation and natural lighting and convenient for movement in and out. In order to ward off winter cold, a heated adobe sleeping platform, the *kang*, was invented in northern China. Finally, the tent-style dwelling was created by nomads of northern China as most suitable for their life of constant movement. Siheyuan (a compound with houses on all four sides) is an old architectural style that still exists. Those in northern China differ in style from those in the south. The siheyuan of Beijing eventually became the chief representative of the north China style. Chinese people attached great importance

Women's garment of the Manchu ethnic group of the Qing Dynasty (1644-1911).

to the location of dwellings from fairly early times, forming geomancy in the Qin and Han Dynasties, commonly known as feng shui. A geomancer would always be called in to choose the best location for a house for the living and burial place for the dead, and many Chinese continue this practice today. Geomancy refers to making an overall evaluation on various architectural conditions such as climate, landform, ecology and view.

Costume Culture. Clothing made constant headway throughout human development, moving from primitive leaf and bark coverings to sophisticated textile materials. Correspondingly, shoes, embroidery, hats and various ornaments and hairstyles appeared. People wore different clothes on diverse occasions and in various seasons, thus forming a diverse costume culture. In the Xia, Shang and Western Zhou Dynasties, the decorative function of clothes was prominent, and a clothing system in accordance with the hierarchy emerged. In the Western Zhou Dynasty, clothes differed by grade

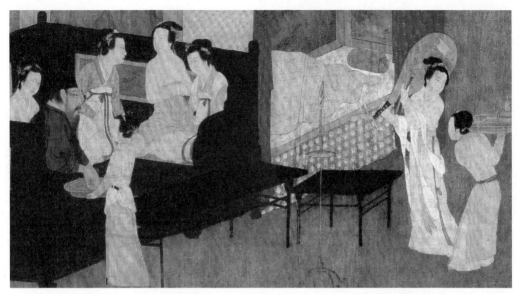

Women of the Tang Dynasty (618-907) in the Painting of Han Xizai's Evening Banquet.

in terms of texture, shape, size, color and decorative patterns. There were strict grades for the robes of kings, feudal princes and ministers. Uniformity in costume culture, however, emerged in the Qin and Han Dynasties. People generally wore *shenyi*, a kind of full-length, one-piece robe. The Jin and the Southern and Northern Dynasties stressed the beauty of clothing, with garments, hats and footwear displaying typical decorative patterns. The clothing in the Sui and Tang dynasties included officials' robes, civilian apparel, men's and women's clothing. The officials' robes showed were strictly delineated by rank in terms of style and color. Women's clothes of the Tang Dynasty mainly comprised a frock, skirt and cape. The skirt was big enough to cover the ground, and the cape hung over the shoulders and fell to the waist. Women of the Song Dynasty commonly wore a frock and skirt. A pomegranate-red skirt was most popular at that time. In the late Song Dynasty, the custom of binding feet began to prevail among noble women. In the Qing Dynasty, people of the subjugated Han ethnic group were compelled to tonsure their hair and meet various clothing requirements. Hence, great changes took place in costumes and a costume system with not only characteristics of the Manchu but also the traditional grading symbols of the Han was finally formed. A long gown and mandarin jacket were typical male apparel in the Qing Dynasty. Han women's costumes were the same with those of preceding dynasties, but the Manchu wore the cheongsam, which is still quite popular today. Han women mostly bound their feet, but Manchu women did not.

Main Traditional Festivals in China

Date	Festival	Activities
The 1st Day of the 1st Lunar Month	Spring Festival	The Spring Festival falls on the first day of the first lunar month of the lunar new year. On that day people in new clothes congratulate each other or go to friends' or relatives' home to pay a new year call. They also offer a sacrifice to their ancestor and have the reunion dinner. Lighting fireworks and lion or dragon dances add festival atmosphere.
The 15th Day of the 1st Lunar Month	Lantern Festival	The Lanten Festival falls on the first moon-rounded day of the lunar new year. Eating boiled rice dumpling symbolizes reunion. There are other activities on that day such as hanging colorful lanterns, guessing lantern riddles, walking on stilts and doing the Yangko dance.
The 2nd Day of the 2nd Lunar Month	Dragon Head Festival	On the day, people offer sacrifice to dragon to pray for good weather for the crops and bumper harvest.
April 5 (or 5 or 6) on the Gregorian Calendar	Pure Brightness Festival	The festival falls on the late period of the spring in which everything on earth are clear and bright. People always go to outskirts to drink wine, indite a poem, sing and dance, and fly kites. Sweeping tombs and worshiping ancestor are the important activity on that day.
The 5th Day of the 5th Lunar Month	Dragon Boat Festival	The festival commemorates Qu Yuan, a man of letter in the service of the Chu King. On that day every family eats glutinous rice dumpling, fixes flagleaf and argyi leaf to the gate, and drinks realgar wine. Dragon boat races also are held.
The 7th Day of the 7th Lunar Month	Double Seventh Festival	Legend has it that Niu Lang (Cowherd) and Zhi Nu (Weaving Woman) in the heaven meet each other on the night on a bridge that the magpies flock together to form. On the night women would put incense burner table, prepare fruit offerings, and do sewing work to beg for ingenuity and skills from Zhi Nu.
The 15th Day of the 8th Lunar Month	Mid-Autumn Festival	The Mid-Autumn Festival is an evening celebration when families gather together to light lanterns, eat moon cakes, appreciate the round moon and guess riddles. People even prepare various melons and fruits to offer sacrifice to the moon.
The 9th Day of the 9th Lunar Month	Double Ninth Festival	The festival has been marked by climbing heights, enjoying chrysanthemum flowers, and wearing in hair small cornel twigs. Later it was named as the Senior Citizen's Festival.
The 29th or 30th Day of the 12th Lunar Month	Lunar New Year's Eve	On the Lunar New Year's Eve, the families put up Spring Festival couplets, Spring Festival Pictures, and door-god pictures, worship their ancestor, have the New Year's Eve Dinner and bid the farewell to the old and usher in the new among the sound of firecrackers. Elder members of a family would give money to children as a gift during lunar New Year. Some people even stay up late or all night on New Year's Eve.

V. END OF FEUDAL POWER AND ESTABLISHMENT OF A MODERN COUNTRY

China had since the 2nd century BC remained in the forefront in the world. This lasted until 1840 when China went into decline, suffering one catastrophe after another.

It was invaded and plundered by big powers with strong ships and cannons. Subsequently, advanced Chinese people began to seek ways to save the nation and achieve modern development. China experienced Westernization in the aspects of technology, social system and culture until the New Democratic Revolution led by the Communist Party of China. Thanks to more than 100 years of unremitting efforts, the nation finally found its way onto a new road of development.

(I) Closed Doors and the Decline of the Qing Court

From the 17th to the 19th century, the world underwent a tremendous transformation. Britain was the first to become a modern country through its "Glorious Revolution" and the "Industrial Revolution"; the French Revolution overthrew the decadent monarchy and created a republic; America became power-ful after the War of Independence and Civil War; Germany rapidly prospered through unification and industrialization; and Russia and Japan also progressed by copying Western ways. In sharp contrast, the Qing Dynasty gradually declined after more than 100 years of its prime period.

The Qing court repulsed foreign civilization. Before the Opium War in 1840, the Qing court regarded itself as the "Celestial Empire" as well as the largest and most powerful country in the world. In its eyes, other countries were all vassal states, which should submit to and learn from China. During the reign of Emperor Qianlong in the 18th century, the West was going through periods of great upheaval that created the various modern powers. However, the emperor paid no attention to these developments. In 1793, when meeting a British envoy, Emperor Qianlong portentously declared, "My Celestial Empire governs all other states in the world" and "we have abundant products of all kinds, so there is no need for us to trade with foreigners." He was blinded by the visionary Celestial Empire. Meanwhile, despite numerous achievements epitomized by the "four great inventions of ancient China" (papermaking, gunpowder, printing and the compass) that had a huge impact on the entire world, traditional Chinese culture ignored invention as it came under the influence of Confucianism stressing the need to "cultivate one's morality, organize one's own family, father one's kingdom and bring order under heaven". Moreover, it regarded the means for improving production techniques as fanciful tricks and evil skills. Hence, when some missionaries took chronometers and guns to China, most officials of the Qing court learnt no long-term lessons from them.

A closed-door policy was adopted. Though Admiral Zheng He's voyages had penetrated to Arabia and Africa scores of years earlier than the first appearance of Western explorers, the Ming court did not take advantage of this to continue to develop the foreign relations. Contrarily, the Ming court banned ocean voyages, in order to prevent depredations by pirates and other states, strictly restricting contact with external world by sea. China lost a good chance to develop valuable contacts with emerging powers elsewhere. From the 16th century, China initiated virtually no maritime trade with outside world and it was left to others, like Portugal, Spain and the Netherlands, who seized the advantage to expand overseas. The ensuing Qing court enforced a ban even more strictly than the Ming. Previously, there were

New Year picture of the late Qing Dynasty (1644-1911): Foreign Envoys Celebrating Empress Dowager Cixi's Birthday in 1903.

at least 100 ports in Fujian, Guangdong, Jiangsu and Zhejiang Provinces that engaged in external trade, but eventually, the only contact point with foreign merchants became the port of Guangzhou lying far up the Pearl River in Guangdong Province. Furthermore, strict restrictions were imposed on the commercial activities of foreigners in Guangzhou. Foreign businesspeople were restricted to a small area of the city and could only trade through Chinese agents. This not only lost China the trading initiative but weakened its ability to resist aggression, while greatly limiting the views of Chinese people and enlarging the distance between China and the rest of the world.

Cultural authoritarianism was carried out. Imperial government itself is a kind of cultural autocracy, implementing obscurantism, which reached the peak in the Qing Dynasty (1644-1911). In the mid-17th century, for example, the Qing court prohibited scholars from establishing colleges, a free press was forbidden and only books related to imperial examinations were allowed to be published; those who published "anecdotes and obscene words" would be severely punished. In order to strengthen its cultural control, the Qing court regulated that the Confucian classics should be instructed on the basis of the annotations of the Song Dynasty (960-1279) scholar Zhu Xi (1130-1200). Examinees for imperial examinations were required to write doctrinaire, priggish eight-part essays in accordance with these annotations. There was also a "literary inquisition" conducted in a large scale, which would sentence someone to death with book-phrases. During the reign of Emperor Kangxi, a man of letters named Dai Mingshi wrote a book titled *Collection of the South Mountain*, containing disguised anti-Qing sentiments. The book was suppressed and Dai and his lineal and collateral relations of three generations at or above the age of 16 were beheaded, in all several hundred people.

People are interested in the reasons why China declined in modern times just like the great Roman Empire. Of course, there are many reasons, but the followings are a few of the most commonly recognized.

Harvesting Rice, a painting created during the Song Dynasty (960-1279).

First, the small-scale peasant economy which fettered the development of productivity is a fundamental reason. The ancient civilization of China was a typical agricultural one, taking land ownership as the economic base and the autarkic natural economy as the main form. Peas-

Small traditional shop managed by all family members.

ants received land to cultivate from the landlord and turned in ground rent in either cash or crops. At the same time, they also engaged in cottage industry in order to make a living. This kind of production organization taking the household as the unit and an economy closely combining small-scale agriculture and a handicraft industry alleviated social contradictions and maintained low level development for a certain period; but, fundamentally, it went against the optimization of social division, expansion of production scale and elevation of the level of production techniques. The small-scale peasant economy meant people were conservative and lacked entrepreneurial spirit.

Second, the autocratic monarchical system that existed for prolonged period of time. In a certain period, the centralized autocratic monarchy system can accelerate social development, but it contains extremely obvious abuses that finally impede social progress. Among all the countries in the world, the autocratic monarchical system of ancient China lasted for the longest time because the small-scale peasant economy provided fertile soil for it and Confucianism served as its moral pillar. One noticeable phenomenon is that many ideologists emerged repeatedly through the various dynasties, but they worked to interpret Confucianism and merely served to entrench the autocracy rather than creating another school of thought. The monarchical power system had reached its peak in the Qing Dynasty (1644-1911), centered on the emperor supported by a rigid central bureaucracy. Hence, individuals could not gain full development and the whole of society lacked creativity and enterprising spirit for progress.

Third, the implementation of the policy of stressing agriculture and repressing

137

commerce. This meant there was no competition and creativity because of the lack of a market. There is a Chinese saying: "Food is the first necessity of the people and grains are the sources of food". During the Qing Dynasty (1644-1911), the population increased at a fast rate, reaching 250 million in 1750, surpassing 300 million in 1800 and hitting 430 million in 1850. With such a large population, agriculture was regarded as the foundation of the country and commerce as a mere supplement. The social status of business people was extremely low and they were despised for a long time. A person engaging in farming for a lifetime would be regarded as a good man, but a person in business was a shifty individual almost certain to be engaged in fraudulent practice. Due to this policy adopted by all previous dynasties, the government usually monopolized all industry that might have ordinarily been the preserve of merchants, such as salt, iron, wine and even the carrying trade and the handicraft industry. As a result, growth of folk commerce was painfully slow. Meanwhile, the commodity economy of China could not gain much development, so capital, technologies and talented people could not be properly utilized. This was the biggest difference in social development between China and the West.

(II) Endless Disasters Brought by Opium

Opium is not only addictive and a difficult habit to stop, but also endangers people's physical health, making them unable to work, and can cause their death. Unfortunately it is this drug that has been closely linked with the fate of China in modern times. The developing course of China's history was impacted by opium and the relations between China and the outside world changed due to opium. The opium brought wars between China and Western countries such as the United Kingdom. When defeated in the wars, China ceded territory and gave compensation to Western countries and gradually fell into a semi-colonial and semi-feudal society.

Expansion by colonization in overseas areas was common among Western powers after geographic discovery. It was the United Kingdom which first launched expansion by colonization in China and made use of opium as its tool. In the scores of years before the Opium War in 1840, China had always held a favorable balance of trade according to normal China-UK trade. At that time, Chinese exports to the United Kingdom were mostly tea leaves and raw silk, and the goods the United Kingdom imported from China were mainly wool fabric and metal products. In order to plunder more properties from China and obtain staggering profits, the British merchants came up with an idea involving this drug. They actually trafficked in large quantities of opium in China through illegal

Opium smokers.

Signing ceremony of the Nanjing Treaty (drawing).

channels and attempted to further open the market in China.

Early in the 18th century the British merchants started to export opium to China and began their villainous drug trading. By the 1830s opium accounted for more than half the goods exported to China from the United Kingdom and its amount kept increasing year on year. In 1823 the amount was 9,035 boxes (about 65 kg of drug per box), some 19,956 boxes in 1830, some 30,000 boxes in 1836 and about 40,000 boxes in 1838. It is estimated that by 1835 the people abusing opium across China were more than 2 million, and later with the increase in import, more and more people used opium.

The unchecked spread of opium brought serious damage to China's socio-economic development and the health of people, This aroused serious attention from the government of the Qing Dynasty (1644-1911). Emperor Daoguang sent Lin Zexu as an imperial envoy to Guangzhou, a center of foreign trade in southern China, to ban opium. Lin Zexu expressed his determination to ban opium by saying, "If the opium is not banned, I will never return. I swear to deal with the matter from beginning to end and there is absolutely no reason to pause the ban." With the support of the local government and people, on June 25, 1839, Lin Zexu destroyed opium captured from drug traffickers by burning it in public on the sea beaches of Humen. It is known as "Destroying Opium at Humen" in the modern history of China.

The fight to ban opium in China aroused strong dissatisfaction from the United Kingdom. The British merchants required their government to launch a war immediately against China to force the Chinese Government to accept their conditions to open the market in China. In April 1840 the United Kingdom launched the war against China. It was the first Opium War and the Qing Dynasty (1644-1911) was finally defeated. On August 29, 1842 in Nanjing of Jiangsu Province on the lower reaches of the Yangtze River, the representatives of the Government of the Qing Dynasty (1644-1911) signed the first unequal treaty in the modern history of China, the Nanjing Treaty, with the British Government. By means of this treaty, the United Kingdom acquired many rights from China: China ceded Hong Kong to the United Kingdom (which was returned to China in 1997); China opened the five ports of Guangzhou, Fuzhou, Xiamen, Ningbo and Shanghai as trading ports; and China compensated 21 million taels of silver to the United Kingdom (equal to one-third of the financial revenue of the Qing Dynasty in a whole year). The United Kingdom also acquired consular jurisdiction, unilateral most-favored-nation treatment, inhabitation rights and renting-land rights in China by means of the Humen Treaty. After this, the United States and France also acquired the same rights as the United Kingdom by signing treaties with the Government of the Qing Dynasty.

The Opium War, the first war in modern times between China and the West, marked the beginning of the modern history of China. In the period of more than 100 years after this, China got in the position of falling behind and being beaten. Wars, ceding territory, and compensation came endlessly. The major ones are shown as follows:

The second Opium War in 1856. In order to further open the market in China, the United Kingdom and France launched an invasion and China was defeated again. The allied forces of the United Kingdom and France fought into Beijing, where they plundered without restraint and set fires in the Yuanminyuan. In June 1858 China was forced to sign the China-UK Tianjin Treaty and China-France Tianjin Treaty. Major contents of the two unequal treaties: Foreign envoys residing in Beijing; opening 10 additional ports as trading ports, i.e. Yingkou, Yantai, Tainan, Danshui, Shantou, Qiongzhou, Hankou, Jiujiang, Nanjing and Zhenjiang today; and compensating 4 million taels of silver to the United Kingdom and 2 million tael of silver to France. After this, China also signed the China-US Tianjin

Ruins of the Yuanmingyuan Park.

Treaty and China-Russia Tianjin Treaty, and the United States and Russia got same benefits as United Kingdom and France.

The first Sino-Japanese War in 1894. China's near neighbor Japan launched this aggressive war against China and China was defeated again. As 1894 was Jiawu Year in the Chinese traditional calendar, so it is called the Jiawu War. The war occurred on the Yellow Sea in northern China. During the war, the Beiyang Naval Fleet which was of an advanced level and was operated elaborately by the Qing Government was almost totally overwhelmed. It was an important action of invading foreign areas taken by Japan after setting a new course of development after its Meiji Reform in 1868, and was the first time that a neighboring island country of China, which had learned from China for a long period of history, defeated China. The whole country of China was astonished. In April 1895 in Shimonoseki, Japan, the representatives of the Qing Government were forced to sign the Sino-Japanese Shimonoseki Treaty. This treaty stipulated: China ceded Liaodong Peninsula, the whole island of Taiwan and its attached islands and the chain of islands of Penghu to Japan. After this Japan controlled Taiwan for half a century and was taken back by the Chinese people in 1945 when China won the War of Resistence Against Japan (1937-1945); China compensated 200 million taels of silver to Japan as its military funds (equal to 3 times the annual revenue of China at that time, and 4 times the annual revenue of Japan); China opened four additional trading ports of Shashi, Chongqing, Suzhou and Hangzhou today; and China allowed Japanese people to operate factories in trading ports of China. The Shimonoseki Treaty further deepened the semi-colonial status of China.

The Eight Powers Allied Forces War that invaded China in 1900. Eight countries of Russia, the United Kingdom, the United States, Japan, Germany, France, Italy, and Austria launched the war in order to maintain and expand their profits in China and the war ended with China's defeat again. The eight powers put about 100,000 troops together in the war; they not only occupied Tianjin and other important northern cities and regions but also occupied Beijing and forced the Qing Government to escape to Xi'an. The Eight Powers Allied Forces slaughtered Chinese people unscrupulously in Beijing, plundered properties, burned down

War Indemnity Foreign Countries Imposed on China	
1841	China paid 6 million taels of silver to Britain who threatened Guangzhou
1842	China paid 21 million taels of silver to Britain
1858	China paid 4 million and 2 million taels of silver to Britain and France respectively
1860	China paid 8 million taels of silver to Britain and France each
1862-1869	(Due to the church incidents between foreign missionaries and Chinese residents) China paid 400,000 taels of silver
1870	(Due to the Tianjin Church Incident) China paid 490,000 taels of silver to France
1873	China paid 500,000 taels of silver to Japan
1878	China paid 9 million taels of silver to Russia
1881	China paid 9 million taels of silver to Russia in order to take back the sovereignty of its partial territory in the drainage area of Yili River
1895	(After being defeated) China paid 200 million taels of silver to Japan
1897	China paid 30 million taels of silver to Japan for its evacuation from Liaodong Peninsula
1901	China paid 450 million taels of silver to Western allied forces
1922	China paid 66 million gold francs to Japan for its evacuation from Jiaozhou of Shandong Province

Source: *A History of Chinese Civilization* by Jacques Gernet (France), first edition in 2006 by China Tibetology Publishing House.

houses and made common people destitute and homeless. A great number of ancient classics, cultural relics and treasures were looted. In September 1901 the representatives of the Qing Government signed treaties formally with representatives of 11 countries, including those of the Eight Powers Allied Forces as well as Spain, Belgium and the Netherlands. As the year was Xinchou Year in the traditional Chinese calendar, the treaty was also called the Xinchou Treaty. It involved China's compensation, establishment of "embassies" in Beijing and foreign forces stationed inside the embassy regions, foreign forces allowed to be stationed in 12 key strategic places along the railway from Beijing to Shanhaiguan, Chinese people prohibited from founding organizations opposing foreigners, and the departments exercising general supervision over foreign affairs changed into the ministry of foreign affairs. The Xinchou Treaty further strengthened the Western powers' forces and impact on China. Regarding compensation, the treaty stipulated that the Qing Government make compensation of 450 million taels of silver to all countries concerned, with customs duty and salt tax as guarantee, and pay it off in 39 years. The annual interest was 0.4 percent and the total amount of principal and interest was 982 million taels of silver. It is customarily-called the Gengzi Indemnity (as the year when the Eight-

Eight-Power Allied Forces Invading Beijing (painting).

Power Allied Forces launched the invasion was the Gengzi Year in the traditional Chinese calendar) and was the biggest indemnity since the Western powers invaded China. Hence the Qing Governments' finances were exhausted, and the burden on Chinese people was greatly aggravated.

Celebrating the Victory of Anti-Japanese War in Shanghai.

Japanese invasion of China during the 1930s and 1940s. On September 18, 1931, the Japanese forces stationed in northeast China attacked Shenyang City, Which was known as the "September 18th Incident". In the following months, they occupied the three provinces of Liaoning, Jilin and Heilongjiang in northeast China. On July 7, 1937, the Japanese invaders fabricated the Lugouqiao Incident outside Beijing City with the excuse that a soldier was lost. They launched an all-around invasion of China, large pieces of Chinese territory fell into the Japanese hands, the Chinese nation faced a crowning calamity and people suffered miserably. Once occupying a piece of land, the Japanese fascist invaders would adopt various brutal and outrageous methods and exerted their control by burning, killing, plundering and raping to the utmost. The Japanese invaders implemented a colonization policy in China, supported a puppet regime, developed a cultural invasion and plundered resources and properties. The Chinese people did not submit but united and attacked back. The Communist Party of China and the Chinese Kuomintang as well as various patriotic political powers and groups organized a broad anti-Japanese national united front, associated with the world anti-fascist forces of the United States, the Soviet Union and the United Kingdom to conduct an anti-Japanese war that lasted for 14 years. On August 15, 1945 the Japanese invaders declared their surrender and the Chinese people won the anti-Japanese war. It was the first victory won by the Chinese people in opposing foreign invasion after 1840. China paid a huge national sacrifice to strive for the victory in the anti-Japanese war. According to statistics, the casualties of Chinese people were more than 35 million and the property loss and battle consumption reached more than US$500 billion.

(III) From Opening Eyes to See the World to Seeking for Self-Improvement

From the defeat in the Opium War, some Chinese people came to understand that China had fallen behind the Western countries in aspects of technology and had to strive for self-improvement.

Lin Zexu was the first man to open his eyes to see the world in modern China. Before the outbreak of the Opium War, like most officials in the Qing Dynasty (1644-1911), Lin Zexu had little knowledge about the outside world. After being appointed to deal with the affairs related to opium, he set to study the Western world and finally proposed the idea of "learning the strong-points of enemies to overwhelm them." He organized people to translate foreign newspapers and books, including *Records on Four Continents* (published in London in 1836) written by a British man Hugh Murray, and introduced the Chinese people to the history, geography, economy, laws, military technologies, sciences and culture of the Western countries. Wei Yuan was another official of the Qing Dynasty (1644-1911) who advocated learning technologies from the Western countries. He opposed blind arrogance, criticized the conservative idea of refusing to learn the "good technologies" of the west, advocated using the Western technologies as reference, and definitely proposed the opinion of "learning good technologies of foreigners to overwhelm foreigners." On the basis of *Records on Four Continents* by Lin Zexu, he added a great deal of information and completed the famous *Records on Overseas Countries* which introduced in detail the geography, history and current situations of the countries in the world and had a comparatively big impact on the Chinese people.

In the 1850s and 1860s a new crisis occurred in the rule of the Qing Dynasty (1644-1911). In 1851 a peasant uprising led by Hong Xiuquan broke out in Jintian Village, Guiping County, Guangxi in southwestern China and the Taiping Heavenly Kingdom was established. In 1853 Hong's army known as the "Taiping Forces" occupied Nanjing, He changed the name of Nanjing to Tianjing, and made it the capital of the Taiping Heavenly Kingdom. After 1860 the Qing Government suppressed the Taiping Heavenly Kingdom. In 1864 the Qing forces captured Tianjing (Nanjing) and the Taiping Heavenly Kingdom was defeated.

After the 1860s in the suppression of the Taiping Heavenly Kingdom, a group of important officials of the Qing court such as Zeng Guofan, Li Hongzhang, Zuo Zongtang and Zhang Zhidong implemented the ideas of learning Western technologies proposed by Lin Zexu and Wei Yuan in order to maintain the power of the Qing court. They operated "foreign affairs", started the "self-improving new power", and defined the developing mode as "Chinese knowledge is the foundation while the Western knowledge is learned to be put into practice." As they studied the West which was taken as the world of "foreigners", this was known as the "Westernization Movement in the history of China."

The Qing Government operated "foreign affairs" for more than 30 years:

Establishing foreign-affairs organizations dealing with foreign countries. In January 1861 the Qing government formally established "yamen (government office) exercising general supervision over affairs of all countries" (Ministry of Foreign Affairs of the Qing Dynasty (1644-1911), in charge of such affairs as foreign negotiation, having trade relations and customs duty. Later Minister of Nanyang Trade Relations and Minister of Beiyang Trade Relations were established to take charge of the trade and foreign negotiations in the south (the region to south of the Yangtze River and the Yangtze River drainage area) and the coastal provinces in the north respectively. Meanwhile the Qing government established the General Bureau of Taxation Affairs in 1861, appointing one main official and one deputy official. The positions were taken by Westerners who took charge of managing all customs duties. A British man named Hurd was in charge of the General Bureau of Taxation Affairs for 48 years.

Running schools and sending students to study abroad. The modern education in China started from the "Westernization Movement." Since the 1860s the Qing Government had run a group of new-style schools teaching "Western languages" (languages of Western countries) and "Western arts" (technologies of Western countries) to cultivate various talents dealing with foreign affairs. In 1862 a school called "Tong Wen Guan" (School of Combined Learning) was founded in Beijing, and an American man Ding Weiliang (W.A.P. Martin) was appointed as its first president, and managed the school affairs for 32 years. According to statistics, officials of foreign affairs opened more than 20 new schools and cultivated a group of persons with abilities in foreign languages, engineering, telegraph, ships, mining affairs, weapons and medicine. The first group of students of modern China studying in Europe and the United States were sent in the course of the Westernization Movement.

First group of children sent by the Government of the Qing Dynasty (1644-1911) to study in America.

Training new-style armies and building up military industry. It was held by foreign affairs officials that the ancient laws and regulations of China were much superior to the west, and only the "firearms" were inferior. By studying advanced foreign military technologies, China could become stronger. From 1861 to the 1890s, officials advocating the Westernization Movement operated more than 20 military factories (bureaus) across China, mainly producing guns, artillery and ammunition, as well as steel and iron and ships. The modern industry of China started from there.

Running modern civil industries. Officials advocating the Westernization movement combined "striving to become stronger" and "striving to become wealthy", with the latter one as the tenet. From the 1870s to the 1890s officials advocating the Westernization movement ran more than 20 civil enterprises, mainly in industries such as mining, metallurgy, and textiles and such causes as shipping, railway and telecommunication.

The Westernization Movement was the first time China studied the West after experiencing two defeats in the Opium Wars in modern times, as well as an industrialization movement within the system of the ruling group. As this movement was limited to the aspect of technologies, its limitation was very obvious. With

Modern capitalist firm.

the defeat of China in the First Sino-Japanese War, the Westernization Movement was declared bankrupt. The history made it clear that it was impossible to find the fundamental solution for China by only operating the Westernization Movement.

After the Westernization Movement, however, the Chinese people really changed their views on the world. Before the Opium War in 1840 when Westerners came to China, the officials of the Qing Government were disdainful of them and would not want to have contact with them. They only ordered merchants to contact them. And those people maintaining contact with foreigners were held in disdain by people. Due to lack of knowledge about outside world, no person of the Qing Government was willing to deal with foreign affairs outside of the country. The Qing Government did not send Chinese people to the United Kingdom and France as envoys until 1876. After scores of years of the Westernization Movement, the contacts between East and West increased and the Chinese people changed their views on the outside world. In eyes of common Chinese people, Westerners gradually became "Yangren" (with a meaning of holding foreigners in esteem) from "Yiren" (with a contemptuous meaning).

(IV) Establishment of a Modern Country System

The Northern Fleet operated by officials advocating the Westernization Movement with painstaking efforts was almost completely destroyed in the First Sino-Japanese War in 1894, and the Chinese nation was confronted with a severe crisis. Some advanced Chinese people came to understnd that it was hard to become prosperous and strong only by learning Western technologies as it could not change the fate of China from being beaten by others. It was a necessity to carry out reform to establish an advanced country. Hence the Hundred Day Reform and the Revolution of 1911 at the end of the 19th century and the early 20th century.

The Hundred Day Reform occurred in the Wuxu Year (1898) of the traditional Chinese calendar. It was an imperialistic reform geared to reform the autocratic system of the Qing Government through such ways as the "Glorious Revolution" in the United Kingdom and the Meiji Reform (1868-1912) in Japan. The decorum of monarchism was maintained while the parliamentarianism was carried out to divide imperial power and administrative power. The leaders of the movement were Kang Youwei and his student Liang Qichao. They publicized the theory of Western society and politics, held evolutionism in esteem, and solemnly contradicted the feudalist obstinate thoughts and the people advocating the Westernization Move- ment which only advocated studying Western technologies without carrying out reform. It was hard for traditional Chinese culture and society to accept the reform geared to change the thousands of years of autocratic system. In order to make the theoretic basis for reform, Kang Youwei said in his works that the thoughts of civil rights, democracy and equality of the modern West and the political rules of parliaments and election were created by Confucius and dressed himself up as the true inheritor of Confucian orthodoxy.

In April 1895 Kang Youwei collaborated with more than 1,300 successful candidates in the imperial examinations at the provincial level in Beijing to submit a written statement to Emperor Guangxu proposing to develop modern industry and implement the constitutional monarchy system. This had important impact on the modern history of China. The event showed that the intelligentsia started to become the mainstream in the movement to save the nation from extinction. Emperor Guangxu supported Kang Youwei's reforming proposal which, however, was opposed by the obstinate and fogeyish school of Empress Dowager Cixi who held the real power. The obstinate school represented by Cixi held that "ancestral regulations cannot be changed", and claimed that "the nation could be subjugated but reform could not be carried out", as "the theory of civil rights had a hundred harms without a benefit." On June 11, 1898 Emperor Guangxu issued the imperial decree declaring the reform. The reform lasted for 103 days until September 21 when Empress Dowager Cixi started a coup d'etat to abolish the "reform", so it was called the Hundred Day Reform.

The Hundred Day Reform ended in failure, but after the movement the modern democratic theory of the West began spreading in China. The failure of the Hundred Day Reform also declared that it was impossible for China to carry out a constitutional monarchy like the United Kingdom or Japan, and the only choice was to put down imperialism through revolution in order to save China from extinction and establish a modern state. It was Dr. Sun Yat-sen and his revolutionary school that shouldered this historical duty.

Portrait of Dr. Sun Yat-sen.

Strictly speaking, the revolutionary movement to found a modern country in China started from Dr. Sun Yat-sen. It was the Revolution of 1911 led by Dr. Sun Yat-sen that put down the absolute monarchy controlling China for more than 2,000 years and made a democratic republic the political choice of China.

Dr. Sun Yat-sen was born in 1866 in Xiangshan County (Zhongshan) in Guangdong Province in southern China. This region was open to foreign countries very early and people had more contact with the outside world. The elder brother of Dr. Sun Yat-sen once went to Hawaii to develop and became an overseas Chinese capitalist. In his youth, Sun Yat-sen went to the United States where he accepted a complete

Western education supported by his brother, including natural science and political science. A will of "reforming China" came into being in his mind. In 1894 Sun Yat-sen associated with some people with ideals and integrity to found a revolutionary group called the Revive Chinese Society, put forth the revolutionary proposal of "driving out foreign aggressors, renewing China and founding a united government", and took an oath to put down the autarchy of the Qing court and establish a democratic republic.

From the end of the 19th century to the early 20th century, the movement to save China from extinction gathered force. "Guang Fu Hui" (Restoration Society), "Hua Xing Hui" (the Society for the Revival of the Chinese Nation) and other revolutionary societies emerged one after another and there came into being a requirement to found a national revolutionary party. In August 1905 Sun Yat-sen collaborated with Huang Xing and Song Jiaoren, who were leaders of revolutionary societies, to found "China Tong-meng Society" (China United League) ("United League" for short, and the latter Chinese Kuomintang evolved from it) in Tokyo, Japan with "driving out foreign aggressors, renewing China, founding a democratic republic and averaging land ownership" as its guiding principle. They set up a headquarters and nine branches inside and outside China, making it a national revolutionary party. In his foreword to the official periodical of the Tong-meng Society, *Min Bao* (Civic News), Sun Yat-sen summed up the guiding principle of the Tong-meng Society and elucidated it to "the Three Principles of the People dealing with the questions of nationalism, democracy and people's livelihood". Nationalism covers two aspects, i.e. "driving out foreign aggressors and renewing China," to overthrow the Qing and make China an independent country; democracy covers "founding a republic", i.e. putting down the autocratic system and founding a modern Western democratic republic; and Principle of People's Livelihood covers "averaging land ownership", by which the land price was appraised and determined, after the success of revolution, the land price which increased due to development of social economy was taken back by the State, and gradually the State would buy land from landlords. As the above-mentioned idea of the Three Principles of the People proposed by Dr. Sun Yat-sen aimed at overthrowing the feudal rule and replacing it with a republic, it is called the "Old Three Principles of the People."

The founding of the Tong-meng Society and the birth of the Three Principles of the People indicated the forthcoming of a new stage of China's revolution. On

October 10, 1911 an armed uprising broke out in Wuchang (a part of Wuhan City), in central south China. This was the Revolution of 1911. As 1911 was the Xinhai Year in the traditional Chinese calander, it is also called the Xinhai Revolution, which overthrew the Qing court. On January 1, 1912, after the election by representatives of 17 provinces, Sun Yat-sen took his oath in Nanjing as provisional

Opening ceremony of the First Congress of the Republic of China (1912-1949) on April 18, 1913.

president. He declared the founding of the provisional government of the Republic of China, viewed the year 1912 as the first year of the Republic of China and changed the Chinese calendar to the Gregorian calendar. Then a provisional Senate was established as a legislative organ.

At this point, in this old oriental country of China the absolute monarchy lasting for more than 2,000 years collapsed at last and a democratic republic with modern meaning began.

At that time northern China was still controlled by the forces of the Qing court. In order to end the opposing situation between the north and south and establish a united republic state soon, the south conceded to the north and transferred the position of provisional president to an important minister of the Qing court Yuan Shikai with the abdication of the emperor of the Qing Dynasty as the precondition.

On February 12, 1912 the emperor of the Qing Dynasty declared his abdication. On April 1, Sun Yat-sen formally relinquished his leadership as provisional president. On the 2nd, the provisional Senate decided to move the provisional government to Beijing instead of Nanjing as expected by Sun Yat-sen.

After this, south and north China were under the control of different forces. The revolutionary party had their activities basically in south (with Guangdong as the center) and the warlord forces changed from the army men of the Qing Dynasty (1644-1911) were basically in the north (also called as the Northern or Beiyang Warlord). Such a situation lasted until in 1928 when the Nanjing National Government united the whole country.

(V) New Cultural Enlightenment Movement

The progress of any society is actually the progress in thoughts and culture. The development of thoughts and culture in modern China was accompanied by the movement of saving China from extinction. The course of saving the country from extinction was also the course of enlightenment.

The ancient thoughts and culture established on the basis of natural economy had their rationality in previous history and played an active role in social development and progress, but fundamentally they did not suit the demands of the development of modern social productivity. In the society of absolute monarchy,

Bronze statue of Yan Fu and his *Theory of Evolution* carved in stone tablet.

people were oppressed gravely by regality, divine power, clan authority and husband authority. They enjoyed no freedom and equality at all. To break the old culture and replace it with the new culture is the necessary demand for the modernization of China.

The Enlightenment Movement of modern China started from the Hundred Day Reform at the end of the 19th century. When publicizing the need to reform, people involved in the Hundred Day Reform took pains to explain the thoughts and culture of the West. For this purpose, they translated and published a large number of books to introduce the Western theories on social and political science, and the most influential one was the book *Tian Yan Lun* (Theory of Evolution) translated by Yan Fu from *Evolution and Ethics* by a British biologist Huxley. In the book Huxley made use of Darwinism to explain the social development rules and the relations between people and held that the biological evolution rule of "survival of the fittest in natural selection" could also be used to explain the development of human history. In human society, there are competitions between peoples and races, and only the fittest one can survive. Such theory was used by the Western powers to expand overseas. But it coued aslo urge the Chinese to save the nation from extinction and survive. According to the theory, China can become strong instead of being weak only by reforming, or else it would be eliminated through selection.

Provisional Constitution of the Republic of China (1912-1949).

New Youth, an influential revolutionary journal in the 1920s.

Dr. Sun Yat-sen pointed out that, when abolishing the autarchy and establishing a republic had become the general course of development and the popular sentiment, the revolution in laggard nations and states would select the advanced democracy out of necessity, and the Chinese nation would never lack the capability of adopting a democratic republic. Dr. Sun Yat-sen developed the Western theory of separation of powers and proposed "constitution of five powers" (adding examination and supervision powers on the basis of administrative, legislative and judicial powers), with emphasis on selecting officials by means of examinations and on supervision of officials. After the founding of the the Republic of China in 1912, Dr. Sun Yat-sen went all out to publicize such ideas as freedom, equality and philanthropy and tried to establish a democratic constitutional government according to the principles of the Western countries. He also made efforts to make the democratic republic the will of all citizens in the new country.

In 1916 Yuan Shikai who had taken the position as president of the Republic of China publicly called himself emperor of the "Chinese empire". He was condemned by the people and died after 83 days of being emperor. The event showed that it was still an important historical duty to completely eliminate the impact of old thoughts and culture.

A movement broke out in 1919. Known as the May 4th Movement of 1919 it was an anti-imperialist, anti-feudal, political and cultural movement launched under the influence of the Russian October Revolution and led by the intellectuals having the rudiments of Communist ideology. Before and after it, a group of radical democrats represented by Chen Duxiu, Li Dazhao, Lu Xun and Hu Shi held high the banners of "democracy" and "science" and launched a New Culture Movement to attack fiercely the old culture by running the magazine of *New Youth*. Then the enlightenment movement of modern thoughts and culture in China reached a peak.

During the New Culture Movement in the 1920s, radical democrats denounced the crimes of the autocratic system and called on the younger generation to fully understand China's position in the world so as to fight for a bright future. They advocated equality between human rights and scientific spirit, denied such fallacies as "regality was granted by gods" and "misfortune and fortune are decided by heaven god", and opposed the obscurity adopted by rulers. Aiming at the adverse current of worshipping Confucius and restoring ancient ways, Chen Duxiu pointed the critical cutting edge directly to Confucianism, the supporter of an autocratic system, which he said is incompatible fundamentally with the democratic republic system.

Opposing old culture and advocating new culture was an important content of the New Culture Movement. Hu Shi and other scholars called for "literary revolution". He opposed the classical style of writing and advocated writing in vernacular Chinese. Writer Lu Xun wrote many works to criticize the old Confucian ethic and morality. His *Diary of a Madman* and *True Story of Ah Q* made the anti-feudalism struggle of the New Culture Movement reach an unprecedented profundity.

Just at the time when the New Culture Movement in China showed its momentum like a raging fire, there came the news that the Communist Party in Russia had won the Revolution of 1917 and the laboring people became masters of their own fate. This was a shot in he arm of those advocating the New Culture Movement. They vowed to follow the Russian road. A group of intellectuals with initial Communist ideas emerged; they included Li Dazhao, Chen Duxiu, Ma Zedong and Zhou Enlai.

(VI) Ups and Downs of National Revolutionary Movements

Although the Qing Dynasty was toppled during the Revolution of 1911, the Western powers still held sway in China.

In March 1913 Song Jiaoren, a leader of the Kuomintang, was assassinated in Shanghai. Dr. Sun Yat-sen launched the "Second Revolution" to complete the causes that had not been fulfilled by the Revolution of 1911. In 1916 Yuan Shikai restored the emperor system and Dr. Sun Yat-sen and others launched the movement to safeguard the system of the Republic of China. Later, the Northern Warlords annulled the Provisional Constitution, and Dr. Sun Yat-sen and others launched the movement to protect the Constitution for two times. In a short while, the systems of parliament, president and cabinet were introduced one after the other, but none of them could solve the problems plaguing China.

Site of the Huangpu Military School of Land Army of KMT.

Given this, Dr. Sun Yat-sen summed up successful experience of the Russian Revolution and came to the conclusion that the Chinese revolution failed mainly because of the lack of a powerful and strong political party that could lead the revolution to victory. He decided to "learn from Russia as teacher", and adopted the "three great policies" of associating with Russia, associating with the Communist Party of China and assisting peasants and workers. He gave a new explanation to the Three Principles of the People, and took opposing imperialist aggression and "controlling monopoly capital and seeking development of the national capital" as the important contents. In January 1924, after plenty of preparation, the First National Congress of the Kuomintang of China was held in Guangzhou in southern China. At the conference Dr. Sun Yat-sen declared the need to build up the Kuomintang of China according to the mode of the Russian Communist Party, and vowed to "found a country on the basis of the Party" and "administer China on the basis of the Party." He absorbed the Chinese Communist Party members into the Kuomintang to start the first cooperation between the Kuomintang and Communist Party of China. After the First National Congress of the Kuomintang, Dr. Sun Yat-sen adopted the organizational system of the Soviet Union Red Army School, and founded the Chinese Kuomintang Military Academy in May 1924. As the site of the academy was on Huangpu Island in a suburb of Guangzhou, it was also called the "Huangpu Military Academy."

Under the cooperation and joint efforts of the Kuomintang and the Communist Party in the period from 1924 to 1927, the national revolutionary movement in China showed new development. Workers movements and peasant movements reached their climax, the Guangdong revolutionary base was united, the National Government was founded in Guangzhou, and the National Revolutionary Army launched a northern expedition. On March 12, 1925, Dr. Sun Yat-sen died of illness in Beijing. Various factions within the Kuomintang scrambled for power, and some in the Kuomintang even declared to kick the Communist Party members out of the Kuomintang. In April and July 1927, Chiang Kai-shek and Wang Jingwei, who held the military power and party power of the Kuomintang respectively began to carry out a party purge, and the first cooperation between the Kuomintang and the Communist Party failed.

On April 18, 1927, the Nanjing National Government of the Kuomintang was founded. In April 1928 the Nanjing National Government declared to keep up the northern expedition. In early June, the National Government armies marched into Beijing, and the Beijing Government controlled by the Northern Warlords for 16 years running was tumbled. On June 15, the Nanjing National Government announced that China was united. On December 29, the local government of northeast China declared to "submit to the National Government and change its banner." At that point the Nanjing National Government of the Kuomintang achieved national unification.

After Japan fabricated the September 18th Incident in 1931 and the Nanjing National Government adopted the policy of non-resistance, large pieces of Chinese territory were occupied by the Japanese invaders, and the anti-Japanese democratic movements of the Chinese people gradually gained momentum. After Japan invaded north China in 1935, the Chinese nation fell into a new crisis. On December 12, 1936 the patriotic generals of the Kuomintang, Zhang Xueliang and Yang Hucheng, initiated "armed remonstrance" to force Chiang Kai-shek to resist the Japanese aggressors, which was the famous "Xi'an Incident". After efforts made by the Communist Party of China and other parties, the incident was solved peacefully, laying a good foundation for cooperation between the Kuomintang and Communist Party to resist the Japanese aggressors. On July 7, 1937 Japan launched an all-around invasion of China and the National Government declared war against Japan and accepted the CPC proposal of cooperation between the Kuomintang and the Communist Party of China. The second cooperation between the Kuomintang and Communist Party started. China was the major battle field in the anti-fascist war during World War II. It held down two-thirds of the forces of Japanese fascists and strongly supported the anti-fascist war in Europe and on the Pacific Ocean. As the Chinese people played an important role in the world anti-fascist war, China was elected as one of the five permanent members of the UN Security Council when the

General Zhang Xueliang and Genal Yang Hucheng.

The Eighth Route Army led by the Communist Party of China ready to ambush the Japanese invaders. (Photo by Sha Fei)

United Nations was founded later.

On August 15, 1945, the Chinese people won the War of Resistance Against Japan. In the ensuing years, the Communist Party of China and the Kuomintang were locked in vehement political and military struggle for establishing a democratic or an autocratic country.

(VII) Founding of New China under the Leadership of the Communist Party of China

On May 4, 1919, a group of young students in Beijing started a demonstration in protest against the treasonable actions of the Northern government. Subsequently, a series of patriotic demonstrations broke out in many cities across the nation, leading to strikes of workers, shopkeepers and students. This was the epoch-making May 4th Movement in modern China. From then on, China's working class entered the political arena, and the Communist Party of China was founded in 1921 as their representative. The May 4th Movement was led by the leaders of this Party, and their names were Li Dazhao, Chen Duxiu, Mao Zedong and Zhou Enlai.

Chen Duxiu and Li Dazhao were the original founders of the Communist Party of China, laying its earliest foundations in Shanghai and Beijing. On July 23, 1921, the First National Congress of the Communist Party of China was held in Shanghai (July 1 was later made the CPC's official anniversary). Twelve delegates representing approximately 50 Party members participated. They discussed the Party program and decided that its official title be the "Communist Party of China". The historic founding of the CPC meant that at long last China's working class had its own political party, and the calamity-ridden China a new political hope. All at once the revolution in China had taken on an entirely new and significantly more favorable aspect.

After its birth, the CPC took on the task of building China into a "real democratic republic", and fighting against imperialism and feudalism by promoting cooperation and forming a democratic united front together with the Kuomintang. From 1924 to 1927, the CPC firmly led the worker-peasant movement, pushing forward the national revolution under the cooperation of the Kuomintang and the CPC. However, after the 1927 purge of Communists in the Kuomintang, the Communist Party-led revolution faced difficult and uncertain times. To restore the

Site of the First National Congress of the CPC in Shanghai.

situation in their favor, the Communists, under the leadership of Mao Zedong, combined the theories of Marxism-Leninism with the day to day reality of life in China. They launched the agrarian revolution and established revolutionary bases in the rural areas. From 1927 to 1937, the CPC, with its rural power-bases, found itself locked in confrontation with urban-dominating Kuomintang. However, in October 1934, the Worker-Peasant Red Army led by the CPC began the unprecedented large-scale strategic shift, which is known in history as the 25,000-*li* (12,500 km) Long March. The Long March lasted until october 1935. In January 1935, the leadership of Mao Zedong was established during an important meeting held in Zunyi of Guizhou Province.

A group of Chinese students dressed up as Long Marchers pose for a picture at the Luding bridge in Luding of Sichuan. During the Long March (1934-1935) an epic battle took place over the Luding bridge. Now the bridge has become a tourist attraction for many Chinese.

In 1937, after the outbreak of the War of Resistance Against Japan, the united front between the CPC and the Kuomintang was reestablished in order to fight more effectively against the common enemy, a truce that lasted until Japan's ultimate defeat in 1945. In the early days of the war, Chinese Communists headed by Mao Zedong analyzed the fundamental characteristics and the law that governed the progress of the war, and set out to demonstrate that only by launching a people's war could China emerge victorious. The CPC correctly implemented the policy of forming an Anti-Japanese National United Front, developing the progressive forces, winning over the middle classes, and isolating the reactionary forces, thus protecting the fundamental interests of the Chinese nation and the Chinese people. Moreover, the CPC built up a series of anti-Japanese bases, and organized the people to fight the invaders behind enemy lines. This strategy pinned down Japanese forces and wiped out large numbers of Japanese invaders. Meanwhile, as the war progressed, Mao Zedong and his Communist Party comrades had also been improving the Theory of the New Democratic Revolution, the fundamental theory that would lead to the revolution in China. According to the theory, the revolution at this stage would be the New Democratic Revolution; afer the revolution China would become a new democratic country, but not a Western country or a socialist country.

In July 1945, shortly before victory in the war was finally achieved, the CPC held its 7th National Congress in Yan'an of Shaanxi Province. The CPC was by this time already a national political party that had over 900,000 Party members, 1.2 million armed forces, and many revolutionary bases. The 7th National Congress of the CPC was already mentally and organizationally prepared for the ultimate and inevitable success of the Chinese revolution, but pointed out that the future of the Chinese revolution lied in efforts to abolish the fascist dictatorial regime, practice democracy, consolidate and expand the anti-Japanese forces, finish off the few remaining Japanese invaders, and, most importantly, rebuild China into an independent, free, democratic, united, prosperous and powerful country.

After winning the War of Resistance Against Japan, the Chinese people hoped peace would remain and an independent, democratic, united, prosperous and powerful new China would be founded. However, the Kuomintang, under the leadership of Chiang Kai-shek, attempted to destroy the CPC-led people's army and its liberated areas. In June 1946,

A shot of the First General Assembly of the Chinese People's Political Consultative Conference.

the Kuomintang's attack on the liberated areas brought about a full-scale civil war. The CPC, calling on all the progressive forces in the country, and managed to seize the military initiative. At last the strategically decisive battle was fought, the Kuomintang was defeated, and its leaders retreated to Taiwan.

On September 21, 1949, the First Chinese People's Political Consultative Congress was opened in Beijing, with delegates from the CPC and other non-CPC parties invited to participate. Mao Zedong chaired the meeting and announced, "The Chinese people, who account for one-fourth of the world's population, have raised themselves up on their feet. The days when the Chinese people were considered uncivilized are now over." On October 1 of the same year, Mao Zedong announced on Tian'anmen Rostrum the founding of New China and the Central Government of the People's Republic of China.

VI. ENDEAVORS OF NEW CHINA AND REFORM AND OPENING-UP

Since the People's Republic of China was established in 1949, the Chinese people have enjoyed much success along with suffering setbacks and making mistakes in the course of creating a modern nation. After arduous exploration, the CPC led the Chinese people to eventually create a modernization road suited to national conditions, namely socialism with Chinese characteristics.

The year 1978 marked a turning point in the history of New China through the introduction of reform and opening up. Since then, the Chinese people and the Communist Party of China have both undergone huge changes, and the relationship between China and the world has entered a new period of development.

(I) The "Poor and Blank" Foundation of New China

The establishment of the PRC opened a new era in Chinese history. Chinese people celebrated the birth of New China with pride and enthusiasm. But it was established on a foundation of old China's economy and culture and extreme backwardness; Chinese people commonly used the expression "poor and blank" to describe this low starting point.

Taking the development level between the 1930's and 1940's as the standard, China's modern industry accounted for only about ten percent of the national economy, while agriculture and the handicraft industry accounted for more than

Chairman Mao Zedong declared the founding of the People's Republic of China on October 1, 1949.

90 percent. At its inception, New China was a backward agricultural country.

In 1949, China's population ranked first in the world; hence, on a per capita basis, its industrial and agricultural output ranked low in the world. Industrial machinery production was almost zero. Large machinery such as aircraft, automobiles and tractors could not be manufactured. Culture and education were backward. The illiteracy rate reached 80 percent; average life expectancy was only 35 years due to the low level of medicine. New China also had to face the devastation left by the old regime.

At the beginning, the People's Government and the CPC as the ruling party put major efforts into consolidating political power and economic development. By October 1951, the people's governments at provincial, city, county and township levels were set up throughout the country, and some regions introduced regional ethnic autonomy progressively for ethnic minority groups. Economically, they confiscated the monopoly capital of old China to launch a State-owned industrial system (accounting for about 66

Peasants were allotted land to till during the Land Reform.

percent of the country's industrial capital) in order to establish a socialist State-run economy. At the founding of New China, among the serious difficulties it faced were rampant speculative capital, chaotic economic order and runaway inflation. To cope, the State took various measures to combat speculation, enhance market management, stabilize the price system, and reunify national fiscal revenue and expenditures, so as to ensure continuous improvements to the financial and economic situation.

A nationwide land reform movement was launched. Old China's land system was extremely unreasonable as landlords and rich peasants, accounting for less than 10 percent of rural population, held 70-80 percent of the land. The landlords rented out their land and exploited farmers through land possession, acting as loan sharks and other such means. Land reform put an end to feudal land ownership, liberating productive forces so that more than 300 million landless farmers could gain access to farmland without exploitation, greatly arousing their productive enthusiasm.

A determined effort was made to clear the pernicious influences left over from the old society, including the social vices of prostitution, drug trafficking and addiction, and gambling. China suffered a lot from opium. During over 100 years following the First Opium War, opium smoking intensified and remained at epidemic proportions until the founding of New China. The number of drug abusers reached 20 million; nearly a quarter of local people in some places were opium addicts. By the end of 1952, opium smoking had basic ally been eliminated. In old China, visiting prostitutes was even more common and many rural girls were tragically sold into prostitution in particular. The people's governments took effective measures to close brothels, banned prostitution and rehabilitated prostitutes.

After three years of hard work, the national economy had been restored and seen initial development. In 1952, industrial and agricultural output value reached 81 billion Yuan, a growth of 77.6 percent over 1949, with an average annual growth rate of about 20 percent. The output of major industrial and agricultural products surpassed the highest level before liberation. People's living standards were generally improved. Compared with the average level in 1949, workers' wages increased 70 percent in 1952, and farmers' income grew 30 percent.

On the basis of overall recovery in the national economy, the Chinese people launched large-scale economic construction in 1953. According to Mao Zedong, after the establishment of the PRC, there would be a very long transitional period towards building a new democratic society, strengthening national industrial development and ensuring a dominant State-owned economy; this would be followed with the nationalization of the private capitalist economy and individual agricultural collectivization. After three years of construction since the founding of New China, the CPC changed its mind as to how long it would take to achieve socialism. In September 1952, Mao Zedong proposed to basically complete the transition to socialism within 10 to 15 years. The main task of the transition was to basically complete national industrialization and the socialist transformation of agriculture, the handicraft industry and capitalist industry and commerce.

To achieve national industrialization had been the dream of many Chinese in the previous century. The Central Government put forward the First Five-Year

(1953-1957) Plan on development of the national economy. It planned to start a large-scale industrial construction, and determined 156 industrial projects including the construction of the steel, aircraft, machine tools, automobile and petrochemical sectors. By the end of 1957, various indicators were significantly overfulfilled. Industrial and agricultural output value amounted to 124.1 billion Yuan, a gain of 56.9 percent from 1952. The output of main products of heavy industry grew significantly and the extremely backward situation of old China's heavy industrial base was obviously changed.

From 1953, socialist transformation occurred in all areas of agriculture, handicraft industry, and the capitalist industry and commerce. Its mission was to transform private ownership into a mode of belonging to the public owership, and to transform labor-based private ownership of farmers and craftsmen into the collective ownership of the laboring people. By 1956, the socialist transformation of private ownership of the means of production was basically completed. In the national economy, the two forms of public ownership— ownership by the whole people and laboring masses collective ownership — achieved a dominant position, and the socialist economic system in China was thus established.

Premier Zhou Enlai delivering a report at the First Session of the First National People's Congress.

In 1954, the first session of the National People's Congress was held in Beijing; it was attended by 1,226 deputies. Before that, deputies to the People's Conqresses at the township, county, municipal and provincial levels had been elected and the People's Congresses at all levels had been convened. The NPC formulated the Constitution of the PRC, discussed and approved the Report on the Work of the Government, and elected new national leaders. Mao Zedong was elected President of the PRC, Liu

Shaoqi, Chairman of the NPC Standing Committee, and Zhou Enlai Premier of the State Council. The PRC Constitution stipulated that the PRC is a people's democratic State led by the working class and based on the alliance of workers and peasants; all power in the PRC belongs to the people; the people exercise power through the National People's Congress and People's Congresses at local levels; the highest organ of State power is the National People's Congress, it is the only State organ exercising legislative power; the State Council is the Central People's Government and is the highest executive organ of State power.

In 1956, the PRC entered a new era of socialist construction. In September 1956, the CPC held its Eighth Party Congress in Beijing. This was the first such gathering in 11 years. The Congress decided that the principal contradiction facing China was contradiction between the requirements to establish an advanced industrial country and the reality of backward agricultural development, and the contradiction between the people's requirements for rapid development of the economy and culture and reality of an existing system unable to meet these needs. The main task of the CPC and the people was to focus efforts on resolving such contradictions and thus transform China from a backward agricultural country into an advanced industrial one as soon as possible.

(II) The Setbacks and Mistakes in Exploration

It was an arduous and tortuous task to undertake modernization in a country like China with its vast land, large population, backward economy and culture, and uneven regional development. This was an unprecedented situation. In the 1950s, the CPC was still in the exploratory stage.

The CPC adhered to the theory of class struggle to guide national construction and pursue pure socialism. In 1957, the CPC launched a national campaign against what was called "Rightists". It proved to be a bad mistake to allow national construction to be guided by the class struggle theory.

To overcome bureaucracy, subjectivism and sectarianism, in March 1957, the CPC decided to carry out a rectification campaign within the Party to sweep away wrong ideas in order to better shoulder the leadership in building a new nation. During the rectification campaign, the CPC attached particular importance to inviting non-Communist Party persons to become involved. Some leaders of the democratic parties and non-party democratic personages provided criticisms to the CPC. But there were also some people taking the opportunity to criticize the Party leadership and the socialist system. Mao Zedong believed a small number of right-wing elements wanted to overthrow the CPC's leadership and overthrow the socialist system, and so the Party must counterattack. Therefore, he launched the anti-rightist struggle. Its enlargement, however, seriously damaged the people's enthusiasm for nation-building and, damaged socialist democracy, so that social and political life became abnormal.

The 1958, the "Great Leap Forward" movement was designed to shake off poverty and backwardness and promote the advance to communism. But it was a painful lesson in failure.

With the establishment of the socialist system and the First Five-Year Plan completed, large-scale construction was in full swing. The CPC thought it possible to speed up economic construction to overcome China's backwardness in a short time and achieve national prosperity. To that end, it formulated a general line called Great Leap Forward along with creation of people's communes. The contents of the general line were as follows: Go all out, aim high and achieve greater, faster, better and more economic results in building a socialist country. This general line focused on the urgent demand of the CPC and the universal desire of the people to overcome the country's economic and cultural backwardness, but also contained impetuosity and over-anxious thinking, excessive emphasis on the pace of economic construction, exaggeration of the people's will and the role of the subjective efforts, all of which ignored objective law.

Steel smelting furnace erected during the "great leap forward".

In November 1957, Mao Zedong led the CPC delegation to Moscow to attend a meeting of world Communist Parties. During this meeting, the Soviet Union proposed to catch up and surpass the United States in 15 years. In regard to China,

Mao Zedong proposed to catch up with or surpass the United Kingdom in steel output within 15 years. That winter, the Great Leap Forward movement began. In 1958, steel output was set to double that of the previous year to reach 10.7 million tons. To achieve this goal, the whole country began iron and steel production. In agriculture, it constantly raised grain production targets; again, in 1958, the Second Five-Year Plan envisaged a gain in grain output from 250 billion kg to 350 billion kg. To achieve this objective, people's communes were set up in rural areas along with cancellation of small-scale agricultural production cooperatives. The rural people's commune was both a government and economic organization, the most prominent feature being "large in size and collective in nature" and certainly large in population, which would make it easier to undertake the mammoth tasks set. Nationwide, there were more than 50 large communes each containing over 20,000 families. Collective in nature meant public ownership and the cancellation of individual household production, household sideline production and trade fairs; instead, there was unified accounting system and distribution by the commune.

The blind pursuit of speed regardless of objective fact, and fundamentally contrary to the law of economic construction, showed the CPC had underestimated the arduous and long-term nature on building socialism in China. The essence of the movement of people's communes was to establish a so-called universal equality, an average, fair and equitable society on the basis of underdevelopment in productivity. It was an unrealistic fantasy beyond the stage reached by the nation. The result of the Great Leap Forward movement and people's communes was not the development and progress of Chinese society, but rather retrogression. The Chinese economy sharply declined for three consecutive years and the people faced serious difficulties. This collective ownership of rural people's commune in China lasted more than 20 years until 1978, when the reform and opening-up policy was introduced.

From 1959 to 1962, the CPC adopted many policies and measures to correct the errors made earlier and to adjust the national economy. By 1965, through the efforts of both Party and the people, China's domestic economic situation had considerably improved. By the end of that year, calculated in constant prices, the national industrial and agricultural output value increased 59.9 percent over 1957; agricultural output value grew 9.9 percent, industrial output value 98 percent. The consumption level of urban and rural residents increased 7.7 percent in 1965 over 1957. However, the Left-deviationist thinking in CPC guiding ideology wasn't corrected, and the mistakes of expanding the class struggle continued to develop resulting in emergence of a guiding ideology of "taking class struggle as the key link".

In 1966, when the national economy was showing good momentum of development after years adjustment, another major downturn occurred with the outbreak of the "cultural revolution" (1966-1976), resulting in great suffering.

After more than 10 years of exploration and practice since the founding of New China, some senior Party and government leaders gained new understanding as to how to build socialism in the country. But this clashed with the ideas of Mao Zedong. He thought the differences revealed a class struggle between the proletariat and the bourgeoisie, and that within the CPC there were revisionists and those who took the capitalist road; thus, China faced a serious danger of capitalist restoration. In order to ensure the CPC leadership remained in true Marxist hands, Mao

University students in the early days of the 1980s.

determined to launch a public, comprehensive, bottom-up nationwide political revolution involving mass participation.

Mao Zedong always sought to ensure that China hewed to its own road of socialist construction based on his longstanding political ideals. But, because his political ideals and practices were somewhat divorced from the reality of the actual situation then prevailing in China, the desired results in strengthening the nation could not be achieved. Some people within the Party, acting for ulterior motives, attempted to use the "cultural revolution" (1966-1976) to further their own political ambitions. This was totally against Mao Zedong's desires and it meant a great loss to Chinese society.

(III) Reform Injecting Vigor and Vitality into the Development of China

Undergoing a chaotic decade of "cultural revolution" (1966-1976), China's economy was almost brought to the brink of collapse in 1976.

Chairman Mao Zedong passed away on September 9, 1976. He was a principal founder of the Chinese Communist Party, the People's Liberation Army and the People's Republic of China. The CPC's second generation of central collective leadership with Deng Xiaoping as its core put an end to the precarious situation left by the "cultural revolution" and blazed a path of socialism with Chinese characteristics.

The end of the "cultural revolution" provided China a chance to return to the road of sound growth. At that time, a discussion on the problem of the criterion of truth was launched. Its central issue was: What exactly is the criterion for judging what was right and what was wrong, the directives of the late Chairman Mao Zedong or the practice? At last, all the members of the CPC unanimously agreed that practice is the sole criterion for testing truth. Through this discussion, people's minds were emancipated from traditional socialism with rules and regulations and people's thinking

Taking photos before the statue of Deng Xiaoping, chief architect of China's reform and opening-up program, at the Shennan Avenue in Shenzhen, Guangdong Province.

was not shackled to the cult of the individual. The Third Plenary Session of the Eleventh Central Committee of the Communist Party of China, convened at the end of 1978, rectified some mistakes of the guiding ideology made by the CPC in the past and denied completely the erroneous theory and practice that took class struggle as the central task. At the same time, the session decided to shift the focus of the work of the Party and the State to economic development and implemented the historic decision of reform and opening up. It created a new period of China's modernization. After this, the State began to work to set things right, redress the unjust and false or wrong cases in all respects, and solve appropriately problems throughout the country which had been left over by history. In June 1981, the Resolution on Certain Questions in the History of Our Party Since the Founding of the People's Republic of China was adopted after discussion and approval at the Sixth Plenary Session of the Eleventh Central Committee of the CPC. The resolution drew the correct conclusions to the CPC's major events in history, particularly the "cultural revolution", since the founding of New China, and evaluated Mao Zedong's place in history based on facts.

China's rural reform began in Xiaogang Village, Fengyang of Anhui Province when 18 farmers vowed to contract land to till.

While striving to set wrong things right and sum up historical experience, the CPC began to push forward the cause of reform and opening up. Since 1978, China has carried out a comprehensive reform from the countryside to the city and from the economic sector to all other sectors. Furthermore, China has opened to the outside world in the areas along the coasts, the rivers and the country's borders, as well as east, central and west China. The unprecedented large-scale reform and opening-up fully motivated the initiative and creativity of hundreds of millions of people, and created a successful great historical transformation from a highly concentrated planned economy to a viable socialist market economy and from a closed and semi-closed State to a State open to the outside world.

China began to carry out the restructuring of the rural economic system at the end of the 1970s. Since 1982, the responsibility systems of fixing farm output quotas on a household basis and work contracted to households rapidly spread across the countryside of China. The work contracted to households (later renamed the rural household contract responsibility system with remuneration linked to output) enjoyed great popularity among farmers. This form of agricultural production and operation established a direct link between the fruit of farmers' labor and their interests. As a result, the practice of the household contract responsibility system not only aroused enthusiasm for production to the fullest extent, but also enabled China to make continuous gains in grain production. From 1979 to 1984, the average annual growth rate of the gross agricultural output value was 8.9 percent, per-capita grain production rose to 395.5 kg in 1984 from 319 kg in 1978, the output of major agricultural by-products quickly increased and people's living standard was improved considerably. The success achieved by the rural economic reform solidified people's confidence in reform, and provided a good example for comprehensive reform of all other sectors.

China's urban economic reform started up at approximately the same time as the rural economic reform. Due to irrational structure arising from the planned economy that China had adopted for a long time, problems arising in the urban economic reform were more complicated than those in the countryside. China adopted a system of pilot sites to conduct the reform which firstly commenced to increase the decision-making power of enterprises. With the scope of pilot sites extending, the state embarked on some reforms in the managerial responsibility system and ownership structure of enterprises. These reforms gradually broke down the single ownership economy and realized diversified forms of economy. With the deepening of reform and opening up, China made efforts to learn extensively from the beneficial achievements of the development of human civilization, China kept exploring economic theory and modes of economic development which conformed to China's reality and actual development conditions in practice during the 1980s and 1990s. In 1981, the China rectified incorrect notions that were traditionally not in accordance with the facts and confirmed that a market economy could exist in a socialist society. In1982, China put forth the theory that "planned economy was primary and regulation through the market was secondary." Under the premise of upholding the leading position of public ownership, the State strives to develop diverse forms of economy by encouraging the development of cooperative economy and allowing the appropriate development of individual economy. In 1984, China declared that private economy and for-eign-invested enterprises (sino-foreign joint ventures, sino-foreign co-operative enterprises, and solely foreign-funded enterprises) were a neces-

Farmers gained benefits during the ongoing rural reform

sary and beneficial complement to the socialist public economy. In 1992, China put forth the establishment of a socialist market economic system which made market forces play an essential role in the allocation of resources under the State's macroeconomic control. In 1997, China emphasized the country would achieve the transformation in the economic system and the means of economic growth as quick as possible. In other words, China would change from the planned economy to the socialist market economy and from extensive economic growth to intensive economic growth. Thus, China came into an important period of development for deepening economic restructuring and speeding up the socialist modernization drive. Entering the 21st century, in terms of economic development concept, China began to strengthen macroeconomic regulation and control. By readjusting eco-nomic structure and transforming the mode of economic growth, China stepped up its efforts to promote reform and opening-up. Over the past 30 years, under the guidance of a full set of economic theories and modes of economy, China had undertaken an omni-directional reform of State-owned enterprises and other sectors including finance, taxation, investment, pricing, foreign trade, commerce, labor, education, healthcare and transportation. At present, China's socialist market economy has taken shape initially and is being made perfect. The introduction of market competition mechanisms will invigorate new vitality in China's economic development.

While carrying out the reform of economic structure, China has never relaxed the reform of the political structure. Efforts have been made to establish and improve the political system corresponding to the socialist market economy system. Proceeding from the system of Party and State leadership, China carries through the

Organizational Structure of the CPC Central Committee

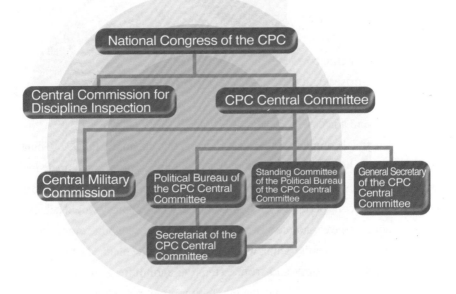

reform of the political structure. Deng Xiaoping held that the drawbacks of the CPC and State leadership, that required getting rid of, mainly included bureaucracy, over-concentration of power, patriarchal methods, life tenure in leading posts, privileges of various kinds, and remaining thought of feudalism. Deng said that some serious problems which appeared in the past may arise again if the defects in the present systems are not eliminated.

(IV) China Opens Wider to the Outside World

China was once a closed or at least a semi-closed country. Despite the Silk Road, which served as a channel for cultural exchange, China, on the whole, didn't realize the necessity of opening out. Since 1978, however, the Chinese Government has specified opening up as a basic State policy and has unswervingly integrated China's development with the development of the rest of the world.

This process of opening up began with the establishment of the Shenzhen, Zhuhai, Shantou and Xiamen Special Economic Zones in south and southeast China in 1980. They were set up to attract foreign investment and advanced technology with the specific purpose of developing the national economy. In 1984, a total of 14 coastal port cities were officially opened, including Dalian, Qinhuangdao, Tianjin, Yantai, Qingdao, Lianyungang, Nantong, Shanghai, Ningbo, Wenzhou, Fuzhou, Guangzhou, Zhanjiang and Beihai. In 1985, the Yangtze River Delta, Pearl River Delta, Xiamen-Zhangzhou-Quanzhou Triangular Area, as well as the Liaodong Peninsula and Jiaodong Peninsula were set up as the coastal economic open areas. They are expected also to promote economic development in inland China. In 1988, Hainan Province was founded to become the largest economic special zone in China. In the following decade, China accelerated the pace of opening up. The

Lujiazui in Pudong of Shanghai before the reform and opening up introduced in late 1978.

Foreign-Funded Enterprises' Contribution to China's Imports and Exports in 2000-2006

	2000	2001	2002	2003	2004	2005	2006
Value of Imports and Exports (US$100 million)	4742.9	5096.5	6207.7	8509.9	11545.5	14219.0	17606.9
Foreign-Funded Enterprises	2367.1	2590.6	3302.4	4721.9	6630.4	8316.4	10364.0
Proportion (%)	49.9	50.8	53.2	55.5	57.4	58.5	58.9

Source: National Bureau of Statistics of the People's Republic of China

year 1990 saw the official opening of the Pudong New Area in Shanghai. Within only a brief period of time, an export-oriented, multi-functional and modern district emerged spectacularly on the horizon, stimulating the economic development of Shanghai and other regions in the Yangtze River Delta.

In the spring of 1992, Deng Xiaoping, the chief architect of China's reform, went to Wuchang in central China, Shenzhen and Zhuhai in south China and Shanghai in east China. In his talks with leaders there, Deng outlined the need to stick to the path of socialism with distinct Chinese characteristics. Henceforth, the third-generation leaders of CPC, headed by Jiang Zemin, led the next stage of China's reform and opening up. In 1992, some border cities in northern China were opened, including Heihe, Suifenhe, Huichun and Manzhouli. The same year saw construction of bonded zones in some of the coastal open cities, which follow a policy more preferential than the one followed by the special economic zones and operated according to international conventions. Meanwhile, nearly 60 cities, counties and towns were granted approval to be opened-up and a further 10 major central cities along the Yangtze River were all given the go-ahead to open to foreign investment and trade. As of the late 1990s, a multi-directional and multi-tiered pattern of opening up had been created covering the broadest possible area.

On November 10, 2001, after 15 years of negotiation, China's accession to the World Trade Organization was agreed unanimously through deliberation of the fourth WTO Ministerial Conference held in Doha, the capital of Qatar. This played an extremely important role in the process of China's opening-up to the outside world. Being a WTO member helps China to maximize its potential in the global market place, turning its regional opening up policy towards a multi-directional one, extending the traditional market economy to embrace the modern service industry, and increasing transparency and regulating the market access conditions.

Attracting foreign direct investment (FDI) is a basic element of the fundamental State policy of opening up. It has played an important role in promoting China's economic development. By the end of 2006, over 600,000 foreign-invested enterprises had been set up in China, covering virtually all sectors including agriculture,

Lujiazui in Pudong of Shanghai after the reform and opening up.

manufacturing and service industries. At present, China has attracted more than US$700 billion of foreign direct investment, ranking it the number one among all developing countries over the past 15 years. In 2005, industrial added value made by foreign-invested enterprises reached 1,900 billion Yuan, accounting for 29 percent of the national total. Also in 2005, advanced technologies introduced by foreign-invested enterprises were worth approximately US$8.3 billion, or 43 percent of the national total; and tax revenue paid by foreign-invested enterprises stood at 634.9 billion Yuan, taking up nearly 21 percent of the national total. By the end of 2006, these enterprises had directly employed more than 25 million people, or over 10 percent of the total workforce in all Chinese cities and towns.

Attracting foreign investment both actively and rationally has resulted in many gains. They include: effectively making up the domestic construction fund shortage;

technological advancements; transference of management mode and experiences; the introduction of modern concepts of circulating and marketing; and the implementation of international competition mechanisms, international regulations and concomitant international standards. In short, the pace of change was greatly speeded up in the formation of China's new open economy, while its investment actively and effectively also helped the Chinese to broaden their international perspectives and free themselves from antiquated ideas and concepts.

On July 13, 2001, Beijing won the bid to host the 29th Olympic Games in 2008. The relationship between China and the outside world has entered a new stage in its development.

(V) Create a New Miracle in Economic and Social Development

Since 1978 China's economy has developed quickly, the society has advanced comprehensively and the construction of modernization has achieved great accomplishments due to continuously deepened reform and expanded opening-up.

China's GDP increased from US$140 billion in the early period of the reform and opening-up to US$2,630 billion in 2006, with the average annual rate of increase above 9.6 percent. In this aspect China is listed as No.4 in the world, rising from No. 15. The GDP per capita increased from less than US$200 in 1978 to US$2,000 in 2006. China leads the world in the production of some important products.

Output of China's Main Industrial and Agricultural Products and Their Ranks in the World in 1978 and 2006

Name of Product	Unit	1978		2006	
		Output	Rank	Output	Rank
Corn	10,000 tons	26546	2	49746	1
Cotton	10,000 tons	217	3	467	1
Rapeseed	10,000 tons	187	2	1270	1
Meat	10,000 tons	856	3	8100	1
Steel	10,000 tons	3178	5	47339	1
Coal	100 million tons	6	3	24	1
Crude oil	10,000 tons	10405	8	18400	5
Electricity generated	100 million kwh	2566	7	28344	2
Cloth	100 million meters	110	1	550	1
Cement	10,000 tons	6524	4	124000	1
Chemical fertilizer	10,000 tons	869	3	5592	1
TV	10,000 sets	52	8	8375	1

Source: National Bureau of Statistics of the People's Republic of China.

Foreign trade increased from US$20.6 billion in the early period of opening up to US$1,760 billion in 2006, and China's ranking rose from No.32 in the world to No.3. Since 2002 the growth of foreign trade has been above 20 percent for five successive years. From 2002 to 2004 the total trade volume rose every year; in 2002 it was listed as No.5 in the world, in 2003 it rose to No.4, in 2004 it exceeded Japan and listed as No.3 in the world, and in 2006, it approached Germany which was listed as No.2. By the end of 2006, the national foreign exchange reserves reached US$1,066.3 billion, exceeding Japan and leaping to No.1 in the world.

The Chinese people rode the reform tide to affluence. Since 1978 the per-

Contrast Between Countries Ranking World Top Ten in Gross Domestic Product in 2001 and 2006

(Unit: US$100 million)

Rank	2001			2006		
	County and Region	Gross Domestic Product	Proportion in the World's Total (%)	County and Region	Gross Domestic Product	Proportion in the World's Total (%)
1	USA	100759	31.9	USA	132446	27.5
2	Japan	41624	13.2	Japan	46593	9.1
3	Germany	18913	6.0	Germany	28970	6.0
4	UK	14313	4.5	China	26301	5.5
5	France	13398	4.2	UK	23737	4.9
6	China	13248	4.2	France	22316	4.6
7	Italy	10904	3.5	Italy	18526	3.8
8	Canada	7051	2.2	Canada	12691	2.6
9	Mexico	6221	2.0	Spain	11280	2.5
10	Spain	6084	1.9	Brazil	8820	2.2

Source: Database of the World Bank.

capita disposable income of urban residents has multiplied by more than 30 times; the per-capita net income for rural residents has increased by more than 23 times; the number of people living in poverty has decreased from 250 million to 23 million in 2006 and more than 200 million poor people have shaken off poverty; the Engel coefficient per urban and rural resident decreased by more than 20 percentage points and the Engel coefficient per urban and rural household was 36.7 percent and 45.5 percent respectively in 2005. At the end of 2007, in China there are more than 570 million mobile phone subscribers, ranking first in the world; and more than 210 million Internet subscribers, ranking second in the world; and the consumption of automobiles was listed as No. 2 in the world, only behind the United States.

The undertakings of science, technology and education have developed quickly. From 2001 to 2005 the expenditure on scientific research across China was 820.3 billion Yuan, accounting for 1.16 percent of the GDP of the same period, higher than the average level of 0.7 percent in developing countries. In 2006 alone, this figure reached 294.3 billion Yuan, a proportion of 1.41 percent of the GDP. At present the number of professional technical people and scientific researchers in China is listed as number one in the world. In 2006 the overall enrolment rate of compulsory education exceeded 95 percent, and the gross enrolment ratio for high school education and higher school education respectively was 59 percent and 22 percent. According to UNDP, in 2003 the literacy rate of people aged 15 years old and above was 88.4 percent, higher than the world average level of 79.1 percent, and the education index was 0.84, higher than the world average level of 0.77.

Medical treatment and health care shared by the Chinese residents exceed the

Development of National Education in 2006

(Unit: 10,000 persons)

Education	Enrolled Students	Students in School	Graduates
Post-graduate Education	40	110	26
General Higher Education	540	1739	377
Secondary Vocational Education	741	1809	476
Senior High School	871	2515	727
Junior High School	1930	5958	2072

Source: National Bureau of Statistics of the People's Republic of China.

world average. The pilot range for a new rural cooperative medical service system was expanded to 2,429 counties (cities, districts), or 84.87 percent of all counties (cities, districts) across China, and 720 million farmers participated in the system. At present there are about 5.5 million doctors of various types and 3.22 million hospital and clinic beds, both listed as number one in the world; the expected life-span per capita is above 72, higher than the world average level 67.1; the infant mortality rate dropped from 200 per thousand before the birth of New China to 21.5 per thousand in 2005; and the mortality rate of women in child-birth dropped from 1,500 out of 100,000 in 1949 to 48.3 out of 100,000. All these indexes are listed at the top among developing countries.

The social security level in China has also been enhanced continuously. In towns 22.41 million residents have received the minimum living guarantee from the government. In rural areas the minimum living guarantee for rural residents has been initially established in 31 provinces, autonomous regions and municipalities directly under the Central Government, and 23.11 million rural residents have received the minimum living guarantee from the government.

The socio-economic development has enhanced China's international competitiveness year on year. It was shown in the *World Competitiveness Year Book of 2006* by the International Institute for Management and Development, Lausanne, Switzerland that China's international competitiveness rose to No. 19 in 2006 from No. 31 in 2005. Among 30 countries and regions each with a population of above

First group of students who do not have to pay for studying in the Beijing Normal University.

20 million, China ranked 6th, next only to the United States, Australia, Canada, Japan and China's Taiwan. Among 25 countries and regions each with per-capita GDP less than US$10,000, China ranked first. And among 15 Asia-Pacific countries and regions, China ranked 6th, next only to Hong Kong of China, Singapore, Australia, Japan and Taiwan of China. In 2006, among the four category-indicators, except for economic development which was still No. 3 in the world, the other three items of governmental efficiency, enterprises' profits and infrastructure were improved. Among them, the governmental efficiency rose up to No. 17 from No. 21 in 2005, enterprises' profits to No. 30 from No. 50 and infrastructure to No. 37 from No. 42.

(VI) Build a Democratic Country under the Rule of Law

In the past 100-odd years, the Chinese people had made unremitting efforts for democracy, freedom and equality. Due to different national situations, the Chinese people chose the path of building a socialist democratic legal system with distinct Chinese characteristics under the leadership of the Communist Party of China.

Since the adoption of the reform and opening-up policy in late 1978, China has entered a new era of developing socialist democracy and building a socialist country under the rule of law. The national democratic systems such as the system of People's Congresses, the system of multi-party cooperation and political consultation under the leadership of the Communist Party of China, the system of regional national autonomy, and the system of grass-roots people autonomy have been developed and improved, the basic rights of citizens are respected and safeguarded, the Party's democratic governance capability has been further enhanced, the

Promoting democracy and legal system.

government's democratic administrative capability has been strengthened, and the construction of the judicial democratic system has been promoted continuously. The reform of the political system has been advanced unceasingly, and the reform of the State's leadership system, legislation system, administrative system, decision-making system, judicial system, personnel system and supervision and restriction system have had obvious effect. With the aim of carrying out the rule of law and building a socialist country under the rule of law, the construction of institutions, standards and procedures for the socialist democracy has been strengthened continuously, the Constitution-centered socialist law system with distinct Chinese characteristics has been formed basically, and there are laws to follow in the major aspects of political, economic and social life in the country.

According to its own national situation, China adopts the unicameral system instead of the bicameral system adopted by Western countries. In China people exercise the national power through the National People's Congress and local People's Congresses at all levels. All citizens of China who have reached the age of 18 have the right to vote and stand for election, regardless of ethnic groups, race, sex, occupation, family background, religious belief, education, property status or length of residence, except persons deprived of political rights according to law.

State Organs of the PRC

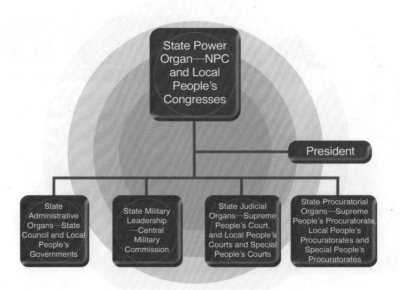

There are more than 2.8 million deputies to the People's Congresses at all levels across China. The deputies have the right to put forth proposals, examine and discuss all proposals and reports, and vote on all proposals according to law, and they may not be called to legal account for their speeches or votes at all meetings of the People's Congress. In China all administrative, judicial and procuratorial organs of the State are created by the People's Congresses to which they are responsible and under whose supervision they operate. The major issues of the State are decided by the People's Congresses. Administrative organs are in charge of implementing the laws, resolutions and decisions passed by People's Congresses. Courts and procuratorates shall exercise respectively judicial and procuratorial power independently and are not subject to interference by administrative organs, public organizations or individuals. The functions and powers exercised by People's Congresses mainly include legislation, supervision, appointment and removal of personnel, and decision-making on major issues.

Since the adoption of reform and opening-up in 1978 the National People's Congress and its Standing Committee have adopted more than 230 laws currently in effect, the State Council has adopted more than 680 administrative regulations, local People's Congresses at different levels and their standing committees have adopted more than 7,500 local regulations currently in effect, and the People's Congresses of national autonomous regions have adopted more than 600 autonomous rules and rules implemented separately. The socialist law system with Chinese characteristics has been formed basically, in which the Constitution holds the core and commanding position. The Constitution prescribes the political system, economic system and citizens' rights and freedom of the state and is the fundamental law of the state. The socialist law system with Chinese characteristics is composed of seven law departments and laws and regulations at three different levels. The seven law departments are the Constitution and laws related to the Constitution, civil and commercial laws, administrative law, economic law, social law, criminal law, and procedure law. The laws and regulations at three different levels are laws, administrative regulations, local regulations, autonomous rules and rules implemented separately.

China's system of political parties is different to both the two-party or multi-party system adopted by the Western countries and the one-party system adopted by some countries. It is a system of multi-party cooperation and political consultation under the leadership of the Communist Party of China. At present, there are nine political parties in China. Besides the Communist Party of China, there are the Revolutionary Committee of the Chinese Kuomintang, the China Democratic League, the China Democratic National Construction Association, the China Association for Promoting Democracy, the Chinese Peasants and Workers Democratic Party, the China Zhi Gong Dang, the Jiu San Society and the Taiwan Democratic Self-Government League. As most of these political parties were founded during the War of Resistance Against Japan (1937-1945) and the Liberation War (1946-1949) for striving for national liberation and democratic freedom, they are also called "democratic parties". The political parties system of China is distinctively characterized by: Multi-party cooperation under the leadership of the Communist Party of China, and the Communist Party of China in power with multiple parties participating in the administration of State affairs. All the democratic parties are friendly parties and parties participating in the administration of State affairs in unity and cooperation with the Communist Party of China, instead of opposition parties. All the democratic parties participate in the State political process, the consultation on the major policies and guidelines and leaders of the State, the management of State affairs, and the stipulation and implementation of State guidelines, policies, laws and regulations. The Chinese People's Political Consultative Conference is an organization of the untied front, an important organ of multi-party cooperation and political consultation under the leadership of the Communist Party of China, and an important form which carries forward democracy in the political life of China.

China is a unitary multi-national State today, and there are 56 identified ethnic groups affirmed by the Central Government. Among them the Han ethnic group has the largest population and the other 55 ethnic groups have less population and are customarily called ethnic minorities. According to the Fifth National Census in 2000, the total population of the 55 ethnic minorities is 104.49 million, occupying 8.41 percent of the total population of China. The multi-national States in the world have different modes of dealing with national issues. In accordance with its historical development, cultural characteristics, national relations and distribution of ethnic groups, China adopts regional national autonomy. Regional national autonomy means that under the unitary State leadership, regional autonomy is adopted and autonomous organs are established to exercise autonomous power in the places where the ethnic minorities inhabit. The national autonomous areas are divided into three levels of autonomous regions, autonomous prefectures and

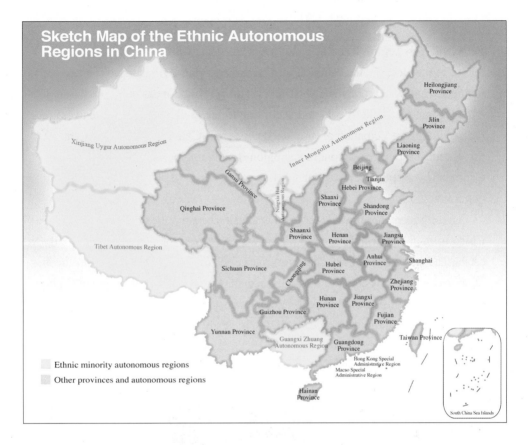

Sketch Map of the Ethnic Autonomous Regions in China

autonomous counties. At present, 155 national autonomous areas are established across China, including five autonomous regions, 30 autonomous prefectures and 120 autonomous counties. Of the 55 ethnic minority groups, 44 have set up autonomous areas and the population of the ethnic minorities with regional autonomy is 71 percent of the total population of ethnic minority groups. Meanwhile, the State has set up 1,173 ethnic townships in places where ethnic minorities inhabit as supplement to the national autonomous areas.

Among the 1.3 billion population of China, more than 800 million people live in rural areas. How to develop the grass-roots democracy in the rural areas and enable farmers to really hold the position as masters of the country and fully exercise their democratic rights is a significant question in the construction of democratic politics in China. After years of exploration and practice, the Communist Party of China has led hundreds of millions of farmers on the path to grass-roots democratic political construction in rural areas that accord with the national situation of China, implementing villagers' self-government. The villagers' self-government organization is villagers committees whose members are elected directly by villagers. In the course of the election, the candidates for membership in a villagers committee are nominated and voted for by villagers and the voting result is made public on the spot. Villagers are ebullient to vote and according to incomplete statistics the average ratio of voting participation of rural residents across China exceeds 80 percent. At present most provinces, autonomous regions and municipalities directly under the Central Government have completed five to six sessions of election of villagers committees.

In the governance practice for more than half a century, the Communist Party of China formed a series of important thoughts on democratic governance, initially established the system of democratic governance and explored new ways and methods of democratic governance. In China the leadership of the Communist Party of China is mainly materialized in such aspects as politics, ideology and organization. By means of stipulating major guidelines and policies, it puts forth suggestions on legislation, recommends important cadres, and conducts ideological publicity, plays the role of Party organizations and members, sticks to the governance according to law and carries out the Party's leadership of the State and society. In practice, the Communist Party of

China has continuously reformed and improved the leadership system and working mechanism, made efforts to explore the practical form of democratic governance, and standardized the relations between the Party committees and the People's Congresses,

In September 2007, the Zhengji Village in Haimen, Jiangsu Provnce elected its own village commttee

Governments, the Chinese People's Political Consultative Conference committees, and people's organizations according to the principle that the Party in power assumes overall responsibility and coordinates all parties involved. To drive people's democracy by developing inter-Party democracy is an important content of the democratic governance by the Communist Party of China. After unremitting efforts over a long period, the Communist Party of China has gradually found a set of systems, mechanisms and methods to oversee and restrict powers and effectively undertake the work of combating corruption and upholding integrity, which accord with the national situation of China, and initially established and improved a system of punishment and corruption prevention paying equal attention to education, system and oversight.

In accordance with the requirement of democratic governance, the Chinese governments at all levels strengthen powerfully the construction of the capability of democratic administration. The Chinese Government attaches importance to the exercise of power strictly in accordance with the statutory limits of authority and procedures, and in the course of administrative law-enforcement, the rights and interests of parties concerned and stakeholders should be safeguarded according to law and various illegal actions in administrative law-enforcement such as pursuing private interests through power should be firmly corrected. While accepting the oversight from the People's Councils, the Chinese People's Political Consultative Conference, judicial organs, public opinion and common people, the Chinese Government has also established and improved a series of administrative oversight systems. According to the requirement of democratic governance, the Chinese Government sped up the transformation of governmental functions, powerfully promoted the innovation in the management system and mechanism, made efforts to construct a government with integrity, high efficiency and practicality, and made the government's administration full of efficiency and vitality.

China has continuously established and improved the judiciary system and working mechanism, strengthened the judiciary democratic construction and made efforts to safeguard citizens' and legal persons' legal rights and interests by judiciary activities so as to realize fairness and justice in the society. At the same time, China has also set up independent judicial and procuratorial organs and carries out the judiciary system with separation between judicial and procuratorial organs. The judiciary organs view facts as basis and laws as criteria, and handle affairs strictly according to law, punish crimes and safeguard citizens' legal rights and interests. In the aspect of system and procedures, the justice in China persists in the principles that all people are equal before laws, and charges and punishment are stipulated by laws, and maintain and realize the judiciary justice and democracy and safeguard people's democratic rights by carrying out the trial classification system, withdrawal system, open trial system, people juror system, people supervisor system, lawyers system, legal aid system and people's mediation system..

In recent years, along with the development of the state's modernization, the democratic system in China has been improved continuously, the forms of democracy become more colorful, the channels for democracy have been expanded gradually, and democratic election, decision-making, management and oversight have been carried out more widely, and people's rights to know the facts, participate, express and supervise have been further safeguarded.

● The democracy in legislation in China has been pushed forward continuously and almost every draft of a law was adopted after soliciting opinions of experts and holding special disccussions. Some important drafts of laws concerning personal interests of people, including the Property Law, had publicized the drafts to the public in order to seek opinions.

● The Law on Lawyers promulgated in 1996 confirmed the basic framework of the lawyer system in China.

● In March 2004 the Second Session of the Tenth National People's Congress examined and passed the amendment of the Constitution in which it is formally stipulated that "the State respects and protects human rights."

● The transparency of the government's work has been continuously enhanced by promoting electronic government administration with governmental portals as windows, building and improving the system of governmental spokespeople and the mechanism of news reports on incidents occurring suddenly.

● The social hearing and public demonstration have gradually become the methods usually adopted by governments at all levels at the time of decision-making.

● On July 1, 2004, the Administrative Licensing Law of the People's Republic of China was implemented formally, which stipulated a series of principles and systems of administrative licensing.

VII. THE LARGEST DEVELOPING
COUNTRY IN THE WORLD

China is the most populous developing country in the world. Large population, relative lack of resources, and weakness in environmental bearing capacity constitute the basic national situation of China at present, which is hard to change in a short time. Problems tormenting China are manifested mainly in the contradiction between underdeveloped economy and people's increasingly growing material and cultural demands and in the contradiction between economic and social development and the comparatively large pressure from population, resources and environment.

China's modernization drive calls for efforts of more than ten and even scores of generations. At present, the Chinese people are striving to build a well-off society.

(I) Huge Burden of Population

China has a large population The food consumed by its people in a day is enough for people in New Zealand to consume for a year, the people in Japan for 13 days and the people in the United States for 4 days. The population issue is a key factor in China's economic and social development and it is also a significant issue

Railway travelers during the Spring Festival.

that China will face for long time.

By the end of 2006 China had a population of 1.31448 billion, about 22 percent of the total population of the world and more than four times of that in the United States, ten times that of Japan and scores of times of that in Canada and Australia. In China any issue disregarding how small it is will become a very big issue when multiplied by 1.3 billion; and any financial and material resources disregarding how considerable they are will become a very low per-capita when divided by 1.3 billion. If counted per capita, China is listed behind in the world in many aspects. The area of territory of China is listed as No.3 in the world but the per-capita tillable field is only 0.103 hectare, about one-tenth of that in the United States and one-thirtieth of that in Canada; and the per-capita fresh water resource is only one-fourth of the average level in the world. The GDP of China at present is listed among the top in the world, but the per-capita GDP is very low, below No. 100 in the world.

After 30 years of reforming and opening-up, the wealth of China is increased and the people's living standard has been enhanced, but China is still listed in the range of underdeveloped countries in the world. At present more than 20 million poor people are enjoying the minimum living guarantee for the urban residents across the country. By the end of 2006 more than 20 million people in the rural areas in China have not solved the

Morning exercises.

issues related to having enough food and clothing, and 35.5 million people have just had enough food and clothing but with unstable and low incomes. In the whole country there are more than 60 million persons with a disability and nearly 2 million migrating children are unable to go to school or continue their studying.

Thanks to the family planning policy adopted in the 1970s, the current population of China is 1.3 billion instead of 1.7 billion. Due to the correct population

Population in Different Age Groups in Recent Years and Their Proportion

(Unit: 10,000 person)

Year	Year-End Population	Various Age Groups					
		0-14 years		15-64 years		65 years and older	
		Population	Proportion(%)	Population	Proportion(%)	Population	Proportion(%)
1990	114333	31670	27.70	76260	66.70	6403	5.60
1995	121121	32218	26.60	81393	67.20	7510	6.20
2000	126743	29024	22.90	88847	70.10	8872	7.00
2005	130756	26504	20.27	94197	72.04	10055	7.69
2006	131448	25961	19.80	95068	72.30	10419	7.90

Source: National Bureau of Statistics of the People's Republic of China.

policy, not only the day that China's population reached 1.3 billion came 4 years later, but also the developing track of China's population was successfully changed and the growth of the total population in the world was delayed. China has entered the range of low birth-rate countries, but, due to the inertial effect of increasing population, China's population will increase at the speed of 8-10 million per year at present and in future scores of years. According to the current total birth rate of 1. 8, it is predicted that in 2010 and 2020 the total population of China will increase to 1.37 billion and 1.46 billion respectively; and the peak of gross population will occur around 2033, reaching about 1.5 billion.

The huge population exerts impact on various aspects of economic and social development in China. While offering abundant labor resources for the economic and social development, it also puts heavy pressure on economic development, social progress, consumption of resources and environmental protection.

China has entered into an aging society. In 2006 there were 104.19 million people above the age of 65, or 7.9 percent of the population of the country. It is predicted that by 2020 there will be 164 million people above the age of 65, or 16.1 percent of the population of the country, and there will be 22 million people above the age of 80. The aging in China is presented by such characteristics as high speed, large scale and "becoming old before getting rich."

Regarding the gender structure of the population, in 2006 the male population was 51.5 percent, 677.28 million; and the female population was 48.5 percent, 637.2 million. The sex proportion of total population is 106.29 and the sex proportion of birth population is still very high, reaching 119.25, much higher than the normal level of sex proportion of birth population recognized in the world (103.07).

The overall level of scientific and cultural qualities of the Chinese population is not high: first, the gross illiteracy rate of the population is much higher than the level of developed countries which is below 2 percent; second, the gross enrolment ratio for colleges and universities is much lower than developed countries; and third, the average number of years receiving education is lower than that of developed countries and even than the world average. Meanwhile, the degree of education received is obviously different between urban people and rural people. In 2004 the average number of years receiving education is 9.43 years and 7 years in urban and rural areas respectively; and the illiteracy rate is 4.91 percent and 10.71 percent in urban and rural areas respectively.

Among the 1.3 billion population of China, there are more than 900 million people aged between 15 and 64, at least 300 million more than the total population of developed countries. It is predicted that by 2016 the population between the ages of 15 and 64 will reach its peak—1.01 billion, and will be still around 1 billion by 2020.

The population of laboring age continues the trend of growth. At present in urban areas in China there are nearly 10 million new laborers every year and in rural areas there are more than 200 million surplus laborers. The growth of employment is mainly in cities. From 2000 to 2005 the growth of employment in rural areas in China was negative and every year tens of millions of people migrated from rural to urban areas for employment. In urban areas there were more than 9 million increased employment opportunities every year, which could hardly satisfy the demands of new laborers and unemployed persons. The current growth rate of the population in China has dropped obviously and the total women birth ratio has decreased below the replacing level, but due to the inertial effect of population growth in the past, the total population and the population of laboring age are both in the trend of rising, and the employment situation is tense on the whole with more supply of laborers than demand. By 2030 in this situation the total population of laboring age every year in China will not be lower than the current level.

The urbanization level in China has been enhanced continuously. Due to the accelerated promotion of population urbanization and efforts made to upgrade the industrial structure, the population urbanization ratio grows at the speed of more than 1 percentage point every year. By 2006 the urban population in China was 577.06 million, about 43.9 percent of the total population of the country.

In the course of quick urbanization, as the change in the use of agricultural lands became an important source for driving economic growth and increasing financial revenue, there was an impulse for large-scale land requisition and the speed of land

Like other small and medium-sized cities in China, Manzhouli City of Inner Momgolia sees constant expansion of its urban area.

urbanization was accelerated. But, meanwhile, as the farmers, who lost land due to requisition, entered the urban society from rural society, broke off the traditional mutual-assistance network in villages, entered the urban society with strange human relations, and did not complete the course of becoming townspeople soon due to change of domiciliary register. The land urbanization was vastly quicker than the citizenization of farmers, which tends to cause social contradiction and conflicts.

China is and will be in the situation of underdevelopment for a long time and the contradiction will exist for a long time between the fast growth of people's demands for welfare and the satisfaction of such demands. The social security in China faces a comparatively severe situation; there is much work to do in social insurances, social welfare and social relief. With the development and changes of the society, the mode of providing for the aged by family generations which has lasted for thousands of years in China is facing an unprecedented challenge. The

A shot of a Job Fair.

current system of basic old-age insurance in China can only cover about 20 percent of all the employees in the whole society and most farmers cannot receive it. Even for the urban employees, about 40 percent of them have no old-age insurance, including a great number of migrant rural workers and informal employees. The medical security system is not sound. The urban medical security system has a small coverage and the strength of the rural cooperative medical service system is not enough. The security of basic rights and interests of nearly 150 million migrant people requires strengthening. At present, the Chinese Government is adopting a series of measures to change the situation gradually.

(II) Disparity and Imbalance in Development

In China today, whereas people's income level and standard of living are continually improving, there is still a growing disparity between the financial circumstances of different social members. The development of a range of social undertakings is moving comparatively slowly, and various issues relating to the day-to-day interests of the people, such as education, health care and housing, have not been adequately taken care of.

The excessively large disparity of income is a serious issue in the social development of China. According to relevant statistics, at the present time in China the richest people, who represent 20 percent of the total population, hold 50 percent of the total social income, while the poorest 20 percent only hold 5 percent of the total social income; the income disparity between the two groups is ten to one.

The issue of income disparity in China is manifested collectively in the following aspects: Firstly, the income disparity between the urban and rural areas. In 2006 the per-capita net income for urban residents in China was 11,759 Yuan while the per-capita net income for rural inhabitants was 3,587 Yuan, resulting in a ratio of urban to ru-

Good Harvest in Kaifeng, Henan Province.

ral net per-capita income of 3.28:1. Secondly, there is the income disparity between different regions. In 2005, of the provinces and autonomous regions in China, Zhejiang Province had the highest per-capita net income for urban residents of 16,239 Yuan, and Xinjiang the lowest, 7,990 Yuan; furthermore, Zhejiang Province also had the highest per-capita net income for rural residents, 6,660 Yuan, while Guizhou Province had the lowest, 1,877 Yuan. Lastly, there is the income disparity between different sectors. In 2005, the service sector offered the highest annual income of 72,000 Yuan, while the textile sector offered anannual average

Primary school for children of migrant workers in Beijing.

income of 11,000 Yuan, less than one-sixth of the former.

The imbalance in social development is caused by the imbalance in economic development, itself mainly manifested in the imbalance of economic development between the urban and rural areas (between industry and agriculture). In 2005, among investment in fixed assets in the urban and rural areas, that for urban areas maintained a level of 87.75 percent whereas the level for rural areas was only 12.25 percent. The issue of agriculture, rural areas and farmers is the most problematic in the economic and social development of modern China. When closely analyzed, the situation with regard to agriculture, rural areas and farmers is the result of a dualistic economic structure with the long-term separation between the urban and rural areas in China, manifested in the contradiction between a superabundant rural population and the limited and continuously decreasing agricultural production materials such as suitable farming land. At present, agricultural workers account for 56 percent of the total population in China, but although this means that more than 300 million people are engaged in agricultural employment, the production yield thus created only accounts for 11.8 percent of the GDP.

The imbalance in economic development is also manifested in the imbalance between different regions. In 2004, the per-capita GDP for west China was 7,219 Yuan, that for east China 18,217 Yuan, the absolute margin between west and east being 10,998 Yuan, representing a ratio of 1:2.52. The economic development is also uneven between different sectors. From 2000 to 2006, the steel industry increased by 260 percent, automobile production by 251.2 percent, microcomputers showed an enormous 1,289.2 percent increase, while agricultural fertilizer and cotton cloth only increased by 75.5 and 98.6 percent respectively.

Some problems also exist in the development of education. First, the investment in education is not sufficient. In 2006 the fiscal funds on education in China accounted for 2.86 percent of GDP whereas the proportion in developed countries mostly exceeded 4 percent and those in developing countries were approximately the same. Second, the allocation of education resources shows an imbalance between urban and rural areas and between different regions and schools, and, furthermore, the opportunity of receiving education is not equal and in particular it is difficult for the children of poor families and migrant rural workers in cities to go to school. Third, the phenomena of "arbitrary collection of charges" cannot be prevented despite repeated attempts at its prohibition. At present, the average number of years during which a child receives formal education in China is eight, compared with 13.4 in the United States, 11.7 in the Republic of Ireland and 12.3 in the Republic of Korea.

The problems in medical treatment and health care are most prominently manifested in the unreasonable allocation of health care resources. Across the country 80 percent of the health care resources are concentrated in cities. Whereas high-quality medical treatment and health care resources are excessively concentrated in big city hospitals, there is a concomitant shortage of community health care service resources, and the service system characteristic of "giving priority to prevention" and reasonable access to a doctor has not come into being. In the rural areas there is a shortage of medical treatment and health care resources, and a large number of rural inhabitants only receive about 20 percent of the total medical treatment resources. And the shortage of doctors and medicines is significantly greater in remote and poorer regions.

China is now expected to see its a per-capita GDP growth increase from US$1,000 to 3,000. It is a period full of opportunities and challenges.

(III) Contradiction between Economic Development and Resources and Environment

China has 122 million hectares of fields suitable for the planting of crops. According to the development strategies, by 2010 the nationwide reserve of these tillable fields is forecast at 120 million hectares, which is the bottom limit at which the economic and social development of China may be guaranteed.

China enjoys fast economic development, but the economic growth featurs high investment, high levels of energy consumption, high materials consumption, high pollution and large requisition of land. And such a situation remains unchanged today. Moreover, China is currently in a period of fast industrialization and urbanization. Due to a comparatively high consumption of energy and various resources and a heavy emission of pollutants, the conflict between economic development and the conservation of natural resources is becoming ever more prominent.

China's economic growth relies to a very great extent on secondary industry, whereas the tertiary industry, characterized by its low energy-consumption, has lagged behind, this disparity leading to huge energy consumption and heavy pollution. In 2006 the added value of the tertiary industry in China accounted for 39.5 percent of its GDP, whereas the pro-

Financial street of Beijing. The Government encourages development of the tertiary industry featuring low energy consumption.

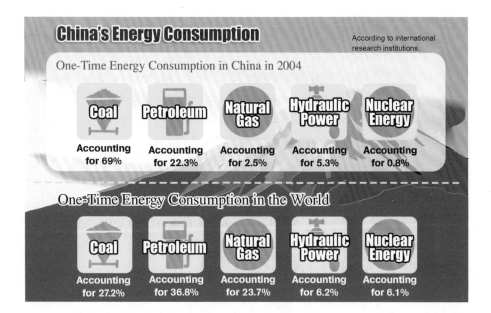

China's Energy Consumption

According to international research institutions,

One-Time Energy Consumption in China in 2004

Coal	Petroleum	Natural Gas	Hydraulic Power	Nuclear Energy
Accounting for 69%	Accounting for 22.3%	Accounting for 2.5%	Accounting for 5.3%	Accounting for 0.8%

One-Time Energy Consumption in the World

Coal	Petroleum	Natural Gas	Hydraulic Power	Nuclear Energy
Accounting for 27.2%	Accounting for 36.8%	Accounting for 23.7%	Accounting for 6.2%	Accounting for 6.1%

portion in developed countries generally exceeds 70 percent— 75.3 percent in the United States and 75.1 percent and 51 percent respectively in Brazil and India, which are at approximately the same level of development as China.

China is the world's third largest energy producer, next only to the United States and Russia; and it is also the second largest energy consumer after that of the United States. However, due to its large population, China is a country with a comparative shortage of energy resources and its consumption structure is not sustainable at current levels.

At present, China's per-capita petroleum resource is 17.1 percent of the world average, and the per-capita natural gas resource 13.2 percent. Though China is a major coal producer in the world, its per-capita share of coal resources is only 42.5 percent of the world average.

In China there is a wide but imbalanced distribution of energy resources. Coal is mainly found in north and northwestern China, hydraulic resources are principally distributed in the southwestern regions, and petroleum and natural gas are mostly concentrated in the eastern, central and western regions as well as under territorial waters. The major regions with regard to energy consumption are concentrated in the southeastern coastal areas which have the more developed economy. The large-scale and far-distant transportation of coal from north to south, of petroleum from north to south, of natural gas from west to east and of electricity from west to east represents the distinctive and basic structure of the flow of China's energy transportation.

The demand for resources in China has grown fast. In the 1990s petroleum consumption increased by 99 percent from 118 million tons to 235 million tons, with an annual average growth of 7.2 percent; that of natural gas increased from 11.4 billion cubic meters to 27.7 cubic meters, an annual average growth of 9.3 percent; that of steel increased from 67 million tons to 163 million tons, an annual average growth of 9.3 percent; and that of copper increased from 729,000 tons to 2.11 million tons, an annual average growth of 11.2 percent. According to statistics supplied by the relevant international research institutes, from 2001 to 2004 energy consumption in China grew by an average of 15.95 percent every year, as opposed to the world average of just 3 percent.

China has made great progress in energy technology, but compared to the growing demands for development and the international advanced level, there is still a significant gap. New technology in such fields as recyclable energy, clean energy and alternative energy develops comparatively slowly and the application of such technology as energy-saving, consumption-reduction and pollution treatment is not nearly so wide as it might be. Regarding major energy-consuming industries and energy-consuming equipment, when compared to the most advanced international levels, the cement industry consumes 23.6 percent more energy, the large and medium-sized steel enterprises consume 15.1 percent more eneergy, and the thermal power industry consumes 20.5 percent more energy. In 2004 the energy consumption per unit of production in China was 2.4 times higher than the world average level, 3.2 times higher than that of the United States and 6.6 times higher than that of Japan. The output efficiency of a ton of standard coal is equal to 28.6 percent of that of the United States, 16.8 percent of that of the European Union, and 10.3 percent of that of Japan. In China the usage coefficient of water used in agriculture is 0.4, or 50 percent of advanced international levels, and the water used in industry is ten times the advanced international level.

Such a kind of economy results in low efficiency and low output. The labor productivity in China is obviously lower than that of Western developed countries. Taking the secondary industry as an example. The labor productivity of China is only 3.3 percent of that of the United States, 5.6 percent that of Japan, 6.3 percent that of France, 8.3 percent that of Germany and 14.3 percent that of the Republic of

Korea.

The serious pollution is the result of an extensive development of the Chinese economy. At present, the annual emission of sulfur dioxide reaches more than 25 million tons, that of chemical oxygen over 14 million tons, and the nitro-oxide per unit of GDP is higher than that of developed countries.

China's ecological environment is deteriorating, a trend which shows no significant sign of being reversed. Fifty-two percent of China's land mass is made up of either arid or semi-arid regions; the high, cold, oxygen-rare Qinghai-Tibet Plateau covers an area of 2.4 million square km; the Loess Plateau, afflicted by serious soil erosion, covers an area of some 640,000 square km; and the desert Karst region covers an area of 900,000 square km.

(IV) Set up a Scientific Outlook on Development

In recent years the Communist Party of China and the Chinese Government have put forth a new strategy known as scientific outlook on development after summarizing the experiences and lessons of economic and social development since the beginning of reform and opening up in late 1978, the experiences and lessons of the modernization drive in the world, and the situation China faces in the new century.

As to the scientific outlook on development, development is the first essential, putting people first is the core ideal, being comprehensive, balanced and sustainable is the basic requirement, and overall consideration is the fundamental method.

● As to "development", we must firmly commit ourselves to the central task of economic development, concentrate on construction and development, seek for development whole-heartedly, and keep emancipating and developing the forces of production.

● "Putting people first" means prioritizing the interests of the people as a whole, focusing on promoting the all-around development of the people, satisfying their demands, and safeguarding their interests.

● As to "comprehensive, balanced and sustainable development", we must promote economic, political, cultural and social development, harmonize economic growth with the needs of the population, the best use of resources and the greatest benefit to the environment, and encourage the whole of society to follow the kind of enlightened approach to development that results in expanded production, a better standard of living and sound ecological and environmental conditions.

● As to overall consideration, we must correctly understand and handle the major relationships that occur in the construction of modernization in China and consider the overall situation and planning process as a complete entity.

According to the requirements of maintaining a scientific outlook on development, China has in recent years made great efforts to achieve healthy and sustained socio-economic development.

Given the problems in development such as the excessively fast growth of investment in economic operations, excessive currency credits put on the market, and too high a favorable balance in foreign trade, the Central Government adopted a series of measures on macro-regulation. By strengthing land control, management on currency credits, the regulation of economic operations by finance and taxes, and regulation and supervision over the real estate market, the Chinese Government avoided violent ups and downs in economic development. The Chinese Government also adopted policies to optimize the industrial structure, carried out policies and measures aimed at adjusting the structure of 11 principle industries including steel and iron, coal and cement, and eliminated a previously sluggish production capacity. Efforts have been made to develop the service sector, enhance industrial levels and standards, and promote the national economy and levels of public information; accelerate the development of hi-tech industry, rejuvenate equip manufacture, actively develop recyclable energy, and move in the direction of renewable energy. State key scientific and technological projects were undertaken, to overcome outdated core and key technologies concerning the national economy, people's livelihood and national security. China has also strengthened both basic research and the more advanced avenues of research in frontline technology and social welfare.

The past few decades have seen China work hard to build up a stable, economical and clean energy supply system, and construct a resource-efficient society. In pursuit of these goals the Chinese Government has carried out the strictest land management system. The energy supply in China mainly depends on domestic sources and for a number of years the self-support ratio has been maintained at over 90 percent.

During the reform and opening-up, China has learned to reduce energy consumption, protect the environment and reduce intensive land use. Efforts have been made to improve policies regarding energy-saving, consumption-reduction, and the concomitant reduction in the emission of pollutants, and establish a system of target responsibility on energy-saving and emission reduction; actively promote the work of energy saving in key industries, enterprises and projects, and develop experimental units of recyclable economy; improve and firmly maintain standards on energy consumption and environmental protection, eliminate sluggish production capabilities with a firm hand, and accelerate progress in energy-saving and environmental protection technologies. In recent years the governments at all levels have done a great deal of work in the field of energy-saving and emission-reduction. In 2006 the energy consumption per GDP unit dropped by 1.2 percent, whereas in 2003, 2004 and 2005 it rose by 4.9, 5.5 and 0.2 percent respectively.

As a measure taken to strengthen pollution treatment and environmental protection, from 2006 to 2010, China will close down small-sized thermal power generation units with a combined generating capacity of 50 million kilowatts and 100 million tons of inefficient iron-making production capacity and 55 million tons of poor-performance steel-making production capacity.

China takes energy saving as a significant strategy, and makes effort to develop a recyclable economy with a view to seeking development based on the minimum consumption of resources. According to the requirements of State development plan, in the five years from 2006 to 2010 China will realize its objective that the energy consumption per-unit GDP be reduced by approximately 20 percent. China is currently persisting in its multiple developing strategy on energy, a strategy that features the systematic development of coal resources, the active development of electric power, and equal importance attached to petroleum and natural gas. In

Wind power plant in Urumqi, Xinjiang Uygur Autonomous Region.

recent years, the State has put a great deal of effort into developing new forms of energy and renewable sources of energy such as wind, biological, solar, geothermal and tidal wave energy. China has announced that by 2020 the proportion of renewable energy in the overall energy structure will be increased from the current 7 percent to approximately 16 percent.

While promoting economic development, China has adopted a series of measures to protect the environment. China has persisted in giving priority to preventative and comprehensive treatment, emphasized the prevention of pollution and the protection of the environment at source, and fully applied the methods of laws, economy, technology and necessary administration in the interests of environ-

mental protection. It has also achieved a comprehensive pro-motion with break-throughs in key points, and made special efforts to solve problems that exert adverse im-pact on the sustain-able development in the future. China has also persisted in saving resources,

More and more residents adopt solar water heaters.

actively advocated consumption of environment-friendly energy, and combined the prevention and treatment of pollution with the work of ecological protection.

The work of environmental protection in China is making extremely positive progress. Satisfactory results have been made in controlling pollution in some river drainage areas, the air quality in some cities and regions has been enhanced, and the emission of pollutants in the industrial sector has shown a small but encouraging decrease, and the air quality in some cities has improved. Of 559 cities monitored in 2006, 62.4 percent had a level of air quality reaching or exceeding the State air quality standard, an increase of 28.6 percentage points compared to 2002. The growth in gross emission levels of major pollutants correspondingly slowed down.

A sewage treatment company in Ningbo, Zhejiang Province.

In 2006 the growth of emission of chemical oxygen and sulfur dioxide decreased to 1.2 and 1.8 percent respectively from 5.6 and 13.1 percent in 2005. The ecologically motivated planting of new forest areas underwent steady development over the same period, coinciding with a decrease in the level of desertification. Across the country forests cover an area of 174.91 million hectares, with wetland accounting for a further 3,849 hectares. China has announced that by 2010, while seeking a continuation of stable growth in national economy, the quality of the environment in key regions and cities will have been significantly improved, the deterioration of the environment will have been kept within predefined basic limits, the gross emission amount of major pollutants will have been decreased by 10 percent, the conversion ratio of rendering urban garbage harmless will be at least 60 percent, the forest coverage rate will be enhanced to at least 20 percent, and results will have been achieved in decreasing the emission of greenhouse gases.

The State has persisted in the implementation of an overall strategy of regional development. The program of the western region development has been steadily promoted, and key ecological projects such as protection of natural forests and prevention and treatment of desert areas have been carried out. The work of rejuvenating the old industrial bases in northeast China has been successfully carried out, the adjustment of industrial structure solidified, the construction of commercial grain bases strengthened, and the renovation of old towns accelerated.

Those policies aimed at speeding up the development of central China have been implemented to boost the grain production and the production of energy and raw materials. The eastern region has made significant progress in leading the way in development; the industrial structure continues to be optimized and international competitiveness has been very much strengthened.

(V) Make Efforts to Build a Harmonious Society

In a large country with a huge population and imbalanced development such as China, modernization should be conducted according to the overall requirements of democracy and the rule of law, according to fairness and justice, integrity and fraternity, vitality, stability and order and harmony between man and nature. Importance should also be attached to those issues relating to the actual day-to-day interests of the people as a whole, efforts should be made to develop social undertakings, accelerate social fairness and justice, construct a harmonious culture, improve social management, strengthen social creative vitality, and follow the path of common wealth. Efforts should also be made to promote a balanced development between social construction and economic, political and cultural construction.

An office was set up in Nangang District, Harbin City, Heilongjiang Province, in December 2007 to help solve problems local people have.

China has developed a significant strategy of building a harmonious socialist society. The main objectives and tasks for building such a society by 2020 are as follows: the socialist democracy and legal system must be further improved, the fundamental principle of administrating the country according to law must be generally implemented, people's rights and interests should enjoy concrete respect and be guaranteed; the widening gap between urban and rural development and between different regions must be steadily reversed, a reasonable and orderly income distribution pattern must take general shape, and household wealth should increase across the board, thus enabling all people to lead more affluent lives; employment rates must be relatively high and a social security system covering both the urban and rural population be established; the basic existing public service system should be further improved and the Government attain relatively significant improvements in administrative and service levels; the ideological and moral standards, scientific and cultural qualities, and health and welfare status of the whole nation must be markedly improved, and further progress made in fostering a sound moral atmosphere and encouraging harmonious interpersonal relationships; the overall creativity of society must reach a new level, and an innovation-based nation be established; the public administration system must be further improved and social order given a stronger platform; resources must be used more efficiently and the environment visibly improved; and finally the objective of turning a society with more than a billion population into one that has a moderate but achievable prosperity and standard of living within a harmonious social framework is the responsibility of everyone to try and achieve.

In recent years both the Central and local governments in China have adopted various powerful measures and made significant progress towards building a harmonious society.

Regarding developments in education, the Chinese Government has persisted in prioritizing education policy, accelerating its development at various levels, and has had the general desire of popularizing and solidifying compulsory schooling, accelerating the development of vocational learning, and sparing no effort to enhance the quality of higher education. In 2006 expenditure on education, health care and cultural undertakings by the Central Government increased by 39.4 percent, 65.4 percent and 23.9 percent respectively from the previous year. In 2007 rural students were exempt from the tuition and miscellaneous expenses of the compulsory education stage so that the economic burden of the families of 150 million secondary and primary school students were lightened, and students of poor families in rural areas continued to get free schoolbooks and subsidies on boarding expenses.

Regarding developments in the sphere of health care, efforts were made to build up a basic health care system covering urban and rural residents. A new rural cooperative medical service system is being actively promoted, and in 2007 the pilot

Blind students of the Jiangsu Taizhou Special Education School were taken to a park for "sightseeing."

areas were extended to over 80 percent of the counties (cities and districts) across the country. By the end of June 2007, some 720 million people participated in the rural cooperative medical service system. Meanwhile, efforts were made to develop a new urban health care service system based on communities was being accelerated. The State has already started experimental units offering basic medical care for urban residents with the overall emphasis on treating major diseases, and is offering financial aid to poor people in respect of medical treatment.

Regarding employment and social security, the State follows the policy geared to create more job opportunities and encourage self-employment. Laid-off employees of State-owned enterprises now enjoy unemployment insurance, and the labor contract system has been comprehensively overhauled to safeguard workers' legal rights and interests. Efforts were made to speed up construction of a workable social security system. In 2007 the central finance put aside 210.9 billion Yuan for necessary expenditure on social security, an increase of 24.7 billion Yuan from the year before. The system of basic pensions for retirees from enterprises has kept on improving, and a social security system geared to the demands of migrant rural workers has been established. The urban and rural social assistance system has been improved; the basic framework of a social assistance system established, and procedures to take into account a minimum living guarantee for urban residents, urban and rural medical assistance, and assistance for urban vagrants and beggars put into place. In 2007 the system of a rural minimum living guarantee started to be established across the country.

In 2006 the agricultural tax and agricultural specialty tax, which had been collected in the rural areas for over 2,600 years, were abolished. The Government also subsidized farmers who planted grain. The result is that China enjoys increased grain production for three successive years. Investment in infrastructural develop-

Medical workers go to the rural areas to serve the farmers.

ment in rural areas has been increased, and the construction of irrigation works, roads, power grids, telecommunications, safe drinking water, and production of marsh gas. Farmers now enjoy higher income from crop cultivation and forestry, and by engaging in secondary and tertiary industries.

Regarding the reconstruction of the judiciary system, the Government has tried to safeguard the independence and fairness of judicial and procuratorial power according to law by implementing systems that take full account of protecting people's democratic and legal rights and interests and maintain the balance of social fairness and justice. The Supreme People's Court has taken back the power to approve the death penalty, and the handling procedure for capital cases has been further improved. Transparency in trial and procuratorial affairs has been targeted and the mechanism of procuratorial jurisdiction over litigation activities much improved, especially in respect of that concerning malfeasance by judiciary staff. A uniform judiciary authentication system has been set up.

During the 17th National Congress of the Communist Party of China held in October 2007, the goal of building a moderately prosperous society in all aspects by 2020 was again definitely advocated. By 2020, the goal of building such a society will be attained, and China will become a country where industrialization is basically realized, comprehensive national strength has been distinctively enhanced, and the domestic market is among top ones in the world. By then, the Chinese people will lead a much better life and share a greater degree of democratic rights. The Chinese society will be more active, safe and united, and will be further opened up; it will have more affinity with the people, and make an even greater contribution to human culture.

VIII. CHINA AND THE WORLD IN THE ERA OF ECONOMIC GLOBALIZATION

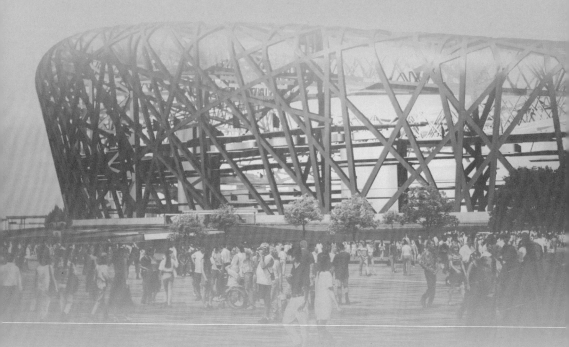

Before China's introduction of the reform and opening-up program in late 1978, the Chinese economy was one featuring basically self-sufficiency and separation from the world economic system. In the past three decades, China, following developing trend of economic globalization, set itself upon the path of peaceful development.

China has become an important member of the contemporary international system and plays a significant role in international affairs. As a large, responsible, developing country, China has committed itself, along with the other nations of the world, to building a more harmonious global environment with long-lasting peace and common prosperity for all.

(I) Join the Process of Economic Globalization

Better economic and trade relations between countries is a basic trend that has been in progress for several decades. From 1950 to 2005, the world trade dependency rose from just 5 percent to 28.4 percent. It can be said that, except for a few countries, almost all countries in the world are involved in the global division of labor, and commercial systems. Foreign trade has become an important engine for the economic growth of most of the countries in the world.

The Principal Speaker of the Asian-Pacific Policy Center of the American Rand Corporation has passed the following comments on China and Japan's accession into the process of economic globalization: "Although arriving late, China has acceded to the system of globalization with a far greater ardor than Japan. The opening degree of China's economy is much higher than that of Japan. In 2004 China's foreign trade value accounted for 70 percent of its GDP whereas Japan's

The CBD in Beijing is home to many of Top 500 corporations in the world.

foreign trade value was only 24 percent of its GDP; China introduced a direct foreign investment of US$60.6 billion whereas Japan, despite having an economic scale several times that of China, actually acquired a direct foreign investment of only US$20.1 billion. The reason for the disparity was that China was just then at a time of economic adjustment, introducing a considerable amount of foreign investment." (*China and Globalization*)

The policy of reform and opening-up, coinciding with economic globalization, made relations between China and the rest of the world much closer and the trade dependency rose proportionately. In 1978 China's foreign trade dependency was only 10 percent, but in 1994 it reached 42 percent. In the next few years it dropped a little but still never dipped below 30 percent, and in 2002 it reached 43 percent, further rising until, in 2006, it attained its highest historical level of 67 percent. The large-scale increase in foreign trade dependency showed that trade was playing an ever-stronger role in China's economic development. As a consequence, China's participation in the process of economic globalization was becoming continually more important.

The level of China's opening-up has entered a new stage and the degree of internationalization is all the time increasing. In the five years subsequent to its accession to the World Trade Organization, China abided by the WTO rules, carried out its undertakings as set down at the time of its entry, adjusted and reformed its economic system according to the correct timescale, amended and improved relevant laws and regulations, and became a fully integrated member of the world economic system. At present, China's general tariff level is 9.9 percent, lower than the world tariff level of 39 percent; China's non-agricultural products and agricultural products tariff levels stand at 9 and 15 percent respectively, against global counterparts of 29 and 60 percent respectively. Among all the sectors in China, the greatest degree of opening up occurred in the service sector, and among the 160-odd service departments distinguished by WTO, China made undertakings in 100 departments, representing 62.5 percent and close to the average level of WTO's developed members.

China actively participates in global and regional economic cooperation courses and plays an important and constructive role in this regard. China takes an active part in the multilateral and regional economic cooperation organizations and activities such as the WTO, the International Monetary Fund, the World Bank, and the Asian Development Bank, has held dialogues with the Group of Eight and the Group of Twelve, and has strengthened the macro-policy coordination with major economic entities and dialogues in such fields as finance, foreign exchange, industry, trade and energy. China, as a developing country, has also participated in the international multilateral commercial system and the stipulation of international economic rules. China is actively promoting the Doha round of negotiation of WTO to re-start as soon as possible.

China has made positive progress in the negotiations aimed at facilitating trade and investment under the regional economic cooperation mechanism of the Shanghai Cooperation Organization, the Asian-Pacific Economic Cooperation Organization, the Asian-European Conference, the ASEAN and the China, Japan and Republic of Korea (10+3), the Greater Mekong Sub-Region Cooperation, and the Asian-Pacific Trade Agreement. By means of such activities as the ASEAN and China (10+1) Cooperation, the Sino-Africa Cooperation Forum, the Sino-Arab Cooperation Forum, the China-Caribbean Economic and Trade Cooperation Forum and the China-Pacific Island Countries Economic Development and Cooperation Forum, China has done much to promote strengthened regional economic cooperation with relevant countries and regions. Indeed, by the end of 2006 China had established 178 bilateral economic and commercial cooperation mechanisms with these countries and regions. From 2001 to 2005, China established foreign economic cooperation coordinating mechanism with nearly 20 countries, including Japan and the Republic of Korea. In 2006 China and the United States started the strategic economic dialogue mechanism and successfully held the first of the projected series of dialogues.

The 8th China Forum of Economists was held in December 2006 in Beijing; it was attended by more than 40 foreign embassy officials in China and representatives of international organizations.

China is committed to speeding up the foundation of free-trade regions, expanding fields of cooperation and enhancing cooperation levels. By the end of 2006 China had held negotiations on 11 free-trade regions, involving 28 countries and regions and whose trade value accounted for about a quarter of China's foreign total. Efforts are being made to establish the China-ASEAN Free Trade Region in 2010.

(II) Bring New Opportunities for Development to the World

In the whole of history no one has maintained such a dazzling economic growth rate as China has in the past 30 years. Those words are taken from an article in the British magazine *The Economist* on September 29, 2007. Since 1978 China's economy has maintained an annual average growth rate of nearly 10 percent, much higher than that of Japan and the Four Small Dragons in Asia (Republic of Korea, Singapore, Hong Kong and Taiwan) in the same period.

China's development is an important part of that of the whole world and cannot be separated from the common interests of the global population as a whole. The continuously growing China has a more and more important influence on the world at large.

China's development provides a positive driving force in the growth of global trade. According to the World Bank, from 2003 to 2005 the contribution made by China's economy to the growth of the world economy exceeded 13.8 percent, next only to the United States, and accounted for a growth of international commerce exceeding 12 percent.

Since its accession to the WTO in 2001, China has imported goods worth US$500 billion a year, and this has created 10 million job opportunities for relevant countries and regions.

Throughout 2006 China's imports kept expanding with the total value reaching US$791.6 billion, a twelve month increase of 20 percent, representing a 2.4 percentage point increase on the year before. This includes US$90.32 billion worth of imports from the European Union, an increase of 22.7 percent; US$115.72 billion worth of imports from Japan, representing a rise 15.2 percent; US$59.21 billion worth of imports from the United States, a growth of 21.8 percent; and US$89.5 billion worth of imports from ASEAN countries, an increase of 19.4 percent.

The rapid growth in China's imports offered a significantly broader market for other countries. Statistics prepared by the United States reveal that in the past decade the US exports to China have expanded by an astonishing 350 percent, six times that of the growth in its export market to other regions of the world over the same period. China has become a wide market for American products. Coca-Cola's sales figures in China have already exceeded the mythical target of 100 million cans, while General Motors and Ford have sold a very large number of automobiles to China's drivers.

Meanwhile, the growth of China's export industry also offers good-quality, low-priced commodities to consumers in many countries, not only satisfying the demands of large numbers of those consumers but also reducing their cost of living and helping the importing countries maintain a stable economy. According to (admittedly as yet incomplete) statistics, access to China's cheaper commodities has enhanced the living standard of the average Americans by between 5-10 percent. Such imports, therefore, are of great benefit to the poorer sections of American society.

Chinese-made products, combining good quality with cheap price, help to maintain the inflation ratio in some countries at a comparatively low level, thus extending the upturning cycle of their economy. A considerable part of China's foreign exchange reserves have been used to buy the national debts of western countries such as the United States, a fiscal policy which has helped those countries escape some of the pressure of economic deficit.

China's participation in economic globalization has expanded the space for global optimization in industrial structure, accelerated economic relationships between the countries, and become an important factor in maintaining a healthy world economy. In the course of opening up and entering into the world market, China has offered opportunities and wealth sources to the world. It has been a driving force in effecting changes in the global systems of labor, pricing, and supply-and-demand, and has accelerated the optimization and upgrading of economic structure. What has rapidly become known as the "China factor" has played an extremely active role in the world economy.

China's development soon offered a wide market for international capital investment, and that investment has seen many positive returns. The huge market surrounding infrastructural construction, for example, has provided a large number of foreign companies with major business opportunities. From 1990 to 2005 the profits remitted by foreign-funded companies in China reached US$280 billion. Based on an investigation carried out by the United States-China Chamber of Commerce, it has been shown that about 70 percent of the US companies in China went into profit and 42 percent of them delivered profits exceeding the global average.

The 6th KFC fast food restaurant set up in Zhengzhou, Henan Province.

With the growth in power of Chinese enterprises, investment in foreign countries and regions has also been on the increase. Since 2002 the direct non-financial investment by Chinese enterprises has increased by more than 43 percent as a yearly average, and by the end of 2006 it had risen to US$73.3 billion, and 61 percent of the sum was concentrated in Asia. China's overseas investment not only accelerated the economic growth in developing countries and offered new employment opportunities for some developed countries, but also was instrumental in rescuing some enterprises from serious financial difficulties.

There are 132 destination countries and regions available for Chinese residents to visit, and the People's Republic now accounts for the largest number of outbound tourists in Asia. In 2006 the number of travelers exiting the country reached 34.52 million, with 28.8 million of those doing so for private business, an increase of 14.6 percent on the previous year.

China has huge potential and excellent prospects for developing foreign economic and commercial cooperation.

Motorola, which has been investing in China for 20 years, is the largest foreign-funded enterprise in China.

In the near future, the import value of China will exceed US$700 billion, and it is set to exceed US$1,000 billion by the year 2010. By 2020 the market size and total demand in China will quadruple that of 2000. Meanwhile, all countries in the world can identify and develop their own business potential in their cooperation with China, which will play an important and active role in driving forward world economic growth.

Regarding the development prospects for China's economy in the first half of this century, some worldwide economic research institutions have made their estimations and a broadly common outlook is as follows: China's economy will keep growing at an annual rate of above 8 percent. By 2010 China's GDP will reach US$3,800 billion; and

China's per-capita GDP will approach US$3,000. China will become the No.1 exporter, the No.2 importer, and a major recruiter of foreign investment and an equally important investor in foreign countries and regions around the world. By around 2020 China's comprehensive strength will enhance further and its international competitiveness will stabilize at somewhere between No.10 and No.15 in the world. It is estimated that from 2005 to 2020, based on purchasing power parity, China will have a contribution rate of 37 percent to the world's new GDP growth. China will bring many more opportunities for future development to the world at large.

(III) A Responsible Developing Country

By the end of 2007 China had established diplomatic relations with 170 countries, formed economic and commercial links with more than 230 countries and regions, participated in more than 130 inter-governmental international organizations, acceded to 22 international conventions on human rights and signed more than 300 international treaties. In international affairs China enjoys a broad range of privileges and takes its corresponding obligations seriously. It has become an important member of the international community.

Participate in UN affairs and safeguard UN authority. As one of the initiating States of the San Francisco Conference, China is a founding member of the United Nations, and the first to sign the UN Charter. After its resumption of the legitimate seat in the United Nations in 1971, China actively participated in the work of various fields, continuously deepened its cooperation with the UN, earnestly implemented its international obligations and firmly safeguarded the tenets and principles of the UN Charter. As a permanent member of the UN Security Council, China took part in the work of UN Security Council, strove to safeguard the authority and role of the Security Council, worked hard to solve regional hot issues by means of peaceful methods such as discussion, dialogues and negotiation, and supported the UN Secretary-General in developing preventive diplomacy such as mediating and coordinating. China played a constructive role in helping the Security Council successfully deal with a series of issues such as the Iraq-Iran war, Cambodia and East Timor issues. China supported the UN in its adoption of necessary and reasonable reform in all aspects and various fields, and advocated that the United Nations should develop in the direction that is beneficial to maintaining the tenets and principles of its Charter, to unity of member states, and to the overall and long-term interests of those member states. China supported the leading and coordinating role of the United Nations in the field of international anti-terrorism and nonproliferation, supported the United Nations in its deployment of peace-keeping forces, and actively promoted the solution of regional conflicts within the framework of UN policy. China widely participated in the international dialogues and cooperation held by the United Nations in various fields such as human rights, development, justice, environmental protection and cultural exchange.

Foreign Ministers Meeting of ASEAN and China, Japan and South Korea held in Kuala Lumpur, Malaysia in July 2006.

Participate in cooperation in global energy security and environmental protection. China has actively strengthened bilateral and multilateral cooperation in energy issues and attached great importance to working together with the international community in the field of world energy security. In such spheres as energy exploitation, utilization, technology, environmental protection, as well as new and renewable energy sources, China has in recent years actively developed dialogues and cooperation with a number of international organizations and countries. China has also planned its unified policy of domestic development and opening up, actively participated in the global exploitation and cooperation in regard of such resources as petroleum and natural gas, and maintained energy security in combination with political transparency. China has undertaken effective cooperation with more than 10 international inter-governmental organizations and non-governmental organizations, including the UNEP, has added its signature to more than 50 international treaties involving environmental protection, and has earnestly undertaken the work of implementation. China has signed bilateral agreements or memoranda of understanding on environmental protection cooperation with 42 countries including the United States, Japan, Canada and Russia, has established environmental cooperation mechanisms with the European Union and the League of Arab States, and has helped African countries develop along the path of environmental protection. With a fully committed and proactive spirit of cooperation, China has participated in regional environmental protection, established a mechanism allowing environmental ministers of China, Japan and Republic of Korea to hold regular meetings, initiated the Greater Mekong Sub-Regional Environmental Cooperation Mechanism, and pushed for environmental cooperation under the mechanisms of ASEAN and China (10+1) and ASEAN and China, Japan and Republic of Korea (10+3).

Commitment to the strengthening of international cooperation in arms control, disarmament and nonproliferation. China has always stood for the comprehensive prohibition and complete elimination of nuclear weapons. Since possessing a nuclear capability of its own, China has solemnly announced an unshakeable policy of no first strike use of nuclear weapons at any time and under any condition and it unconditionally undertakes neither to use nor threaten to use nuclear weapons against non-nuclear weapon States. China has always held an extremely restrained

The "Peace Mission-2007 Joint Anti-terror Drill" held by members of the Shanghai Cooperation Operation.

attitude regarding the development of nuclear weapons and the size of its nuclear arsenal is always maintained at the lowest possible level for adequate self-defense. China has never deployed nuclear weapons overseas. China was one of the first States to sign the Comprehensive Nuclear Test Ban Treaty and has maintained its position regarding that Treaty since the suspension of nuclear testing in July 1996. China firmly supports the implementation of the Biological Weapons Convention and the Chemical Weapons Convention and thoroughly carries out its obligations as stipulated in those Conventions. China believes in the peaceful use of outer space, and encourages the international community to adopt practical methods to effectively prevent an extra-terrestrial arms race. China firmly opposes the proliferation of weapons of mass destruction and their means of delivery, and actively participates in the course of international prevention of proliferation. China has acceded to all the international treaties and relevant international organizations in the field of nonproliferation, actively undertaken exchanges and cooperation with other countries and mechanisms related to multinational export control, and has promoted solutions to issues related to nonproliferation by means of peaceful methods such as dialogues and cooperation. China maintains a policy of ever tightening export control laws and regulations involving nuclear, biological, and chemical missiles, as well as conventional military hardware, and has also established an inter-agency contingency mechanism for nonproliferation export control, and has strengthened those powers by which it is enforced.

Strive to maintain neighborhood and regional security and stability. By a series of practical actions, China has sought to establish good relations and mutual confidence with its neighbors, accelerated bilateral cooperation and regional security cooperation, and worked hard to improve the regional security dialogue and cooperation mechanism. Sticking to accepted guidelines for international relations, and in the spirit of equal consultation and mutual understanding and accommodation, China has properly solved its border issues with neighboring countries, dissolved disputes and accelerated stability. China has now signed border treaties with a dozen continental neighboring countries and has solved those border issues which came about for historical reasons. The resolution of border issues with India and Bhutan is already developing in a positive direction. China has signed a series of agreements with relevant neighboring countries to accelerate bilateral mutual confidence, has further signed the Declaration on the Conduct of the Parties in the South China Sea with ASEAN to maintain stability and develop cooperation in this area, and has made a significant breakthrough in the common development of the South China Sea region with the Philippines and Vietnam. China has more actively and practically developed its military relationship with the major powers, strengthened its military communications with neighboring countries and extended its policy of military exchange with developing countries. By brokering reciprocal visits between high-level officials, China has solidified the basis for mutual and friendly cooperation; by undertaking strategic consultation and dialogues, China has promoted mutual communication and confidence; and by enlarging the scope and nature of these meetings, China has broadened mutual dependence, avoided confrontation and helped to realize common security and stability.

Actively promote regional security dialogues and cooperation. China plays a constructive role in such regional and inter-regional mechanisms as China and ASEAN, ASEAN and China, Japan and the Republic of Korea, the Shanghai Cooperation Organization (SCO), the Asia-Europe Conference, ASEAN Regional Forum, and Asian Cooperation Dialogue. Under the framework of SCO, China and other SCO member states have comprehensively strengthened cooperation in defense security, established multi-level cooperation mechanisms in a wide field including meetings of heads of States, prime ministers, foreign ministers and national defense ministers, launched SCO Secretariat and Regional Anti-Terrorism departments, and advocated the setting up of a new global security structure with mutual confidence, benefits, equality and respect. China attaches much importance to the role of ASEAN Regional Forum, has put forward constructive proposals on its sound development, and has either sponsored or jointly held seminars on non-traditional security fields under the framework of the Forum. As a major country in the region, China has taken the lead in acceding to the Treaty of Amity and Cooperation in Southeast Asia, and has injected a new vitality into the peace and friendship between China and ASEAN countries. China actively participates in the regional cooperation in non-traditional security fields such as maritime search and rescue, combating piracy, and cracking down on drug production and trafficking.

Participate in dealing with global and regional hot issues. China holds a strong position on solving international disputes and accelerating worldwide common security by political and diplomatic methods such as negotiation and dialogue. Regarding the nuclear issue on the Korean Peninsula, China has always advocated

The second-stage meeting of the fifth-round Six-Party Talks on nuclear issues in the Korean Peninsula was held in December 2006.

a dialogue-led peaceful solution, with the ultimate aim of denuclearizing the Korean Peninsula and maintaining the peace and stability of the Peninsula and Northeastern Asia. Since 2003 China has actively worked along diplomatic lines with the relevant parties, and succeeded in hosting first the Three-Party Talks between China, North Korea and the United States and then the Six-Party Talks between China, North Korea, the United States, Republic of Korea, Russia and Japan. China was instrumental in getting the participants of the fourth round of Six-Party Talks to issue a Joint Statement on confirming the target of denuclearization of the Korean Peninsula and achieved an important stage in the negotiations. Regarding the problems in the Middle East, China opposes any practice that might threaten regional peace and stability. Along with other countries China persuaded the UN Security Council to pass Resolution No.1701, and called on the concerned parties to return to the conference table in the light of the relevant UN decisions and the principle of "Land for Peace." China's position is to realize as soon as possible a comprehensive and just solution to the problems plaguing the Middle East, including that which exists between Palestine and Israel, and harmonize relations between the relevant countries with the ultimate objective of a lasting peace. Regarding the Iraq issue, China advocates seeking a political solution within the UN framework, and stands for maintaining the independent sovereignty and integrity of the territory of Iraq, respecting the Iraqi people's wish to become masters of their own country, and doing a great deal of work on how the future of Iraq will take shape when the country returns to peace. Regarding the issue of Iran's nuclear capability, China supports and safeguards the international nuclear nonproliferation system, advocates policies in support of peace and stability in Middle East region, opposes proliferation of nuclear weapons, and stands for a peaceful solution to the Iran nuclear issue by means of diplomatic negotiation.

China continuously extends its participation in UN peacekeeping actions. From 1989 to the end of 2006, China deployed 6,000 military personnel, policemen and civilian officials on 16 separate UN peace-keeping initiatives and by so doing became the 12th largest supplier of UN peacekeeping forces. Nine Chinese soldiers lost their lives in the cause of maintaining global peace. By January 2007, nearly 2,000 Chinese army men, policemen and civilian officials were carrying out their missions

In July 2006, Chinese soldiers participating in peace-keeping actions in Haiti mourning those who have died in the cause of maintaining peace in the region.

Expenditure on National Defense in 2005

Country	USA	Russia	UK	France	Germany	Japan	China
National Defense Expenditure (Unit: US$100 million)	4953.3	186.0	578.8	428.9	311.4	453.9	306.5
National Defense Expenditure in GDP(%)	4.03	2.45	2.71	1.93	1.07	0.89	1.35
National Defense Expenditure (Unit: US$1,000)	356.61	16.39	288.03	123.54	122.93	188.47	13.32

Source: *White Paper on China's National Defense in 2006.*

in 11 separate peacekeeping actions. After conflict broke out between Israel and Lebanon in July 2006, China declared its willingness to increase its forces attached to the UN temporary army stationed in Lebanon to 1,000.

Actively participate in the struggle against global terrorism. China adheres to the UN Charter and other accepted international law guidelines as the basis of its anti-terrorism policy. It brings the leadership and role of the United Nations and the UN Security Council into full play, prevents and combats terrorism in partnership with many other countries, roots out the sources of terrorism, strengthens coopera-tion in such areas as exchanges in anti-terrorism information, cuts off the monetary supply of terrorist organizations, apprehends and where appropriate extradites suspects of terrorist crimes, and has put a great deal of effective work into the international anti-terrorism struggle. China has acceded to 10 international anti-terrorism conventions including the International Convention on Stopping Terrorist Explosions, signed the International Convention on Severing Financial Aid to Terrorism, and thoroughly implemented a series of decisions on anti-terrorism issues passed by the UN Security Council. China advocates strengthening regional anti-terrorism cooperation, holds joint anti-terrorism exercises with relevant countries, and is continuously exploring new ways to combat terrorism, a policy which is having an impact on international terrorist forces.

Adhere to a defensive national defense policy. China's national defense is subject to and serves national development and security strategies. It aims at safeguarding national security and unity and ensures the realization of the grand objective of modernization. Since the 1990s, on the basis of its economic development, China has promoted the gradual growth and reconstruction of national defense and modernization of armies, which has suited the developing trend of new military reform in the world at large and yet still satisfied the demands of maintaining national security and protecting national interests. But such growth is still compensatory to make up for a weak national defense basis and is harmonious with national economic development. At present, China's total military budget per-capita is still at a low level when compared with that of most other countries, and especially when set beside that of the super powers. In 2005 the annual national defense expenditure of China was equal to 6.19 percent of that of the United States, 52.95 percent of the United Kingdom, 71.45 percent of France and 67.52 percent of Japan.

(IV) Promote the Building of a Harmonious World

We members of the human race have only one earth. Building a common beautiful home and realizing global harmony is the lofty ideal to which each of us can aspire. But the world in reality is not peaceful. Regional conflicts and major flare-ups occur continuously, economic imbalance becomes wider, the gap between north and south is enlarged, traditional and non-traditional security threats interweave, and the peace and development of our world faces numerous difficulties and challenges.

At the UN Summit on the 60th anniversary of the establishment of the United Nations in September 2005, Chinese President Hu Jintao delivered a speech in which he proposed all countries in the world join hand in hand and make a combined

The International Symposium on Respecting and Promoting Human Rights and Constructing the Harmonious World was held in Beijing in November 2006.

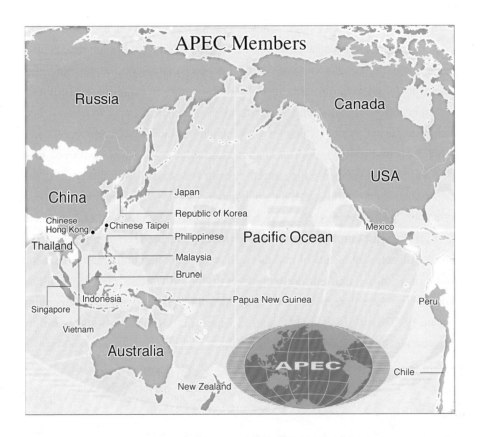

effort to create a harmonious planet with long-lasting peace and common prosperity.

As for the harmonious world advocated by China, the basic conditions are as follows: In politics we should respect each other, negotiation should be carried out on a basis of equality, and together we should promote the democratization of international relations; in economics we should cooperate with each other and take advantage of each other's strength, and promote together the development of an economic globalization, in culture we should learn from each other and seek common ground while respecting differences, working together to accelerate prosperity and progress in human civilization; in security we should trust each other and strengthen cooperation, persist in solving international disputes through peaceful means instead of armed forces, and safeguard together world peace and stability; and in environmental protection we should make a joint effort in protecting our global homeland.

Building a harmonious world is the actual embodiment of the excellent cultural traditions and moral ethics of the Chinese nation. Harmony is an excellent cultural spirit and important concept passed down in China's culture through thousands of years. In the traditional culture of China, the word "harmony" contains multiplicities of profound meanings such as peace, cooperation, equality, consultation, mutual benefits, tolerance, and co-existence. Since ancient times, there have been such precepts as "peace is valuable" and "be harmonious but not homogenous." It is believed that unity, mutual assistance and friendly relations between men, nationalities and states are the supreme realm for social development; it is also stressed that "being harmonious but not homogenous" is the precondition for "peace is valuable". This means seeking for common points while respecting differences, correctly coordinating all the parties involved, and properly dealing with and burying disputes by means of mutual dialogue and cooperation under the precondition of acknowledging pluralism, diversity and difference. By putting these thoughts into social practice, we will pay attention to mutual respect, cooperation, and unity. This will inevitably lead to domestic and international harmony, benevolence to neighbor and foreigner alike.

The 4th ASEAN Fair was held in Nanning, capital of the Guangxi Zhuang Autonomous Region, in 2007. Picture shows the Thai Hall.

China's desire to build a harmonious world is consistent with the common value orientation of the whole human race. The desire to build a harmonious world also accords with the proposals put forward in the UN Charter which advocates that all countries "exist together peacefully by means of good neighborhood," "collect forces to maintain international peace and security," and "accelerate the economic and social progress of peoples around the world by means of international organizations."

The harmonious world that China advocates refers to the process with the actual world as its basis and starting point. There are, there will be, of course, conflicts and differences, as well as contradictions and problems, but it is a key point that all the countries should seek for common goals by negotiation, respect relations between countries and ever increasing global issues, continuously identify and enlarge the harmonious factors in the actual world, and never cease from the task of driving human society forward along the road of development and progress.

In recent years China has made unremitting efforts to build a harmonious world with long-lasting peace and common prosperity.

To build such a world, we should begin by building a harmonious neighborhood. China is surrounded by approximately 30 countries. China shares a border with some of them, and is separated by a stretch of sea from some others, They include 11 small and medium -sized developing countries in southeastern Asia, such as the 10 countries of ASEAN and East Timor. The 10 countries of ASEAN are all close neighbors of China. Based on the principle of "being friendly to and accompanying one's neighbors," China has actively developed a spirit of friendly cooperation with ASEAN countries. At present, the relationship between China and ASEAN shows a positive developing trend of "equality, mutual assistance, cooperation and win-win." In the political field, both sides only took 10 years to establish a strategic partnership; in respect of security, both sides have made efforts to enhance mutual trust by means of dialogue, peacefully solved disputes by means of negotiation, and realized regional security by means of cooperation, signing in the process many documents of mutual assistance; in the field of economics, the cooperation between both sides in trade, investment and economy has developed at great speed: in 2006 both sides became each other's fourth largest trading partner, and the China-ASEAN Free Trade Region will be established in 2010, at which point it will represent a population of 1.8 billion, its GDP will exceed US$2,000 billion, the trade volume will reach US$1,230 billion, and it will be the largest free trade region composed of developing countries in the world; in international and regional affairs, both sides have jointly promoted the sound development of regional and inter-regional cooperation mechanisms such as those between ASEAN and China, Japan and Republic of Korea (10+3), the ASEAN Regional Forum, the Asian Cooperation Dialogue, Asian-Pacific Economic Cooperation Organization and the Asia-Europe Conference. In October 2006 the Summit on the 15th Anniversary of the Establishment of China-ASEAN Dialogue was held in Nanning of Guangxi, and the strategic partnership established there between the two sides has excellent future prospects.

The establishment and development of the Shanghai Cooperation Organization (SCO) is another successful example of how China has committed itself to building a harmonious neighborhood. In 2001 the SCO, composed of China, Kazakhstan, Kyrgyzstan, Russia, Tajikistan and Uzbekistan, was founded in Shanghai. SCO member states possess the natural advantage of being geographic neighbors and sharing a similar history and culture. They also share a commitment to adhering to the tenets of peace and development, abide by democratic principles,

Summit of the Shanghai Cooperation Organization held in Pudong, Shanghai in 2006.

Members of the China-funded research class on anti-poverty in developing countries.

are pursuing the policy of opening up, and actively conduct various forms of dialogue, exchange and cooperation. For years SCO has stoutly practiced and carried forward a mutual policy of trust, benefit, equality, and consultation. It respects cultural diversity, and the "Shanghai Spirit" of seeking for common development has become an important force in maintaining regional and world peace, stability and prosperity. In June 2006, the Summit on the 5th anniversary of the foundation of SCO was held in Shanghai. At the summit, all the heads of the member states put forward their plan for the future, based around the theme of carrying forward the "Shanghai Spirit," extending practical cooperation, and accelerating common development. They subsequently signed the Declaration on the Fifth Anniversary of SCO, which fixed the orientation and missions of SCO for the future.

Development is the key for building a harmonious world. Therefore, China attaches much importance to accelerating world development by the momentum of its own, and realizing common development with all other countries. For years China has been actively promoting better economic and trading relations with developing countries, constantly enlarging the benefits of mutual cooperation, promoted as the ultimate "win-win" situation. Subsequently, as a result of this cooperation with China, a large number of developing countries have realized many more opportunities for development and are scooping the material benefits that development brings. China has extended its cooperation with developing countries by opening domestic markets to a greater degree, importing more products from those countries, and offering them production technology aids. The Chinese Government strongly supports Chinese enterprises in their effort to conduct multi-forms of overseas cooperation in the spirit of mutual benefits.

Despite the sheer domestic ardor of its own development policies, China has nevertheless persisted in supporting developing countries with practical action and has gradually enlarged its economic aid to those nations. From the beginning of 2002 to August 2006, the number of countries and regional organizations receiving China's aid reached 105 and China unconditionally wrote off approximately US$17 billion of overseas debt owed by forty-five countries in Asia, Africa, Latin America and the South Pacific region. In September 2005, at the High-Level Meeting on Financing for Development on the occasion of the 60th anniversary of the United Nations, China's President Hu Jintao announced the significant measures China would adopt to increase assistance to other developing countries: China will give zero tariff treatment for certain products to all the 39 Least-Developed Countries (LDCs) having diplomatic relations with China; exempt or cancel in other ways within the next two years all the outstanding interest-free and low-interest government loans due as of the end of 2004 owed by all the Heavily Indebted Poor Countries (HIPCs) having diplomatic relations with China; within the next three years, provide US$10 billion in preferential loans and preferential export buyer's credit to developing countries; and train 30,000 persons of various professions from the developing countries within the next three years. In December 2005, the Chinese Government gave an undertaking that it would provide about one-third of US$10 billion in preferential loans and preferential export buyer's credit to developing ASEAN countries and increase preferential loans by US$5 billion on the current basis.

Over the years China has implemented nearly 900 infrastructural and social welfare projects for African developing countries, offered nearly 18,000 scholarships, and sent out medical aid teams totaling 16,000 doctors, nurses and medical personnel. Within the framework of the Sino-Africa Cooperation Forum, China tore up debts from 31 nations amounting to 10.9 billion Yuan and yet offered vocational training to approximately 10,000 of their citizens. At the Beijing Summit of Sino-Africa Cooperation Forum held in November 2006, China's President Hu Jintao put forward a policy by which measures would be adopted on eight aspects aimed at increasing assistance to African countries: China's assistance to African countries will double the 2006 figure until 2009; US$3 billion will be provided in the next three years in preferential loans and US$2 billion in preferential export buyer's credit to African countries; a Sino-Africa Developing Fund will be set up and the total amount of funds will eventually reach US$5 billion; there will be an exemption from all the outstanding interest-free government loans due as of the end of 2005 owed by all the HIPCs and LDCs in Africa which have diplomatic relations with China; the tax items from 190 to 440 for commodities enjoying zero tariff treatment exported to China by LDCs in Africa which have diplomatic relations with China will be enlarged; within the next three years, three to five overseas economic and commercial cooperation regions will be set up in African countries; and within the next three years 15,000 persons of various professions from African countries will be given the inestimable benefits to themselves and their nations of further training and education.

(V) Inheritance and Development of Tradition

Thanks to the implementation of the opening-up policy and economic globalization, the contemporary society of China is now undergoing unprecedented changes. China is developing fast to become a modernized society. The history of human beings has never seen such a huge change that improves the living condition of more than one billion people so rapidly.

Today's China maintains its tradition. It is furthermore a country that keeps up with the times and is full of innovation. The development of China's society is at a transitional stage. China is taking a completely new attitude facing the future.

The structure of China's social economy is also undergoing changes. Further development of a socialist market economy diversifies the structure of the economy.

Job fair held specially for rural migrant workers in Chongqing.

It forms the pattern with the public sector remaining dominant and diverse sectors of the economy developing side by side. Meanwhile, the organization of economic activities, means of employment and distribution methods are also diversified. All these factors contribute to diversified relationships of different social interest. People at different social stratum have different understanding about the development of the society as well as different requests not related to their own interest.

Urbanization speeds up the changes in rural areas. The source of ancient Chinese civilization developed through agriculture. The small-scale peasant economy based on family production determined the value of the society and mode of development. Modernization and urbanization develop side by side. As a result of the quick development of modernization construction in China, the number of cities increases and the scale of the cities are enlarged. Thanks to the Chinese Government effort to actively promote the urbanization, update the industrial structure and implement the strategy of "the development of cities bringing along the development of rural area, and the development of industry supporting the development of agriculture", the farmers are no longer confined to rural areas. Some farmers have moved the cities, because living in the cities enables them to have more opportunities and enjoy a more convenient life. Recent years have seen large numbers of surplus laborers moving into the cities. They can earn more in cities and therefore live a better life. Urbanization brings not only the shift in population ratio in urban and rural areas but also the change of concepts. The farmers no longer regard land as their sole source of living. They overcome the old and closed concept of attaching sentimentally to their hometown and fearing changes, and become competitive and innovative.

The concept of value of the Chinese people is also changing. The traditional thoughts, such as the doctrine of the mean, are replaced by modern concepts of value. The development of the society greatly improves people's concept of value. People's understandings about concepts, such as time, efficiency, development, various key elements of production, justice, fairness, honesty and friendliness, etc, are greatly improved. The concepts of democracy, legal system, liberty, equality and fraternity are widely accepted by the whole society and are put into practice by people. The Chinese people used to advocate modesty and prudence. Nowadays, people publicize their individuality. The spirit of innovation runs high. The whole society is full of vigor. In recent years, the Chinese people have more independence and choices in their thoughts, which are varied with obvious differences. All these make greater demands on the political and cultural construction of this country.

Development of culture is characterized by variety. Different forms of culture, no matter traditional or modern, from the east or the west, can be found everywhere in China. It becomes a common understanding that the artistic character of the artist should be stressed and the development principle of art itself should be respected. Art works are more likely to be produced for amusement. Different schools of art coexist. Art and life are mixed together. Literature is popularized. Ordinary people can write books. Web literature becomes fashionable. Pop music becomes an indispensable part of people's life. Songs are created on the websites. Rock and roll can be heard everywhere. Traditional Peking opera is protected and advocated. As people from all walks of life participate in TV cultural activities, TV shows become very successful, marking the coming of the age of popular cultural consumption. Holiday culture is also diversified. People are still fond of traditional festivals such as the Spring Festival and the Moon Festival. On the other hand, young people are also keen on Western holidays such as Valentine's Day and Christmas. China ranks

Voting for new neighborhood committee in Xi'an, Shaanxi Province.

first in the number of netizens in the world. A lot of people write blogs and publish what they write by using DV online.

Chinese opinion about marriage and family also undergoes changes. More women go out to work and earn stable incomes. The strengthened realization on equality between man and woman shook the dominant role of man in the family. The authority of man is downgraded. The traditional Chinese praised

Allhallowmas celebration in the walking street in Jianghan Road, Wuhan, Hubei Province, in 2007.

Ceremony held for the first issue of Harry Potter 7 (Chinese edition).

highly the marriage with only one spouse for the whole life. Now, this situation has changed. Recent years have seen an increase in the divorce rate in China. The uneven divorce rates show that there are more divorces in urban areas compared to rural areas. More than half of the divorces are asked for by women. The majority of the people divorced are above the age of 30. Among them, most are females who have received higher education. Active social life, flow of population and strengthened self-awareness and awareness of freedom result in unstable relationships in families and sexual relationships outside of marriage. The traditional Chinese attached great importance to bringing up children. It was believed that people without children, especially a son, did not fulfill their filial duty. Nowadays, the view of bringing up children is changed. Some young people concentrate more on their career development and seeking of freedom, so they choose a DINK family. The change of view on bringing up children and the implementation of the birth control policy in China leads to a notable decrease in the rate of births and speeds up the aging of the society. The improvement of dwelling conditions and fast flow of population gradually minimizes the size of families. At present, the first "only child" generation is at the age of getting married. The pyramid of the traditional Chinese family is developing in the opposite way. The mode of aged people living with their family, which has a several-thousand years' history, is facing unprecedented challenges. Nowadays, the average size of families in urban and rural areas has decreased to 3.4 persons from 4.8 persons in the 1970s. The average number of people in each family in cities is 3. It is even only 2.8 to 2.9 in big cities such as Beijing and Shanghai. This number is 3.3 at town level and 3.7 in rural areas. The number of single-person households and single-parent families is growing fast.

A family of three is typical in China.

The development of social economy in China enhanced the people's standard of living. Chinese people's life style is undergoing changes. Their view of consumption is updated, level of con-

Foreign visitors on Tian'anmen Square in Beijing.

sumption improved, structure of consumption optimized and method of consumption multiplied. The Chinese people are becoming more and more fashionable and are attaching importance to the current style and color of clothes. Compared to their fathers' generation, Chinese young people are facing too many changes in their life. The older generation experienced a long-time shortage of supply, so they formed the habit of working hard and living plainly. It is more and more popular for the young generation to spend money on luxuries and fashionable products. Some world famous luxuries companies start to make inroads into the market by opening their shops in China. Many Chinese young people are very fond of Western food. The cuisines from various countries can be found in big cities such as Beijing and Shanghai. Youngsters become fans of Western fast food such as KFC and McDonald's. They enjoy having birthday parties with their friends in these fast food restaurants. Some young people buy apartments by installments to build their own "world". Some do not live with their parents after they get married. They regard leisure as important as work and want to fully enjoy the happiness of life.

William H. Overholt describes the changes in China in his article entitled *China and Globalization* as follows:

It is hard to overstate the social adjustment Chinese are experiencing. But because China has been willing to accept such adjustments, no large country in human history has ever experienced such rapid improvements in living standards and working conditions. When reform began, workers in Shanghai all wore the same clothes, looked tired and listless, and seldom owned basic appliances like televisions or even watches. In the countryside malnutrition was widespread. Today Shanghai workers wear colorful clothes and look confident and energetic. Today the average Chinese family owns slightly more than one television. Malnutrition has vanished. As a result, Chinese overwhelmingly support further globalization.